Quality: Achieving Excellence

Edgar Wille

C

CENTURY
BUSINESS

This paperback edition first published in the UK 1993
by Century Business
An imprint of Random House UK Ltd
20 Vauxhall Bridge Road, London SW1V 2SA

Random House Australia (Pty) Ltd
20 Alfred Street, Milsons Point
Sydney, NSW 2061, Australia

Random House New Zealand Ltd
18 Poland Road, Glenfield
Auckland 10, New Zealand

Random House South Africa (Pty) Ltd
PO Box 337, Bergvlei, South Africa

First published in 1992 by Century Business

Typeset by Ɐ Tek Art Ltd, Croydon, Surrey
Printed and bound in Great Britain by
Mackays of Chatham PLC, Chatham, Kent

A catalogue record for this book is available from the British Library.

ISBN 0–7126–5672–3

Quality: Achieving Excellence

SUNDAY TIMES BUSINESS SKILLS
Other titles in this series:

QUALITY: CHANGE THROUGH TEAMWORK
Rani Chaudhry-Lawton, Richard Lawton, Karen Murphy & Angela Terry
ISBN 0–7126–9833–7 (hbk); 0–7126–5677–4 (pbk)

QUALITY: TOTAL CUSTOMER SERVICE
Lynda King Taylor
ISBN 0–7126–9843–4 (hbk); 0–7126–5667–7 (pbk)

EFFECTIVE MEETINGS
Phil & Jane Hodgson
ISBN 0–7126–9873–6 (hbk); 0–7126–5662–6 (pbk)

TIME MANAGEMENT
Martin Scott
ISBN 0–7126–9853–1 (hbk); 0–7126–5657–X (pbk)

QUALITY: SUSTAINING CUSTOMER SERVICE
Lynda King Taylor
ISBN 0–7126–5834–3 (hbk); 0–7126–5519–0 (pbk)

QUALITY: MEASURING AND MONITORING
Tony Bendell, John Kelly, Ted Merry & Fraser Sims
ISBN 0–7126–5829–7 (hbk); 0–7126–5514–X (pbk)

LEADERSHIP: THE ART OF DELEGATION
David Oates
ISBN 0–7126–5819–X (hbk); 0–7126–5651–0 (pbk)

LEADERSHIP: THE ART OF MOTIVATION
Nick Thornely & Dan Lees
ISBN 0–7126–5824–6 (hbk); 0–7126–5646–4 (pbk)

SUCCESSFUL PRESENTATIONS
Carole McKenzie
ISBN 0–7126–5814–9 (hbk); 0–7126–5691–X (pbk)

Each book is carefully co-ordinated to complement *The Sunday Times* 'Business Skills' video training package of the same name, produced by Taylor Made Films Ltd.

Contents

To
Ruth, David and Marion
my children
who grew up to be my friends

Acknowledgements

I am grateful to so many people who have helped in various ways in the preparation of this book.

Bill Pryce, Tim Evans, Ian Mitchell, Richard Smith and David Slater of the Employment Department and Valerie Hammond, director of Ashridge Management Research Group (AMRG), must have the credit for starting me on my journey through British industry. (See Appendix A for details of the 'Investors in People' initiative which was the basis of this journey.)

Many people at Ashridge gave me a helping hand. Anthony Mitchell, who also runs Anthony Mitchell Associates, a Quality Management Consultancy, debated the gurus with me. Kathryn Leishman taught me about statistical process control. Terrylynn Knott gave me a rest now and again from doing my own word processing. Margaret Dawson, the AMRG administrator, dug me out several times. Jackie Ashton sorted out my computer problems. Chris Conway and Martin Bennett participated in some of the organisational visits. Corinne Seymour, on an Ashridge award in connection with her work on the learning organisation, provided the basis for chapter 18, with the help of Michael O'Sullivan, Governor of Holloway Prison, George Harris, Personnel Director of Toshiba and Martin Wibberley, Director of Human Resources, Bosch. Rod Boyle helped particularly with BS5750.

Then there are the people who welcomed me into their organisations: Bob Knox of Stanbridge Precision Turned Parts, Colin O'Neill of Rothmans, Charles Daybell of Braintree District Council, Phil Steele of IBC Vehicles, David Clifford of Seaham Harbour Docks and a number of their colleagues. Also Paul Ruggier of Texaco and Chris Hodgkinson of ICL without whom there would have been no chapters 16 and 17.

Henry Neave of the British Deming Association showed a lively interest which was most encouraging. He clarified my understanding of variations enormously.

Elizabeth Hennessy, Martin Liu, Diana Eliot and Paula Jacobs of Century Business were a pleasure to work with on a very tight timescale. Lucy Shankleman of Century Business launched me on the writing of this book, saying it would be good for my career. As an over 60 I liked that.

EW

A Route Map to this Book

This book owes its origin to visits I made, on behalf of Ashridge and the Employment Department, to scores of organisations. Many of them follow the total quality approach, a revolution in business life.

Chapters 1 and 2 set the scene by looking at definitions of quality and sitting at the feet of the Quality gurus, such as W. Edwards Deming, Joseph M. Juran and Philip Crosby. The sources of some of my information are the subject of chapter 21, where I offer a sample of 69 books which might start you on your own voyage of discovery.

Chapter 3 takes the plunge and gets into the apparently technical subject of 'variations' discovering that in fact it is all about management responsibilities and the folly of nagging operators for what they cannot control. This chapter also links with chapter 9 where some of the techniques used at all levels in a total quality company, not least by shop floor workers, are briefly illustrated. A short chapter 10 fits BS5750 into the scheme of things.

Chapters 4 to 8 deal with how total quality management affects everything done in an organisation. The way in which the whole workforce becomes committed to quality and continuous improvement is discussed in chapter 4; the dangers of preoccupation with quotas, targets, goals and numbers management might spark off controversy in chapter 5. Chapter 6 sees quality achieved by the co-operation of a whole chain of suppliers and customers, both internal and external. Each awaits the results of the work of the other and each expects quality; so we don't have to wait till the end of the chain to get it. It is built in all the way.

QUALITY: ACHIEVING EXCELLENCE

Chapter 7 sees the effectiveness of organising people in self-directed teams and how this empowers them to be involved in the search for quality. No longer a question of leaving their brains at the door and just doing as they are told. Chapter 8 applies all these principles to the service industries, recognising that the staff are more on public display in such organisations, but that the principles of quality and how to provide it are still the same.

Chapters 11 to 18 then invite the reader to accompany me, in retrospect, on some of my journeys round British organisations involved in total quality management. Put together they make it clear that total quality is not an idealistic dream. It *is* happening. Progress is being made. My general feeling about what I saw is one of optimism.

This is reflected in chapter 20 on co-operation, where the principles set out would change not only the face of business, but of society as a whole.

EW

1. Introducing Quality

QUALITY IS ABOUT PEOPLE

The total quality approach is about people and attitudes. It's not about techniques and procedures as such. It includes them, and it needs them. However, it's people who actually use them, inspired with a simple idea that the purpose of work is to provide customers with something that will delight them and make them want to keep paying your salary, by buying the product or service you provide.

MANAGEMENT DEFINED

Providing quality is everybody's job in a company. A lead needs to come from management who should offer frameworks and a sense of purpose. Management can be defined as:

> *Risking yourself in the mobilising of resources and relationships to add value to the enterprise.*

Managers risk themselves because every decision, however well informed, is a risk. They don't know for sure that everything will turn out as they planned. The very word 'decide' implies risk. It comes from a Latin word meaning 'to cut off'. When you chop off the branch of a tree you have stopped any chance of it bearing fruit. When you decide on one course of action, you have blocked off another possibility.

Life is like this – but you try not to risk the business, you choose the best branches to retain and what seem inferior ones to remove. Quality is an essential branch to grow, some would say *the* essential one.

Of the rest of the definition 'relationships' is the most important word. 'Resources' seems to cover everything. People are there as well as money, materials, markets, machines and so on. The word 'relationships' brings people into concert to produce something that is greater than the sum of their individual contributions. We use the word synergy for it (i.e. one plus one equals three or more). The most important single function of management is to foster relationships; between all the stakeholders; suppliers, customers, community, government, as well as employees.

QUALITY IS ABOUT WORKING TOGETHER

Fostering relationships is vital when dealing with quality. Quality is a mindset, but it is not merely an individual mindset; it is a collective one. Quality is attained by people linked with each other. We speak of the chain of suppliers and customers. Everyone and every team is a supplier to someone and a customer of someone else. This applies both within the organisation and outside it. It is the key to quality.

If ever the quotation 'No man is an island' rings true it is in this area. Donne hadn't lived to see the significance of women in this crusade, but his idea is sound. Interdependence – true in every field of life and never more so than when seeking to produce quality goods and services. This is why when the *doyen* of quality gurus, W. Edwards Deming, produced his 14 points about quality, ten of them made explicit reference to people, and people were in the other four by implication.

Quality demands people's energies, enthusiasm and intelligence. It means that everyone in the enterprise is involved in producing the best, as defined by the customer, and perhaps even better than that – the best that the customers will want when they know they can have it.

The implication of this is that the gospel according to Frederick Winslow Taylor is dead. No longer can managers do the thinking and the 'workers' just do as they are told. Everyone's ideas and observational powers are required. Gone are the days when most employees were met by a notice in invisible ink as they came to work which said:

Please park your brains at the gate.

QUALITY NEEDS TECHNIQUES

Of course techniques are required. In Chapter 9, I describe techniques that help the whole workforce to use their brainpower productively – statistical process control, cause and effect diagrams, problem solving, Pareto charts, histograms and so on. These are the tools of self-control and of self-management. These make visible the process of achieving quality; the operators themselves can then monitor progress. They do not have to depend on supervisors.

Increasingly the role of managers and supervisors is changing so that they become the coaches, counsellors and guides for teams of workers in the art of managing and developing themselves and in making the best use of available techniques. We shall see many examples of this new role of management, from a wide range of companies with whom I have had close contact as part of my work for the Ashridge Management Research Group and the Employment Department (UK).

DEFINITIONS

Definitions are always a problem. They usually spring from *your* perception, which of course is wrong, and *mine* which is right! Actually there is often no right and wrong. This was the point made by Humpty Dumpty in *Alice through the Looking Glass* where words meant what he chose: 'The question is which is to be the master – that's all.' As long as we define how we are using words everyone knows where they stand, then we can go ahead and communicate. This is the purpose of words anyway, unless you are a politician dodging a tricky question.

The word 'definition' has a fascinating origin which has a lesson for us when we use it. It comes from a Latin word meaning 'to finish'. You can see it in the *fini* in definition. The word therefore means 'to determine the boundaries of something', to say where something finishes. In the case of words this means to specify their limits, how far we can take them. This will be particularly relevant in the use of the word 'quality', where some gurus want to push the boundaries further than others. It is then not just a matter of words, but of the thinking behind their use.

(Readers will, I hope, bear with me and even share a little of my fascination with words, because they are the only tools we have to engage in this conversation – and I do want it to be a conversation, not a monologue, even though I have the advantage. Or perhaps I don't, because you can always stop reading.)

DEFINING QUALITY

Some of the definitions of quality are a bit uninspiring. BS4778 (1979) reads:

> *The totality of features and characteristics of a product or service that bear on its ability to satisfy a given need.*

This doesn't set many boundaries and leaves all kinds of unanswered questions. A given need. Given by whom, for whom? It is not what Dr Deming would call an operational definition, but at least it envisages people out there in the world with a need to be satisfied.

We are not working to satisfy our own need. Perhaps a product-led business tends to do this because it may still be in love with a product no one wants any more. Its abstract quality might be wonderful, but this is not what quality means in business terms. Gold taps are not quality when all the customer needs and wants are reliable brass ones. The definition does, therefore, have the benefit of directing our attention outside ourselves to the market-place which in the end defines quality.

FITNESS FOR USE

This is the definition offered by Joseph Juran, another of the quality gurus. It has the advantage of brevity and is therefore memorable. It can be used by anybody as an aid to thought. Is the item I am producing fit for use? Does it fit in with the customers' intention for its use? Will they find it works effectively, that they won't lose time and production while they wait for a replacement? Will it fit in with whatever else they are doing?

This last point is important. My heating engineer told me about a wonderful new boiler for a central heating system which was designed and produced by one company. It was economical and effective in hot water production. The only trouble was – it was too powerful for most existing systems. It was not fit for use.

The definers of 'fit' and 'use' are the customers, not the providers, though the latter by their marketing and selling efforts may have contributed to the definitions. 'Fitness', as in our example, means ability to fit into the total activity of the customer.

CONFORMANCE TO REQUIREMENTS

This is the favourite of the evangelist of quality, Philip Crosby. Its advantage is that it points outside ourselves to the customers and the market-place. Somebody requires something, whether goods or services. What they want is defined in their terms. They know what they want and are able to say what it is. That is made clear by the word 'conformance'; the customers have said what they require and the provider has to meet the specification. 'Which of you if your son ask for bread will give him a stone?' The biblical saying can extend to customers as well as sons.

The word 'conform' has the idea of taking the shape of something. In this case it is a question of fitting the mould in the customer's mind. The two main words in the Crosby definition are clear and unambiguous. Something either meets what is asked for or it does not. If you have stuck to the pattern provided by the customers, eliminated all defects, met all deadlines and ensured proper safe delivery, you have conformed.

However, disciples of Deming are less sure of the sufficiency of this definition. 'Requirements' is seen as a limiting word. It means that the provider may settle for just meeting the specification. However, this disregards the competitive nature of the market-place. Someone else may come up with something that is better suited to the underlying requirements of the customers.

The customers may not have the vision to imagine that

something better is a possibility, but when they see it, they will know that it is just what they have been searching for. You may lose future business if you don't pursue the path of improvement beyond customers' expressed wishes.

CONTINUOUS IMPROVEMENT

You have to be thinking all the time (and 'you' means everyone at every level in your organisation):

'There must be a better way to do this' or *'This would suit the customer better if . . .'.*

Continuous improvement is the key to gaining a competitive edge in today's market-place. The Japanese have a word for it – *kaizen*. It means continuously improving everything that everybody does, in every operation in every part of the organization at every minute of the day . . . and if you can think of any more 'everys' just drop them in. It is a word of much greater emphasis than the mere translation 'continuous improvement'.

It isn't only a matter of your ultimate customers. It is the whole chain of customers. If you are working in a plant and you have to provide the traditional widget as a component to the next bay in your work team, then they are your customer. Your widget must be fit for their purposes, so that they in turn can conform to the requirements of the next in line after them, and so on until the ultimate consumer is reached.

If as you work, however, you and your team see a way of reducing rejects or reworks by a little adjustment in methods or procedures, you make the change. Make sure, of course, that you need no one's authority, that you check with customers – the next in line and anyone else who is affected. You may also need to check with someone who is responsible for design or logistics. A major improvement may have to go back to the design board, although there are lot of little things that make a big difference which require no permission from anyone.

We shall later discuss the two different types of variation – one of which is systematic and needs managerial decision – the other being due to special, even one-off causes, which may be suitable for individual action.

The main point, though, is that everyone should be on the look-out for improvement – and improvement means going beyond the mere specification of your internal or external customers. If you can really improve the product or service, then maybe you will not merely satisfy your customers; you might even *delight* them.

DELIGHTING THE CUSTOMERS

John Macdonald and John Piggott in their book *Global Quality* have yet another definition, which encapsulates this aspect of delight.

> *Quality is delighting the customer by continuously meeting and improving upon agreed requirements.*

You may query how feasible this is. You can't let everyone go tampering with what the design department has come up with; you can't have declarations of unilateral independence amongst the work teams. Nevertheless we shall see how clear arrangements can be made to empower people to contribute to continuous improvement and to feel responsible for everything, so that in one sense everything is their job, or at least their concern.

Teamworking particularly helps this and creates the opportunity for multi-skilling, where all members of the team can undertake a variety of tasks and can stand in for one another. This broadens their horizons and enables them to apply their minds to a range of improvements. The team structure also encourages the sharing of ideas and the working out of how to implement the improvements.

ASSOCIATED QUALITY

Another factor in delighting the customer is the kind of quality action which accompanies the main task. Too often we have thought of quality in the purely manufacturing context. Now we extend it to services. Nonetheless there is a large service element in every offering made to customers, especially if we include the whole chain, our next in line internally as well as the external customer.

Cheerfulness in adversity and clear communication of what is needed or of potential difficulties or threats to the next in line, enhance ultimate quality indirectly, but are of themselves quality offerings to those we serve and support.

Then there are those parts of any organisation which are not directly involved in the manufacturing of the product or the provision of the service. Their opportunity to affect quality can be enormous. The invoicing section which bills a worthy customer for goods not required nor sent is guilty of eroding quality. Even worse if, as in an illustration given by Popplewell and Wildsmith in their novel about total quality called *Becoming the Best*, the error is compounded by putting them on the bad debt list and consequently losing a large and respected customer. These are breaches of quality, as are inaudible mumbles when answering the phone or indeed, long delays before answering.

EMPOWERED PEOPLE

Similarly, it is a quality action when an employee uses discretion to bend the normal rules a little to accommodate a long-standing customer's urgent needs. This is where the theme of empowering people is a significant one. Give people at the most junior level the knowledge, information and permission to use their common sense when the rule doesn't really meet the situation.

People should be able to give at least some information about something which is not strictly within their area. This can be done by encouraging employees to work in a broad context where they don't have only one narrow activity, but have a reasonable idea of where they fit in with what other people are doing. Thus BA baggage handlers can usually tell you something that will put you on the track of some other service you require, and are trained courteously to explain your rights and possible actions when your baggage has gone astray.

Another example which will be discussed later is that of Braintree District Council, which I visited during the Ashridge research. There we will meet a refuse collector who sees the job as providing a quality service, and who debates the merits and demerits of the British quality standard BS5750. Quality actions from the Refuse Department include a willingness to take the extra step even if one Monday you have some extra refuse, because you cleared out the attic. How it delights when the refuse collector says 'That's all right, mate', as he humps that awkward non-standard box into the waiting vehicle.

As Macdonald and Piggott put it:

> *The customer's perception of quality includes more than the satisfaction obtained from the primary product or service. Their view of the company that provides the basic need will include how the original enquiry was handled on the telephone, the method of timing of delivery, the clarity and helpfulness of the operating instructions and the timeliness and accuracy of the invoice. Clearly if we are to delight the customer, quality management must be extended to the administrative areas.*

OTHER DEFINITIONS

There are some other rather long-winded definitions of quality about. I give a couple here, not because you could ever remember them, but because in terms of logical thought they do cover a lot of ground.

Armand Feigenbaum defines quality as:

> *The total composite product and service characteristics of marketing, engineering, manufacture and maintenance through which the product and service in use will meet the expectations of the customer.*

There are several good thoughts here. The product or service is used and that is when its quality is tested. It is aimed to meet customers' expectations, but there is no thought here of going further to what he or she might be educated to expect, and therefore buy your product or service in preference to someone else's. There is some recognition that quality is a cross-functional, composite affair, but there is no reference to administration which can create the greatest customer dissatisfaction.

Another and rather general definition comes from John Groocock, who describes quality as:

> *The degree of conformance of all relevant features and characteristics of the product to all aspects of the customer's need, limited by the price and delivery he or she will accept.*

I suppose by referring to customer need rather than expectation the way is open for unexpected improvement which goes beyond what was thought possible.

A FAVOURITE DEFINITION

H.J. Harrington defines quality as:

> *Meeting or exceeding customers' expectation at a price that represents value to them.*

This gets the idea of going beyond what the customer knew they wanted.

In *Becoming the Best*, Popplewell and Wildsmith put a definition into the mouth of the hero of their novel – Neil Johnson, the company's chief executive. He encouraged a lot of debate to define quality at every level of the company. The definition arrived at was:

> *Quality is the degree of excellence by which we satisfy the needs of the customer.*

This led to a lot of employees saying they never saw a customer, which in turn led to discussion of the fact that everyone had a customer, the one served by the process – the next in line.

Furthermore, needs are impersonal; someone suggested making it more personal, so the definition finished up:

> *Quality is the degree of excellence by which we satisfy our customer.*

The 'our' of 'our customer' creates a personal link. I think I would like to retain the idea of delighting our customer. On balance, if I were awarding a prize for the best definition, it would go to Macdonald and Piggott for their:

> *Quality is delighting the customer by continuously meeting and improving upon agreed requirements.*

THE CUSTOMER CHAIN

I have referred to this concept several times and will look at it in chapter 6. It is a crucial part of the concept of quality. It forges a chain in which many links build quality into the process of delivering a product or service. This goes all the way from conception and design to arrival at final destination and subsequent use.

Rarely does one person produce and deliver a product or service. Everyone has a supplier and a customer. Everyone is part of the simple process of receiving an input and transforming it into an output, which then becomes someone else's input. The next person's job is made much more difficult if the transformation of input into output by the previous person has not resulted in faultless input from the perspective of the next in the line.

If, however, it does meet or exceed the agreed requirements, not only is there a chance that work will be a delight for the receiving customers, but also the whole chain, with its many handover points, makes quality a more attainable goal. It is not a question of a once-for-all inspection at the end or at key points in the process. The process is broken down into a number of steps, simple to identify and easy to carry out. Quality is created incrementally and not in one mammoth leap, and because there is a series of handover points at which any dissatisfaction can be expressed by the recipient, inspection as a separate activity is virtually superfluous.

THE DEPENDENCY OF MANAGERS

Everything, we have said in this chapter, depends on people. Quality is a people issue. It needs people who have intelligence and who are empowered to act for themselves without a lot of supervision. In one sense everyone is a manager now. Everyone is a white-collar worker even if blue overalls are worn.

Unfortunately, management, especially senior management, see themselves as responsible for everything that goes on, and in a sense they are. The buck stops with the chief executive or the chairman. Thus the managerial hierarchy think they can co-ordinate everything in such a way that the company will fulfil its objectives. They will issue instructions and if everyone does as they are told, fulfils all the laid down procedures, then mistakes will be minimal and the customer will receive what is required.

This approach cannot succeed. Management have to empower people to do their own checking and co-ordination. They have to share their responsibility. They still have the ultimate responsibility, but they fulfil it by ensuring that people are trained and developed to meet the challenges of their own enhanced responsibilities.

This makes life tolerable for the people at the top, who can then get on with their policy-making activities. It makes life more interesting for the people lower down in the old fashioned pecking order. It reduces the amount of middle level supervision required and enhances everyone's status in the one-time lower orders. All are colleagues with a sense of responsibility and the opportunity to undertake meaningful intelligent work. This is not a question of altruism or being nice to people. It is the only way to survive and progress. To do otherwise would be to waste the vast talent untapped in most organisations.

Management are no longer in control of the complexity of modern business and industry, if they ever were. They have to recognise that they cannot run the business on their own, especially when it comes to ensuring that quality prevails and that continuous improvement is being harnessed to gain competitive edge.

INTERDEPENDENCE

Every single person is vital to the success of the operation. Each has to take responsibility for their part and its relation to all the others. To get it all right we have to lean on each other. It is no longer a matter of workers leaning on managers. Everyone's ability, creativity and intelligence has to be harnessed.

It is a completely different way of working, a different way of organising the business and will involve a substantial re-education effort. People will need to be re-educated in their own jobs; they'll need to understand that they are not working in isolation; that each job is part of a whole process and they have to know how they and the next person fit into it.

No one quality director can be wholly responsible for quality, poring over reports and charts which obscure as much as they reveal. Safety checks, audits, corrective actions, data analyses, none of these track the real issues; often they try to lock the stable door after the horse has bolted. However, if you make everyone responsible for quality and for continuous improvement; fire them with enthusiasm and give the training and the tools to handle it, you will have a committed workforce, mobilised to delight their customers within the enterprise and in the world outside.

It's happening

Quality then is about people. Quality is about working together. Quality uses techniques and gets everyone using them. Quality conforms to requirements, establishes fitness for purpose and above all delights the customer. Quality is produced by empowered people and in turn empowers customers by giving them what they want, and ultimately something beyond their expectations.

All very well, but does anyone do it? Is it happening? Is it feasible? If it's not even feasible, it's not worth writing about. If some organisations are there already, then it is worth writing about to spread the message and get more to join the trail of success – success for customers, for suppliers and for employees. Even if they are only part way there it's worth writing about. Didn't there used to be a saying 'I'd sooner see a sermon than hear one any day'?

Over the last two years I have been privileged to visit some 70 organisations and to have close discussion with as many again to find out what they are doing to link their people development policies and actions with the fulfilment of their business objectives. This was done as part of a project awarded by the Employment Department in the UK to Ashridge Management Research Group (AMRG). One of the outputs of this project was a book *People Development and Improved Business Performance* (Wille 1990). Another was a second project, in support of the 'Investors in People' programme (see Appendix A). These visits showed me that total quality was being adopted in many organisations. Some of the stories are told in chapters 11 to 18.

2. Listening to the Gurus

All subjects have their gurus; Einstein, Jung, Freud, Galbraith, Keynes, Popper and so on. Management has Peter Drucker. Customer care has Tom Peters. Lateral thinking has Edward de Bono. Mind mapping has Tony Buzan. No budding MBA can get an 'A' for a strategy assignment without reference to Michael Porter, or one on leadership without mentioning Warren Bennis.

QUALITY GURUS

A guru was originally a mystical teacher, to whom people went to have their thinking and their lives transformed. The word then came to describe any thinker or teacher who introduced transforming ideas. Quality is as such a system of thought and has its share of gurus.

Three in particular stand out although there are others not far behind. The three are W. Edwards Deming, now in his nineties, Joseph M. Juran, not much younger, and a relative stripling, Philip Crosby, who has been in the quality business for something like 40 years. He survived a heart attack and revolutionised his health by taking a total quality approach to the management of his own life.

When I first met Deming on one of his visits to Ashridge Management College (where he has often led the studies of the British Deming Association) I was somewhat awed to realise that I was in the company of one of the 10 most influential personalities on the world stage since the Second World War. This must be so for he was the major influence in the transformation of the Japanese economy from junk shop of the East to standard bearer of quality and conqueror of Western markets.

Juran must also claim a major share in this revolution. And Crosby must take his place alongside these two for popularising the religion of quality in a way that was accessible to American and Western companies. There are also another half dozen quality experts whose contribution is reflected in the book.

W. EDWARDS DEMING

Deming is an expert in statistics and quality control, who worked in the American Census Bureau and in industry on the American war effort. He had gone to Japan after the war at the invitation of the Japanese Union of Scientists and Engineers (JUSE) to help rebuild the Japanese economy on a peacetime footing. He gave a series of lectures on quality control to engineers and on management's tasks and responsibilities to top managers. Within five years Japanese industry was outperforming the Americans and people all over the world were clamouring for Japanese goods.

The Japanese took notice. The Americans had let quality slide once the war-time need for reliability had subsided. Japan has come to dominate the market in many areas, from motorcycles to consumer electronics, from steel to cameras.

Deming started out on the path of statistical method in collaboration with Dr Walter Shewhart, whose name is perpetuated in the Shewhart Control Chart. As Deming's experience grew, he became convinced that the opportunity for progress lay not in techniques, though these are important, but in management. Wherever he went he found himself talking about management, which had lost sight of quality in the endless search for quantity and cost cutting.

Yet in fact, as Deming has pointed out repeatedly, quality reduces costs (see figure 5.1, p. 61). If you think about it, it ought to be obvious that to do or make something right first time saves all the expense of redoing.

Deming came to popular notice in America as a result of a TV programme in 1980: *If Japan can, why can't we?* Since then he has been giving over 30 four-day seminars a year to American managers, to say nothing of his frequent excursions overseas. He is a guru who could claim, though he is too modest to do so, that thousands of disciples sit at his feet each year.

At the time of writing he still visits Japan most years for the presentation of the Deming Prize, which is a most prestigious award. The message is gradually getting through all over the world, with the Japanese unworried, because they believe that when the West catches up with where they are now, they will be several more years ahead.

THE DEMING PHILOSOPHY

There is a distinct philosophic, almost spiritual, fervour about the Deming message. It is based upon a system of beliefs about people and aspirations for their well-being. The people are employees and everyone who may be called a customer. Happy people, delighted by what you have provided, become loyal customers. They will continue to demand what you supply and you will be on the pathway to profit and growth.

Cutting costs by reducing quality may improve the financial numbers in the short term. Profit is often seen as the difference between numbers – revenue and expenses. If the profit is down, things which don't contribute visibly to the numbers, like training, research and development and customer service, tend to be cut. But without continually improving what you offer your customers you will lose their loyalty and short-term number improvements will backfire. It does not fool customers. Rafael Aguayo calls managers who take this short-term approach VNO managers (Visible Numbers Only).

Similarly, employees are often rewarded on the basis of numbers without regard to the quality of what is being produced or the customer loyalty it is losing. Productivity induced in this way is counter-productivity.

We shall look at other aspects of the Deming philosophy as we proceed. It never departs from the original Deming principle that statistical analysis is essential to the identification of errors and their causes. Nevertheless his main message concerns management and people rather than particular techniques. He propounds a new way of looking at business life and indeed life in general. A popular formulation of Deming's perspective is set out in his *14 Points*, summarised below. They will keep on cropping up.

It is important to understand that the 14 points, which sometimes Deming calls obligations, are a way of thinking rather than writing on tablets of stone. From time to time Deming himself changes the phraseology to make them clearer. Henry Neave produced a good summary of them for the British Deming Association entitled *Deming's 14 Points for Management*. I am indebted to him for enabling me to make sure that I have 'got it right', and for permission to quote from this and his book, *The Deming Dimension*.

He writes of the *14 points*:

> They are not a straightforward, well-defined list of instructions; they are not techniques; they are not a checklist; they are vehicles for opening up the mind to new thinking; to the possibility that there are radically different ways of organising our business and working with people.

CONSTANCY OF PURPOSE

The first of the points stresses the need to keep at it. Continuous improvement of products and services cannot be switched on and off in the light of short-term needs. The striving for improvement must be consistent, inexorable and never ending; it affects everything in the company.

A NEW PHILOSOPHY

The second point describes quality as a whole new philosophy, involving a thorough and radical rethink which will not live with the commonly accepted levels of delays, mistakes, defective materials and defective workmanship. Deming says that this requires a total transformation of the western management style. Otherwise, industry will continue to decline. Continuous improvement of systems, processes and activities will not happen.

AWAY WITH MASS INSPECTION

The third point eliminates the need for mass inspection as a way to achieve quality. Quality has to be built into the product in the first place with statistical evidence available. At first people used to laugh at Deming, doubting whether workers could be relied upon to do their own inspection and to produce things properly in the first place. They have, however, been proved quite wrong.

RELIABILITY OF SUPPLIER

The fourth point ends the practice of awarding contracts to suppliers solely on the basis of price tag. Many companies go for the cheapest supplier. Deming would have us go for quality, without disregarding price. Often his fourth point is regarded as insisting on single sourcing – this is a matter of having one supplier with whom you build up a close relationship. Deming himself recognises that single sourcing may not always be possible and it may take time to reduce the suppliers sufficiently, but it is a distinct aim with advantages which far exceed possible disadvantages of being held to ransom by a single source. The very entertaining of such a thought shows that the quality of mind that Deming is teaching is not understood. The idea is to build a co-operative relationship with the supplier.

FOREVER IMPROVING

Deming's fifth point is never to be content with things as they are, never to give up seeking for better systems of operating, 'improve constantly and forever *every* process for planning, production and service'.

TRAIN AND TRAIN AND TRAIN

The sixth point is training. Training is absolutely fundamental to the Deming philosophy because new skills are required to keep up with the continual changes in materials and methods, design, machinery, techniques and service. Training is productive and not one of the things that should be cut when the financial situation is tight.

LEADERSHIP

The seventh point concerns leadership: leaders are there to help people to do a better job. They are responsible for putting the system right where necessary (and Deming believes that as many as 90 per cent of problems are system ones). The better the systems become, the more chance the workers have of doing a good job. Deming has no patience with the idea of browbeating people to do a proper job when, in fact, the system in which they are working is ill-equipped and ill-designed. To be forced by the system to do a poor job is demotivating indeed.

DRIVE OUT FEAR

The eighth point is succinctly stated as 'drive out fear'. This is a matter of getting away from the 'us and them' approach of confrontation between superiors and others. In fact the language of superiority is not used by Deming and his followers. Resentful compliance will not achieve good work. There have to be joint working relationships rather than management by blame. Quality will not be achieved where people come to work of necessity, but hate every moment of it.

PULL DOWN BARRIERS

The ninth point gets rid of barriers between departments and staff. A company is a system. In fact, the supplier company and customer are parts of the system. Any part of the system which fails will diminish the whole. Thus the people who handle the invoices, the researchers, the designers, the sales desk and the production people are one team as well as part of their own specific teams. Traditionally people have tended to work in their own little fortresses, often fighting their fellow employees instead of the competition. As Neave says it is important to use elementary statistical tools at all levels to provide a common language and mutual understanding.

ELIMINATE SLOGANISING

The tenth point proposes the elimination of slogans, posters or other exhortations to the workforce to do better. In this he is taking a different approach to Philip Crosby who runs zero-defect days and does go in for sloganising. Deming says that these kinds of exhortations create adversarial relations, and just to put up a poster saying 'Do it right first time,' or, 'Increase input by a certain percentage,' can be counter-productive, particularly where the process is set up wrongly. People can only do a good job if they are part of the chain which gives them good materials to start with and a system which works.

GET RID OF QUOTAS

Deming's eleventh point opposes quotas where numbers are often chosen quite arbitrarily as targets. Again it is much better to use statistical methods for continual improvement of quality and productivity which the workers and their team leaders can handle for themselves. Deming is against all measuring methods that pay bonuses when certain quotas have been reached. If the target is too high, you are giving the workers something very difficult to achieve, and it will only be achieved by corner cutting, lowering standards and ignoring the quality requirements. On the other hand, if the targets are soft and easily reached, then people may hang about doing nothing because they have reached their target and fear it will be raised. Better for everybody to work to the limit of their capacity with emphasis on quality.

This elimination of arbitrary numerical targets, quotas and bonuses is one of the most controversial of Deming's points. There are a lot of pressures for what is called 'performance management based on financial incentives'. This is called into question by the Deming approach.

PRIDE OF WORKMANSHIP

The twelfth point wants all workers to have pride of workmanship in their jobs. This means getting rid of annual merit ratings, or performance appraisal, and of management by objectives and a move from sheer numbers to quality. When Deming says no appraisal of performance, he does not mean that leaders and workers should not frequently get together to discuss the personal development of their skills, he means that traditional payment by rating is not conducive to quality. In fact he goes right back to schooldays when marks and competitive ratings were of the essence and meant that only a minority left school with their heads held high, feeling proud of their performance. Most people were marked as second-raters. The barriers to good workmanship also include poor tools, unreasonable targets, bad material and unsatisfactory systems.

SELF-IMPROVEMENT

The thirteenth point makes an appeal for a vigorous programme of education and for the encouragement of everybody in self-improvement. Deming makes the point that it's not enough just to have good people, but people who are improving, and this means education. He uses the word education rather than training as more fundamental. Education to Deming means personal improvement, personal development.

TRANSFORMATION IS EVERYBODY'S JOB

The fourteenth of Deming's points originally read in a 1985 version:

> *Clearly define top management's permanent commitment to quality and productivity and its obligation to implement all of these principles.*

In keeping with what I've said above, that the points are not written on tablets of stone, in 1986, Deming offered a significant rewording:

Put everybody in the company to work to accomplish the transformation. The transformation is everybody's job.

This change is characteristic of the way in which Deming listens to the discussions he sparks off at his seminars. The new rewording to involve everybody does not deny that top management's commitment is vital to continuous improvement of quality and productivity. Deming still believes that top management must take initiatives which go beyond pious aspiration. They must set up the system and the structure which will provide the framework for what, in his later version, Deming calls transformation. The emphasis is now on everybody having responsibility for improvement within their own areas, and in the context of the whole organisation.

DEADLY DISEASES

Deming has also produced a list of 'deadly diseases' of Western management, among which he includes emphasis on short-term profits and short-term thinking, and management by use only of visible figures with no recognition that unknown or unknowable ones may be important.

Deming is often thought of as essentially a statistician. He does start by discussing variability in results, but this leads into a whole management philosophy. (See chapter 3.)

JOSEPH JURAN

Joseph Juran is another nonagenerian, very active and much appreciated in Japan, and now in the United States. Juran's writings are very thorough, though some find them tedious. Nevertheless his 1954 visit to Japan made a significant contribution to what Deming had stated.

I first came across him when I bought a few hundred random second-hand books for £100. Among them was Joseph Juran's book *Managerial Breakthrough*, which defined the work of all managers as follows:

- To break through into new levels of performance, creating change, followed by holding the resulting gains.
- To control (prevent the wrong kind of change).

This philosophy of management echoes many of the points which we have already seen with Deming.

The two gurus, Deming and Juran, do not seem to me to be drastically different in their viewpoints. In *Out of the Crisis*, Deming refers several times approvingly to the work of Juran. In *Juran on Leadership for Quality* , there is only one reference to Deming. They have both contributed much; this book is more interested in their contributions than their supposed rivalry.

MANAGERIAL BREAKTHROUGH

In his book, *Managerial Breakthrough*, Dr Juran defines control as the prevention of unfavourable change, which implies an accepted standard or norm. However, he says:

> It can be a cruel hoax, a built-in procedure for avoiding progress. We could become so preoccupied with meeting targets that we fail to challenge the target itself.

Challenging the target is what he means by breakthrough. It means potentially favourable change:

> A dynamic decisive movement to new, higher levels of performance.

He makes the distinction between 'improvement through better control by making sure standards are adhered to' and 'improvement through breakthrough where a whole system is changed'. This is very close to Deming's criticism of managers who blame workers for inadequate performance when actually it is the system itself which requires improvement. Breakthrough is the creation of good changes, whereas control is the prevention of bad changes. All managerial activity is directed at either breakthrough or control.

Juran uses the human biological organism as an analogy. The body devotes much energy to preventing change, with body temperature as a case in point. But the body also devotes energy to creating change, by exercise and general improvement.

Deming describes occasional and unpredictable deviation in processes as *special causes* of variation and predictable and relatively stable deviation as *common causes* of variation. Juran uses the terms *sporadic* for the former and *chronic* for the latter. It is the responsibility of management to address the chronic and not to blame the workforce for them. It is indeed helpful to recognise that these two giants in the field of quality arrived at similar conclusions via their own routes, both of which started off with a statistical approach. Juran also stresses that breakthrough activity tends to be long term, where control is short term and immediate.

COMPARING JURAN AND DEMING

Juran is the editor of *Juran's Quality Handbook*, which is periodically revised. It is easier to describe it by weight than by number of pages, though these run well in excess of a thousand. Juran has been highlighting managerial responsibility for quality since the 1940s with emphasis on the fact that although techniques are useful, it's people who produce quality. He was probably the first of the gurus to emphasise that quality was achieved by communication, management and people. Like Deming, he emphasises that massive training is essential and has to involve the whole workforce, that senior management have to be committed, and that improvement has to be continual.

Juran is clear that the 'pursuing of departmental goals can sometimes undermine a company's overall quality mission.' Like Deming, Juran believes it is more important to concentrate on the flow of the process and make sure you get it right rather than specific targets and management objectives.

He too is against campaigns to motivate the workforce to solve the company's quality problems by doing perfect work. Such slogans don't set achieveable goals or provide plans to meet them and resources to carry them out. Many believe that Juran was the first to bring a whole number of unconnected approaches into an integrated philosophy.

Juran has a systemic approach to company-wide quality management. It begins with quality policies and goals. It goes on with plans to meet them. Then it provides resources which enable progress to be evaluated and action taken. Finally it motivates and stimulates people to believe in, meet the goal, and improve on it. This is summed up in the Juran trilogy: quality planning, quality control and quality improvement.

Juran sees danger in single sourcing for key purchases. He believes that having several sources keeps the suppliers on their toes. He is, however, in agreement with the idea of maintaining a close relationship with the suppliers.

He does not believe that 'quality is free' or that there is a point where conformance to requirements may be more expensive than what is gained from adhering to these standards.

JURAN'S TEN STEPS

As Deming has his 14 points, so Juran has his ten steps:

1. Build awareness of the need and opportunity for improvement.
2. Set goals for it.
3. Set up an organisation to reach those goals with a quality council in the lead.
4. Training.
5. Problem solving projects.
6. Report progress.
7. Recognise people who produce good quality work.
8. Ensure that everybody is informed about the results.
9. Keep a score of it all.
10. Maintain momentum by making annual improvement part of the company's regular processes.

THE CROSBY APPROACH

Philip Crosby is an evangelist and a populariser who goes in for quite a bit of razzamatazz in arousing interest in quality. He is a frequent broadcaster and a very persuasive speaker. Even though his original contributions are not as great as those of Deming and Juran, he is probably the man who has brought total quality to more companies than anyone else.

In principle most of his message harmonises with the other two gurus, but his approach is less rigorous. He does seem to give the impression that exhorting workers to turn out a perfect product is meaningful, even though most of the problems are systemic rather than operator-created.

Crosby does teach continuous improvement. His aim is to secure zero defects which is sometimes thought impractical. However by zero defects he means defects as perceived by the customer. Deming and Juran would criticise this by saying that it tends to rule out the possibility of going beyond what the customers know they want. In a sense 'zero defects' is not good enough.

Crosby goes in for the celebration of zero-defect days on which the workforce sign a pledge to aim for work which has no defects. Deming and Juran would query the value of that kind of thing.

Crosby's definition of quality is 'conforming to requirements', which again suffers from the criticism that you can conform to requirements without a ceaseless search for improvement.

It has to be said that Crosby has a lot of experience in working on quality in-company. He founded Philip Crosby Associates (PCA), a world-wide company which runs quality colleges. He has sold the company but still operates as a consultant.

THE FOUR ABSOLUTES

Like the other gurus, Crosby has his steps and points. He has four absolutes of quality which are at the root of all his, and PCA's, courses.

- Have a definition of quality, understood by everybody, as part of a common language facilitating communication: 'Quality has to be defined as conformance to requirements, not as goodness.'

- Have a system by which to manage quality and a performance standard which is unambiguous: 'The system for causing quality is prevention, not appraisal.'

- 'The performance standard must be zero defects, not "That's close enough".' In other words, we mustn't plan errors into our operation like the company that one year said it was 'going to halve fatal accidents'.

- 'The measurement of quality is the price of nonconformance to requirements.' That is, all the expenses of doing things wrong from the customer's perspective. (There is also the price of conformance – what is necessary to make things come out right, essential inspection, education and prevention. But these are part of doing a good job anyway.)

Whether you agree with Crosby in detail or not, he has succeeded in creating popular awareness of quality on a grand scale.

CROSBY'S 14 STEPS

His 14 steps, summarised below, emphasise:

1. Commitment from management.
2. A quality improvement team to run improvement programmes (though it's still part of everyone's job).
3. Quality measurement displayed so that everybody can evaluate what is happening and do what is necessary.
4. A definition of the cost of quality used as a management tool.
5. The provision of a method of raising quality awareness so that everyone has an operational definition of conformance to requirements.

6. A systematic method of resolving problems that have been identified in the earlier steps.
7. Launching a zero-defects programme.
8. Training supervisors to lead the quality improvement programme.
9. Having a zero-defects day to help all employees realise that things are changing.
10. Goal setting to turn the pledges that employees are encouraged to make into specific improvement goals.
11. Setting up a means by which, when employees meet a situation they need to communicate to the manager, there is a channel for doing it. Without this, the pledge to improve things and go for zero defects becomes meaningless.
12. Showing appreciation of those who participate.
13. Setting up quality councils.
14. 'Do it over again.' This is to emphasise that quality improvement programmes never end.

The 14 steps are intended as guidelines, but a lot of people who follow Crosby tend to treat them, as indeed Deming's 14 points and Juran's ten, as if they were gospels. In the strict sense of the word 'gospel' meaning good news, they probably are, but they are not absolute laws without the following of which quality cannot happen. Particularly in the case of Crosby, some companies exclude the zero-defects day and some of the stirring up of excitement that Crosby tends to go in for.

Crosby emphasises the ongoing management of quality, but his 14 points don't have the same amount of emphasis on the principles of breakthrough and control or handling variation with statistical process control that we get from Juran and Deming.

Crosby's books make a good read because to a large extent they are novels with live characters grappling with quality in companies. His book *Quality Without Tears; the art of hassle-free management* has a good deal of straightforward guidance, again taking you through his 14 steps.

QUALITY: ACHIEVING EXCELLENCE

SUMMING UP THE GURUS

All three of these gurus are really talking about management. That is what quality is about. The purpose of a business is to create and keep a customer. There is only one way to do this, by giving the customers what they want, and that is a definition of quality. Running a business, therefore, is all about quality. In one way there is no other topic.

3. The Principle of Variation

In the past, and maybe still in many companies, it has been the custom for supervisors to nag the operators for greater speed, higher productivity, less defective work and reduced wastage. The attitude is that if only the workers would try harder, do their best, be careful, concentrate on the job in hand, then output would increase in quality and in quantity.

This chapter explores the view expressed by Deming, Juran and others that this attitude, which makes going to work such a miserable business for many, stems from a misunderstanding of what causes variations in output. A clearer grasp of the fact that there are two sources of variation in outputs would show the folly of blaming people for what they cannot control.

Variations through special or sporadic causes can often be put right by operators. Once these stabilise, however, improvement is possible only by tackling the system, and that is the ultimate responsibility of management. The systemic variations may represent ongoing problems which need addressing, or they may be opportunities to seek ever higher standards of excellence, even though there is no current problem.

Is poor quality the operator's fault?

The reason for poor quality is often not the unwillingness of workers, but the system under which the work is carried out. Incoming material may be defective and operators are trying 'to make a silk purse out of a sow's ear'. Perhaps maintenance is rushed because the quota system means there isn't time to stop production to do it properly.

Such circumstances are outside the control of the operator, who may none the less be bullied because of the poor quality output. The issues are systemic and are the responsibility of management to put right, with help from the operator who may well know best what needs doing.

Rafael Aguayo lists some of these things which affect quality, yet are quite outside operator control. He includes the layout of the plant, the room temperature and the amount invested in research, development and training.

> They don't buy the equipment, tools, and raw materials or determine the design of the product. They don't develop the reward system or the organisational structure. In short they don't determine 90 per cent of the things responsible for the quality of the product.

He goes on to challenge management for holding the workers responsible for all the defects. Only management can provide the framework in which the operators can do a quality job and take pride in it. They will then contribute to the continuous improvement process with a stream of suggestions on how things might be further improved.

There will be some things the operator can do something about. Given the right training, employees can respond to and reduce the number of mistakes which are due to their own carelessness; they can make sure they are working when they should be, that they don't hold things up by being late and that they don't try to make the equipment do what it is not designed to do.

Nevertheless, both Deming and Juran believe that most of the variations in the processing of work are due to the system, which management should address. A small proportion are due to the errors of the operators. Yet it is they who are so often blamed; exhorted to do better and bombarded with slogans.

SPECIAL CAUSES OF VARIATION

Writers on quality categorise the causes of *variation* of goods or services in two main classes:

- Those which the worker is able to deal with.
- Those which require management action.

Deming describes *special causes* of variation as unpredictable or unusual circumstances in a process, which may be due to individual or group mistakes or some exceptional failure of material or equipment. Often the operators can do something about these special causes. Juran describes them as *sporadic*. On process control charts they show up as major high or low points thus displaying a state of unpredictability. (See chapter 9 for examples.) Get rid of the cause and the process settles down to a steady range of predictable variations within the limits of what the system allows it to achieve. *This is described as being in statistical control.*

COMMON CAUSES OF VARIATION

The variations which remain once the results are stable in this way cannot be improved by intervening. Such variations are inherent in the system and to reduce them requires that something be done to improve the process, with action to enable the operators to work within it.

This second category of variations is described by Deming as *common causes* and by Juran as *chronic waste*. The special causes may be dealt with by 'firefighting' activity; but common causes or chronic waste have to be dealt with fundamentally. No amount of bullying or exhortation will change these variations. Try as they might the workers cannot change the shape of the graph. The predictable ups and downs will still occur.

This stable condition still needs comparing with customer specifications. It may or may not be within them, but with special causes out of the way, the continuing 'stable' variations can be addressed. Something can be done to change the system, either to get it into conformity with customer requirements or to improve beyond these. As Juran puts it, chronic waste is an opportunity for improvement. You can improve the supply arrangements, the maintenance arrangements, the complaints procedures, the customer care awareness and so on. A new process is established which will get nearer to the elusive goal of perfection.

Once the system is in statistical control, its predictability enables one to work, for example, to get the control limits closer together and therefore enhance the ability to meet or exceed customer requirements. In some cases the control limits have been brought so close that they have represented a level six times better than that the customer would accept. This means that variations outside the new limits on the chart may still be within the customer's requirements and the scope for maintaining quality is high. The whole system has been tightened and if this is continued in a methodical way continuous improvement will be the result. It is important however to avoid tampering, where although the process is in control, common causes of variation are mistaken for special causes, leading to haphazard chases after every individual variation in sight.

This systemic change has to be tackled by management. It will tend to be more long-term than dealing with the unpredictable special causes. Management should harness the knowledge and experience of the operators who can provide it, based upon their closeness to the job. Usually, however, it is only management who can change the processes in a way which will enable the workers to produce less variable output.

ANALOGY FROM THE SWIMMING POOL

Recently I was doing my mile swim in the Ashridge pool, which I use as a think tank as well as a health centre. It occurred to me that what I was doing provided an analogy to the theme of variations.

I am a slow swimmer, but a persistent one and am quite proud of my mile, as I'm in the second half of my sixties. Yet it does irk a little when I see the younger people and some of those in their fifties swimming two or even three lengths to my one. I therefore went in for some self exhortation. I ordered myself, just as do supervisors on the shop floor, to try harder, to put more effort into it.

I was not swimming correctly. I was not using the techniques I had learned years ago at school. My hands were not correctly parting the water; my legs were not coming properly together, nor were they co-ordinating with my arms. So I gave myself training and eradicated these common causes; I modified my system. After a week or two, instead of doing five lengths in five minutes I was doing seven. After that my rate settled down and I have been unable to improve it at all. Mere effort produces the odd spurt, but over the mile or even half mile there is no real change.

My improvement at first had been a matter of tackling common causes by changing my co-ordination system. There were no special causes at work, such as going in to swim with a hangover or trying fancy strokes. Such special causes could have been dealt with by desisting from such conduct.

So my swimming rate is in statistical control or stable state. The rate will not go up a second time unless I again change my swimming system, the relationship between my body and the water. I will probably need some proper lessons, so that I no longer swim only the breast stroke and with my head sticking up out of the water. I can improve my rate only by adopting a new system, swimming with my head under the water much of the time and using a variety of strokes. Sporadic effort will not do it. The problem is chronic and therefore needs a total revision of methods and procedures.

When I have achieved the second of these system changes, I will again become dissatisfied and will need to change the system by further enlargement of my stroke repertoire. There is a long way to go before there is no further room for improvement.

This constant setting up of systems, enabling people to work within new limits and achieve stability within them is the main meaning behind the term 'continuous improvement', so often used in quality discussions.

ANALOGY FROM A SLIMMING DIET

Just to reinforce the idea of variations and how to handle them, another idea came to me on the same swim. The pool really was a think tank that day.

When first working at Ashridge, I found the meals provided for those working on programmes, tutors and nominees, delicious and tempting. My girth began to show the results. The bathroom scales groaned under the added weight. My eating system might have been in statistical control, but the limits were unacceptable. Two friends separately and in the same week spoke of the benefits they had gained by a vegetarian diet. Always ready to try anything, I thought I would give it a go. I found that I enjoyed my food as much as ever, but with a lower fat and calorie intake my weight dropped. Day after day the pounds disappeared. This was a system change, but quite soon the fall in weight ceased.

Each day, give or take a pound or two, the scales told the same story. I was in statistical control or in stable state once more, albeit within a more satisfactory system with more acceptable limits. If I don't change my regime further, I shall remain between 173 and 175 pounds.

Now that may be all right, but I would still like to lose another six pounds. So what system am I going to use? Well I remember for some ten years keeping my weight under control with the aid of the Royal Canadian Air Force exercises; so if I resume these, perhaps I will be able to get my weight within new limits and achieve a new and better level of statistical control, which will conform more closely with my requirements.

THE FOLLY OF NAGGING

Of course these analogies are not perfect, but may help understanding. The reader will readily think of others. Take for example the audio typist who has to achieve a required speed in spite of the variation in clarity of the person dictating. It is absolutely useless for a supervisor to rebuke a typist for low output when he or she is being required to wrestle with the vagaries of a system which does not train dictators to enunciate clearly and indicate punctuation and new paragraphs, as well as spelling out obscure proper names.

This is the 'common cause' of the typist's variations. If it had happened only sporadically, when the dictator was in a great hurry, for instance, it would have been a special cause, easy to identify and put right, but this permanent variation from acceptable limits will require a new system, involving the retraining of the dictator.

The outcome of nagging, of insisting on higher output in spite of the regularly variable quality of the dictating, can only send quality of output into deeper decline. The typist will not even try to cope with the poor dictation. He or she will just do the best they can. It will go back to the dictator, who will complain about the high error rate, but he or she has set up the system of indistinct input and can expect nothing better until a new approach to dictating is learned.

TWO-MINUTE CUSTOMER CARE

Nagging, bullying or hustling will always result in a decline in quality. Viki Holton, of Ashridge, told me the story of the way in which a customer care department set up a system for dealing with customer queries. Every complaints clerk in a certain company was given two minutes in which to deal with a query. It was held that this was long enough to extract the precise nature of the problem, answer it if it was simple and straightforward, pass it on to an expert if this was not feasible or promise that someone would get back to the complainant within a fixed period. The time of each enquiry was automatically logged and the printouts regularly scrutinised.

What happened when a customer wanted to let off a little steam? didn't get to the point very quickly or in any way took up more than the two minutes allowed to the clerk? The customer would have to be interrupted, hustled to get to the point, and not given the understanding ear which helps to create customer loyalty.

Some clerks were even known to say: 'I'm sorry sir, but I am allowed only two minutes on each enquiry. So may I take your name and address and get someone to call you back.' Such frankness hardly did much for quality customer care. The other ruse was to transfer the customer to the first name that came to mind as the dreaded two minutes approached. This led to the customer being passed round the organisation with ever increasing frustration and a waste of everyone's time.

I suppose this two minute rule and the recording of it would be called quality control by some. But it broke every rule of quality. It was concerned only with one facet – time. It was not concerned with whether, in Crosby terms, it conformed to customer requirements; whether, in Juran terms, it was fit for use. And it certainly did not delight the customer.

Clearly when they exceeded two minutes a call the clerks were the victims of a poor system. If the extent to which they exceeded it was averaged out, it would be found that there was a consistency about the level of variation. It was in statistical control, but not achieving the levels which had been arbitrarily set by the system. The system needed changing, rather than the clerks needing discipline.

DEMING'S SOLUTION FOR THE HUSTLED TELE-PHONIST

Deming gives a way to change the system in a very similar situation. After I had written about the two minute story above, I found a story in Deming's *Out of the Crisis* of a woman in his class at New York University Business School who had worked for an airline as telephone reservation and information representative. She had to cover 25 calls an hour.

She was instructed to be courteous and not rush customers who called. Failure to achieve her quota or to be courteous would be failure; but could she justly be held accountable for it? A statistical control chart would show a persistent and consistent pattern of variation. Nothing she could do would alter it. Either she departed from standards of courtesy or she failed to meet her time budget. The system set her up to fail. That was management's fault. They alone could have changed her terms of reference and the support arrangements she needed.

No provision was made in the 25 calls an hour rule for the

regular inability of the computer system to deliver information with sufficient speed or of the frequent need to consult directories manually. This was on straightforward enquiries, not the more complex ones, which from the start obviously needed to be referred elsewhere.

Deming offers some suggestions for improving the system itself. This would use the computer to monitor all the calls the telephonist undertook, including the delays through information not being immediately available. Presumably this would have to include time taken to placate a particularly irate customer.

Then Deming would have the supervisor plot the clerks' activity on a control chart. It would probably be found that there was a stable pattern of time taken, where the variations were predictable and where nothing the operators did could really alter things. Management would then get down to dealing with the system, defining when a call was to be referred to a specialist and developing procedures which would ensure that customer satisfaction was the prime criterion of success, yet also having regard to the need to minimise costs.

The plotting of information would also reveal where special or individual causes were responsible for variations, such as frequent spikes on the chart well outside the generally stable system, or someone whose individual chart was not in statistical control. These would indicate the the operator was in need of some special help or training or in extreme cases not suitable for this kind of work. Experience shows, however, that this is a minority of cases and that the system is the key cause of variations.

VARIATION A KEY MANAGEMENT ISSUE

The title of this chapter may have created an expectation of a study of statistical process control. 'Variations' in a heading doesn't look as if it is going to get to the heart of management practice. Yet in fact it has already had us traversing a wide range of examples of how to transform the working of a company.

I was puzzled when I first heard that the key to the Deming philosophy was 'variation'. But if you think about it you can say that this is all that management is about. It is about reducing unwanted change and ensuring beneficial change. This goes well beyond variations on a statistical control chart, proper use of which, however, will help the change processes in the wider sense.

Managers have to enable those they lead, producers of goods and providers of services, to maintain the standards which the customer depends on. Simultaneously they have to create systems which will enable improvements to be made to meet needs which the customer may not yet be aware of.

Reducing unwanted change is reflected in attention given to getting rid of special causes shown up on statistical control charts. When we have done that and our activity is in statistical control or stable state we still have to be sure that our new limits enable the employees to conform to customer requirements. We then go beyond this to deal with consistent and predictable variations which do not disturb the customer but signal an opportunity for improvement. This is the philosophy of *kaizen* or continuous improvement. (See chapter 1.)

If we recognise that change is essential to business success, then we should not be surprised that an apparently boring subject like variation is also central to competitive advantage.

LEADERSHIP NOT SUPERVISION

This is the substance of the seventh of Deming's 14 points. It links with the twin division of variations. The principal job of managers is *not* control, making sure that workers do what they have been empowered to do. That is up to the workers themselves, especially with help from their fellow team members. In the main the operators inspect their own work and deal with many of the special causes of variation, though some will require managerial attention.

A major role of management lies in the area of common causes of variation. These provide opportunities for improvement to the systems within which everyone else works.

As illustrated in the previous chapter, Juran saw the main task of management as breakthrough – 'change, a dynamic, decisive movement to new, higher levels of performance'.

Improvement can come through closer adherence to procedures. Juran gives an example of filling customer's orders within seven days. Factors such as blunders, shortcuts, gambles, failure to record correctly or forgetfulness may prolong the period to nine days. These are special causes which can be put right by getting back to the procedures.

But if someone comes up with a new approach based on a new concept or new machinery or procedures there may be a radical improvement down to under two days. This is changing the system; it is the area where quantum leaps are made, but even these build on the incremental steps taken at all levels within the enterprise.

These breakthrough activities should be at the top of managerial priority lists. While management are nagging the operators or getting involved in apportioning blame, they are not paying attention to the areas where they make their real contribution. While they are inducing fear in the operators, they are not harnessing their talents to help in the significant breakthroughs.

QUALITY A HOLISTIC ISSUE

The theme of variation and failure to distinguish between those variations which are within the control of the operator and those which require management attention is a good illustration of the way in which quality issues lie at the root of many company problems and opportunities.

When variation is not understood, statistical information is misinterpreted. This results in a bad effect on people's morale, a misdirection of corrective effort and a misapplication of managerial contribution.

Thus a chapter which aimed at dealing with the statistical issue of variation in achieving quality standards has found itself involved in the whole range of issues by which a company succeeds or fails, nearly all of which concern how you treat people. Give people a sound system and appropriate training and generally they will deliver the goods or services at a quality which meets or exceeds the customer's expectations.

4. Everybody on Board

As we have seen, whatever you talk about when dealing with quality it will always come back to people. In the previous chapter an unpromising subject like statistical variation led us back to people. The majority of the errors and defects stem from the system, yet it's often the operators who get blamed. Only management, however, can change the system. The workforce can point out what needs doing and how, but they haven't the authority to change work flow, supplier arrangements, maintenance schedules, procedures and rules.

This chapter maintains that one of the keys to quality is to empower and encourage people to give input from their knowledge and experience. It is they who actually do the job and know all the idiosyncrasies of the system. They know the weaknesses of machines, the phone responses of customers; it is they who have to wrestle with cryptic instructions or complex computer forms. They are the people to consult if you really want to do a good quality job.

THE LEGACY OF TAYLOR

Instead, companies all over the world are still living in the shadow of Frederick Winslow Taylor. About a hundred years ago he saw the poverty of the workers and the back-breaking effort which had to go into getting such a poor return. He also saw that it meant a poor return to the owners. So he came up with 'scientific management', intending it to benefit both parties.

Jobs would be carefully analysed and broken down into the

minutest of their component parts. A worker would then concentrate on one particular function which became quicker and easier to perform. Taylor genuinely cared about the workers. They would have an easier life and earn more money, while the bosses would have higher productivity.

But there was a price to pay. Workers were not supposed to think about their work. Thinking workers were not time-efficient. Let specialists, called managers and engineers, do the thinking. Let the workers park their brains at the factory gate. This was efficiency.

Initially the workers and management were pleased, but in due course soul-destroying repetition took over from the pride of workmanship, which even the least skilled jobs had required in former days. Interest and sense of responsibility waned and the workers became cyphers with no real interest in their jobs.

Bosses manipulated the numbers quite frequently, when they saw wages rise as workers became more skilled and efficient. The rates would change and so new pressures were introduced to encourage faster work for the same reward. Workers responded by developing norms well below their capacity (and woe betide any colleague who exceeded these). Malicious compliance grew as operators learned to beat the system, while appearing to apply it.

The well-meaning efforts of Taylor gave rise to many decades of confrontation and disharmony between the workforce and management. Mistrust and suspicion prevailed between the parties. 'Labour' had no incentive to feel any pride in the product or service or any sense of ownership in the job or organisation.

REVERSING TAYLORISM

Total quality management seeks to reverse all this, by restoring to people a sense of responsibility for what they do and giving them the opportunity to contribute to improving performance, whatever their level.

As Juran points out (1989), quality requires the participation of all employees. They need to become artisans again. Jobs need redesigning to make this possible. The Taylor system was, in Juran's view, based on the low level of education of the workforce:

The subsequent rise in educational levels has made that premise obsolete. It is now feasible to increase the delegation to the workforce, provided that the jobs are redesigned so as to make it possible for the workforce to accept the delegation.

He comments that under the Taylor system the 'experience and creativity of the workforce were major unemployed assets of the companies'.

PRIDE OF WORKMANSHIP

A number of Deming's 14 points (discussed in chapter 2) are in the same vein.

Number twelve for example:

Remove barriers that rob the hourly worker of his right to pride of workmanship.

Pride of workmanship means that when variations are of the common cause type and the system needs to be changed by management, the operators are part of the process of change. They are the true experts, whose opinion is recognised as worthwhile and whose insights are based on close observation. They have learned over many years 'through the job' and in partnership with the specialists they can form an unassailable team.

Pride of workmanship means accountability and responsibility in a real sense; operators should be held accountable, when they have the tools, the scope and the authority without which accountablility is a mockery. Blaming people for variations which are outside their control completely fails to understand accountability. The avoidance of this is one of the reasons why understanding variations is of such significance to the managing of a business.

The recognition of every worker as part of the decision-making team is fundamental to total quality. An asset long neglected, the worker is now seen as essential to competitive advantage. Where this is so the workforce are empowered, self-managing and given tools for thought and action. They know they can make a difference. They are expected to contribute to innovation and improvement; making suggestions is part of their job.

THIS IS THE REAL WORLD

No doubt some managers will feel cynical about this perspective. When I have discussed it with some of the old school I have been told to get my feet on the ground and that 'in the real world' it is just not like that.

'In the real world' is one of those killer phrases used to stultify rational debate. It is all too easy to be driven into a corner by them, because they are uttered with such confidence. That is why I am glad I was able to visit so many companies and see the success of these more enlightened attitudes.

In fact Martin Wibberley of Bosch in Cardiff has banned the words 'unskilled' and 'semi skilled' from the company vocabulary as an affront to the intelligence of the workforce. (See chapter 18.)

This attitude can and does work, but it means a change in managerial thinking, a new respect for all employees as colleagues and a flight from the 'us and them' mentality. It means this on both sides; when management begin to change, the operators must try to submerge their understandable mistrust, and the managers must prove themselves worthy of trust.

This isn't soft talk, nor is getting people to work together a soft skill. It all relates to hard necessity, often to company survival. But it can happen and is happening 'in the real world'.

SINGLE STATUS

This jibe about the need to live in the real world was doubtless frequent in the days when single status or common conditions of service were first discussed. The other word used – 'harmonisation' – is particularly expressive, fitting into the wider aims of establishing a workforce who work in unity for common objectives.

Yet single status or harmonisation is a fact of life in many companies now. The absence of special parking places for top management may seem a nuisance to a busy chief executive arriving at noon after external meetings all morning; but is it any less of a nuisance to the worker who comes in at shift change time and has to park far away? Both can use the walking time for the improvement of their health and a bit of thinking!

In the single status companies I visited I found no irritation on the part of senior management. Eating in the same place as everyone else has provided opportunity for gaining a sense of greater involvement with the workforce. Bosses are seen as ordinary people after all. The distance between levels of staff is bridged, and cohesion encouraged.

Companies I visited often had identical pension and private insurance schemes for all staff. In one large company the managers all transferred into a less prestigious scheme so that everyone could have the same terms. The company driver, no longer regarded as just the MD's chauffeur, told me of this with great pleasure.

This single status approach has no direct bearing on quality, but it is a quality approach in its own right. It contributes to the ethos of an organisation where pride in workmanship and ownership of results prevail.

SELF-INSPECTION

The reversal of Taylorism by total quality approaches is seen where the workforce inspect quality as part of their job rather than have products or services inspected externally at a later stage. In the case of service industries the latter is all too often after customers have experienced poor quality treatment.

Deming's third point is to cease to be dependent on mass inspection to achieve quality. Quality should be built into the product or service in the first instance. This is a people issue, as we shall see in chapter 12 when we look at the work of the teams in Rothmans where every worker is involved in recording delays and their causes subsequent study.

At Stanbridge Precision Turned Parts everyone understands the statistical control charts on the visual display units. When what appears to be a special cause begins to emerge, eager discussion takes place on whether to stop immediately and put things right or wait and see if a little more time will produce self-correction. (See chapter 11.)

Similarly, workers at the Seaham Harbour Dock Company know when to call in their falconer to stop the contamination of stored products by seagulls. (See chapter 15).

DRIVE OUT FEAR

This is the eighth of Deming's 14 points. Crosby is on the same wavelength, stressing involvement of all work groups in corrective action and never-ending improvement which cannot happen in an atmosphere of fear. Juran also believes that the workforce must be fully informed on the purposes of all action. They must be involved in everything from quality planning to quality control to quality improvement (the 'Juran trilogy').

Deming has the air of an evangelist when he calls upon managers to 'drive out fear'. The man who started out as a statistician makes the most stirring calls to humanistic action, albeit for very practical business reasons.

In his classic *Out of the Crisis* he gives many quotations from people about their jobs in companies where total quality does not predominate. There are fears that the next annual rating may not provide a needed 'raise'; fears of being held guilty of treason if they dare to put forward an idea; fear to shut down production on a line for an essential overhaul, because the production figures would suffer. This last concern contrasts strikingly with those companies, many of them Japanese, which permit *any* worker to stop the line rather than go on turning out a defective product.

Then there is fear of not having an answer for the boss, when the reason for some difficulty is demanded; fear to admit a mistake; fear to ask the reasons for a decision; fear of not reaching the daily quota; fear of contributing to a team effort, because someone else may get the credit and the rating; fear of reporting a problem, because it might mean temporary shutdown of equipment.

There are still managers who do not understand that people need to be respected. If you accept the principle of democracy no person has the right to despise or bully another just because he or she has a different level of decision making authority. Some managers still believe that the only way to get workers to produce is to introduce some sense of fear.

Even Juran believes that fear can bring out the best in people in certain circumstances. So say Macdonald and Piggott – they also have a sly dig at Deming who can create fear at his seminars when he berates managers who ask what he considers are silly questions!

SLOGANISING

Juran is strongly against 'campaigns to motivate the company's workforce to solve the company's quality problems by doing perfect work'. As he sees it, depending on motivation by slogans is management abdication unless they agree 'specific goals, establish specific plans to meet these goals or provide the needed resources'. Blaming operators for poor quality work is pointless in the absence of effective systems, and slogans can make no difference.

Philip Crosby cannot be held responsible for all the sloganising which follows in the wake of his campaigns. However his razzamatazz – with special zero-defects days and people signing the pledge to strive for zero defects – acknowledges insufficiently the distinction between the two types of variation studied in the previous chapter. (Though ICL seemed to make it work as we show in chapter 17.)

'Eliminating slogans, exhortations and targets for the work force' is the tenth of the Deming points. This flows from the two types of variation. If the problem is systemic, what is the use of urging the workforce to do better without changing the system? It will only infuriate them or make them cynical.

Deming quotes one such slogan 'Your work is your self-portrait. Would you sign it?' He counters: 'No, not when you give me a defective canvas to work with, paint not suited to the job, worn out brushes.' Again, we are being directed to an understanding of the true role of the manager to provide the framework in which people can produce quality goods and services.

Posters are mentioned such as 'Getting better together', when no one listens to worker suggestions or invites them to full participation in the journey toward total quality.

Even 'Do it right first time,' while excellent as the aim of the company as a total team, is useless when directed just at operators, who are wrongly assumed to be the cause of the problems. It is just as likely that they are being provided with faulty material or unreliable machinery. Deming is emphatic that such posters are being largely directed at the wrong people. They do nothing to transform attitudes; in fact they demotivate.

Quotas and targets similarly can be impediments to progress. They frequently require from people results over which they have little or no control.

TRAINING FOR RESPONSIBILITY

This is a key issue in enabling people to move out of the Taylor mode into the acceptance of responsibility and involvement in the achievements of their organisation.

It is training which will enable the workforce to contribute to the process of continuous improvement. Training will enable them to deal with the variations that lie within their range of authority, to deal with simple special causes and then go on to help both their team and their manager to work out what needs to be done.

A variety of statistical tools need to be understood and utilised at all levels of the company. These make participation, ownership of the job and pride in workmanship feasible. I found it quite humbling in my early visits to British companies to have people with little formal education explain what they were working on in complex statistical terms that were fast losing me. I was thus challenged to gain at least some working understanding.

This kind of training gives people pride in their own abilities; it enhances their own self-confidence and cultivates teams with individual strengths that complement each other.

Deming's sixth point is a simple one: 'institute training on the job'. I prefer the term 'learning through the job'. Learning goes deeper than training; 'through the job' takes the learning right into the heart of the work that is being accomplished.

'Sitting by Nellie' is a UK term for the haphazard kind of training where you sit by someone else and eventually get the hang of things. It is still widely practised. A more formal kind of training takes time and means temporary loss of production. Short-term thinking doesn't like that; although the temporary loss will be recouped many times over.

Another problem with such unstructured training is that it can instil bad habits. Short cuts may be taught to achieve quotas at the expense of quality. Customer satisfaction and competitive edge are not likely to get uniformly stressed in a company which won't spend money and time on formal training.

EDUCATION AND LIFE-LONG LEARNING

Training deals with skills, but it must go beyond just how to perform a particular operation. It must be set in context. It must enable the learner to know why activities are undertaken and what customer expectations are. Only then can the trainee contribute to quality work.

Deming's thirteenth point, in one of its versions, runs: 'Institute a vigorous programme of education and self-improvement.' Education goes beyond training and seeks to bring out people's potential. Education is linked with a Latin word which means to 'lead out'. Training, on the other hand, is derived from an old French word meaning to 'drag behind in an orderly fashion'.

However, development is probably the most comprehensive word. It too comes from the old French and originally meant 'to unwrap, so as to reveal the germ' of something. It is this wider end of the learning process that Deming has in mind. He is looking for the growth of a workforce who can respond to new things; who can be creative, thoughtful and innovative. The human asset is one which does not depreciate, but rather appreciates in value as it matures.

During my visits to British companies, I was impressed with the work at Lucas where any employee can be supported to learn anything related to work. If it is related to the current job it is regarded as part of the company's normal responsibility. Anything else, so long it has some connection with work, is supported. There has been a high take up. The company rationale is that it needs an adaptable, flexible workforce who will be able to cope with whatever the future may bring forth. Minds which are exercised over a wide range of subjects and skills are more likely to meet that future in a way which optimises its potential.

Some skills being acquired in Lucas are in the realm of foreign languages, so that with closer links with the rest of Europe, people will be ready to seize business opportunities. Wider global opportunities are envisaged too, for example a group of people undertook to learn Japanese so that they could get closer to Japanese people with whom they were already doing business.

Rover and Ford are also investing in people in ways which encourage their overall learning, rather than just the attainment of job-related skills.

When Deming speaks of self-improvement he is also applying to the individual the philosopy implicit in *kaizen* or continuous improvement. It is up to everyone never to be content with what they know and what they can do. There is always more. This is a life quality approach which will have untold repercussions on the quality of life at work and the outcomes of that work.

There is no doubt, from the issues we have looked at in this chapter, that quality is fundamentally about developing people's skills and potential. It concerns the human contribution, which, aided by machines, statistics, procedures and structures, nevertheless goes beyond them. Quality is the most human of subjects. It rests on people; it is defined by people and it can delight people, both customers and providers.

5. Beware of Management by Numbers Only

Let us admit straight away that numbers do matter. Costs have to be controlled, a company has to know what it is producing, how much and of what quality. It has legal obligations which involve numbers. But this is different from managing by numbers only. This chapter will address this issue.

The eleventh of Deming's 14 points advocates leadership in place of quotas on the factory floor, and the elimination of management by objectives, by numbers, by numerical goals.

This has created a good deal of controversy, causing some to say the Deming should stick to his statistics and not meddle in management. It must nevertheless be remembered that statistics led him into managerial considerations, as indeed it did for Juran.

Quotas – enemies of quality

The reasons for objecting to managing by visible numbers lie in several directions.

Take quotas first. They usually make no distinction between the different kinds of variation, whether they are specific, and controllable by the worker or whether they are systemic and therefore the reponsibility of management.

Many quotas are set quite arbitrarily. A decision taken in the boardroom to double turnover in two years may be the translation of the chairman's optimism into policy. Perhaps it gets pushed through on the basis of fear. One of the board members dares to raise objections of a realistic nature. The chairman responds: 'Not you; I thought when I appointed you that you were going to be entrepreneurial and bold; now you're joining the negative thinkers who can always find a hundred reasons for doing nothing. I expected better of you.'

The board member is young and has family responsibilities which quickly flash before his eyes. So he gives in, the decision is recorded and the pressure to achieve it soon permeates every level of the company with everybody knowing its impossibility, but no one daring to say.

Another way of setting quotas is to take the previous year's figures for some activity and just add a percentage. This too can be meaningless, based on hope, not analysis. MBAs are taught analysis at business schools, and then told to forget it when they get into the 'real world'.

This attitude is prevalent at all levels. Quotas are set on a company-wide basis which take no account of special local circumstances. Rafael Aguayo tells the story of an excellent salesperson who was continually under target. Closer examination revealed that her area included the home base of one of the main competitors. It was always going to underperform by comparison with other areas.

Aguayo and Deming both bring out another folly of quotas. They are often set at the average for the whole factory. It is evident that some people are going to be above them and some below, otherwise it wouldn't be an average. As Aguayo puts it: 'We can't all be above average can we?'

Another negative influence of quotas is that people stop work when they have achieved them, for fear that the quota and the pressure will be increased if they exceed it. If the quota has been based on an average then the effect will be to drive production levels down. Those whose performance was responsible for the high average on which the quota is based now have to perform at the new average level, or suffer the wrath of their peers. They dare not do what they did before. In some companies the abolition of quotas must sound like blasphemy. But it is a good illustration of the fact that when you talk quality you are talking of nothing less than a revolution in the way of doing business. All manner of idols fall.

If the quota is set too high then quality will fly out of the window. Short cuts will be taken; defective material will be passed; self-inspection will be skimped; everything will be ruled by the stampede to get the quota out of the door. How much of it comes back as reject is neither here nor there. The quota has been met.

Deming also berates piecework. People get paid for the number of items they turn out and therefore concentrate on quantity not quality. There is no piecework in Japanese factories.

Quotas, piecework and management by measured objectives are all substitutes for everyone working in teams within stable systems, with a common objective to delight the customer and secure the further success of the company and therefore of their own livelihood.

RATING BY APPRAISALS

Appraisals for ranking, rating and rewarding people are seen as divisive and demotivating by those who share Deming's perspective. Divisive because they focus on individuals rather than teams, the true units of quality performance. Demotivating because they usually fail to enhance people's sense of worth. Someone is told that he or she is slightly below average. Apart from our misgivings about averages, this will be taken as a vote of no confidence and can have a disastrous effect on a person's work.

This kind of approach creates winners and losers and motivates no one. If you are in the top quartile you're a winner. Everyone else is a loser, as Aguayo comments when talking of appraisals for rating and ranking people.

This is probably one of the most opposed parts of the teaching of the quality gurus, particularly of Deming. Many managers believe you have to rank and rate people to keep them motivated. Conferences are run on 'performance management', encouraging individual incentives and bonuses for measured performance. I spoke at one myself and asked the audience of human resource specialists why this term 'performance management' was being hijacked to describe incentive, bonus and other reward schemes aimed at relating people's personal achievements to money and other benefits. Surely all management is performance management, not simply that part which aims to manipulate people to work harder by offering rewards.

The Economist for 18 January 1992 carried an article on Performance Related Pay (PRP) which declared that 'belief in its efficacy is based more on faith than hard evidence'. The Institute of Manpower Studies (IMS) found no correlation between PRP and profit growth. There was doubt whether it motivated people to perform better. It could destroy a collegiate atmosphere.

Some writers actually talk of joy in work as motivational. Consultant Roger Harrison put his reputation on the line with a book subtitled *Love in the Workplace*. However soft this may sound, if you think about it, aren't joy and love what even the most hardbitten of us seek out of life? Our worklife is a big part of life, it cannot be separated from the rest of what we are and what we do, so why shouldn't we find some love and joy at work? I retired once for about three weeks. I wouldn't still be working if there wasn't more to it than monetary reward.

As Herzberg recognised we all need money, but he called it a hygeine factor. Our real kicks come from the content of our work and the fellowship we find with others in carrying it out.

Conventional appraisal systems designed for merit rating deny this in practice. They often administer a different kind of kicks. I remember the near terror with which they were approached by managers in the Pakistan State Manufacturing Industries where I was working in 1986. The basis was mainly an attempt to fix numbers to achievement or lack of achievement. The system was judgmental and destructive of good working relationships, unless your boss was easy-going when it was meaningless anyway. There were a few bosses who approached it positively as an opportunity to aid the development of their staff, but that was not how it was generally seen.

PERSONAL MERIT VERSUS TEAM PERFORMANCE

If you are trying to inspire the whole workforce to work as a team, pull together to achieve quality in product and service, accept the interdependence that goes with that approach and optimise the synergies, how then can you proceed to put them on an individual rack for variations in performance, many of which may be systemic, over which they have no real control?

Henry Neave, director of research of the British Deming Association, has some helpful ideas about this matter of performance appraisal in *The Deming Dimension*. He points out that the term 'appraisal' means different things to different people. According to him Deming uses the term to cover schemes which involve judging and ranking people, ignoring the fact that 'most of the variations in performance come from the system in which people live and work, rather than from the people themselves'.

DEVELOPMENT REVIEW

Regular free, frank discussions, on individual development needs (including where people fit into the team and defining roles and functions) are seen as useful by Neave and Deming. My own experience would echo that view. I wrote a manual on how to carry out that kind of developmental review for the Pakistan Institute of Management and seven State Manufacturing Industries. When I managed the Training School of Compower, the British Coal Board's Computer Company, the staff used to put me under pressure to get on with the development discussions because they found them helpful. So I would go along with Henry Neave's perspective.

JUDGMENTAL REVIEW

What is being opposed as detrimental to quality, co-operation and teamwork is the judgmental review. This doesn't mean that there is no place for discipline, but if there is a need for rebuke it should be dealt with straight away and not saved up for an annual reprimand.

Neave and Deming quote Lao Tze who 26 centuries ago said: 'Reward for merit brings strife and contention.' In merit rating of people, because there will be different views of what they can be held responsible for, many will leave the interview smarting under a sense of injustice. The situation will not be one where everyone wins and pulls together. The danger is that everyone will look after their own interests, to get a good rating. The needs of the group and even of the company as a whole will be secondary.

Performance appraisal for rating people will smother innovation, because innovation is risky. People will tend to get rewarded for conforming, for pleasing the boss, rather than for sticking their necks out in support of what they see as best for the enterprise. Much of the judgement will be on short term criteria. And none of it really examines the circumstances under which the performance varied. Attempts to explain that the system caused the variation will be considered excuse making.

Similarly the interdependences without which nothing can be achieved will not normally get a fair hearing. Barriers between departments can be a potent preventer of achievement. They are part of the system which impedes results. The usual response to pointing this out is that it is part of your job to be political and exercise influence where you have no authority; you just haven't been good enough at that part of your job. You haven't been tough enough, persuasive enough, farsighted enough, quick enough on your feet. How does any of this help the growth of teamwork and a company which is united in the aim of delighting customers with quality in the terms that they define?

GOAL SETTING

We have already seen that quotas are based on false premises which ignore the fact that if the systems set up by management are not sound, all the goodwill in the world on the part of the workers will not produce quality goods or services. Looking at goal setting as a whole this fallacy is then compounded by all kinds of absurdities, some of which are now illustrated.

Henry Neave tells of a nuclear plant which averaged 12 serious accidents a year. The edict came one year from top management that the rate was to be halved this year! (In other words we had 12 accidents last year; this year we plan to have only six.)

It is this kind of thing that fuels Crosby's zero defects campaign. He asks how you can plan to have defects. There is nothing wrong with his view that you can't plan to have any defects at all, that the only acceptable standard is zero; but some distinction between sources of imperfection needs to be made, otherwise you are getting people to pledge what does not lie within their power to deliver. It also has to be borne in mind that Crosby defines a defect as something which does not conform to customer requirements. He is not talking of perfection.

Aguayo tells the story of a personnel director who was given two significant goals: to reduce employee turnover and increase the use of training. She noticed that the least capable people and those with the least education stayed the longest, because they couldn't easily get other jobs. So she recruited people with minimum education and put them all through the training two or three times. The chairman commended her for meeting both her goals. But how much damage had she done to the company?

Aguayo also tells the story of a company which set plant production quotas it just couldn't meet. But there was no escape, so the numbers were faked. This had the effect of making the inventory numbers lower than the records said, every time they were counted. Theft was suspected; as a result a very expensive security system was installed.

Deming tells of a conversation he had with a postal service official who was vexed by the number of mistakes his sorters were making. Deming asked how they were paid. The answer was on the basis of sorting 15,000 pieces of mail a day. Obviously the highway to error-making.

We must all have seen in our business lives the way in which goals are set. I remember in one organisation in which I worked there was a scurry every month to explain the variances from budget. I didn't understand then the folly of the exercise, that we were putting all deviations into the same pot, irrespective of whether they were normal fluctuations of a system in statistical control or more fundamental problems involving the whole system.

How are some of these budgets set? At the the time next year's budgets are being set, someone says: 'I reckon we could increase sales by five per cent next year'. No analysis, just a gut feeling, which either leads to a lot of pressure on everyone or is ignored. If it leads to pressure then this is the way in which quality suffers and customers, the arbiters of quality, don't even get what they want, let alone something better.

SQUEEZING COSTS

Another aspect of the numbers game is that of sqeezing costs to increase profits. It has to be done from time to time, and anyway there must be a limit to what is spent. There is never enough money to do everything we would like to do. There has to be some prioritising of expenditure, but the process of containing costs leads sometimes to very unwise steps.

Companies will change suppliers to the cheapest provider of a particular component. Although it is the cheapest and helps initially to keep costs down, its product may be inferior or not fit in with the rest of the system. Goods then begin to be returned under warranty. The hoped for higher margins are not obtained. The cost of replacing faulty parts involves attention to the whole of the finished article, taking it apart and putting it together again. This far outweighs the cost of doing it right to begin with, using high quality parts, fit for use, as Juran would say.

All this seems so obvious. Why do intelligent, well trained managers ignore these truths? Nothing short of a total revolution in the way we think about and do business will put it right. For this reason it is not enough to set up statistical systems for quality control, to get everyone talking quality and even doing their own inspection. Unless we take a total view of how the business is run at every level and in every function we shall fall well behind our competitors in the market-place.

INCREASING COSTS BY REDUCING QUALITY

We have been giving examples of interfering with financial figures under the illusion we are improving the situation, but all we are doing is sacrificing quality and reputation for apparent short-term gain. Of course it is difficult in times of recession, but even then we don't help ourselves by a reputation for shoddy goods or services. We mortgage the future without improving the present situation.

In any case there is a large cost in not aiming for quality. You have to carry out all these reworks and accompanying support activities, credit notes and telephone discussion or meetings, to say nothing of the diminishing of employee morale as they see the standards slipping.

When you have to rework products they incur cost twice. You pay for the initial manufacture or assembly and then you pay again when the job is repeated. Five per cent reworks at each stage of a process through nine steps means about a third of production is lost. This agrees with the IBM estimate that not doing things right first time accounts for 30 per cent of their products' manufacturing costs.

All this runs counter to the view that quality is expensive and too much attention to it will erode profits. Figure 2.1 suggests the reverse is true.

THE COST OF QUALITY

Crosby has plenty to say about the cost of quality in his various books and his colleges study them in depth. He stresses the need to go beyond treating such costs as just a means of measuring defects on the production line. Knowledge of the cost of quality is a management tool.

He divides the cost of quality into two categories

- The price of nonconformance (PONC).
- The price of conformance (POC).

PONC includes all the costs of doing things wrong. This will include the effort involved in correcting sales orders when they come

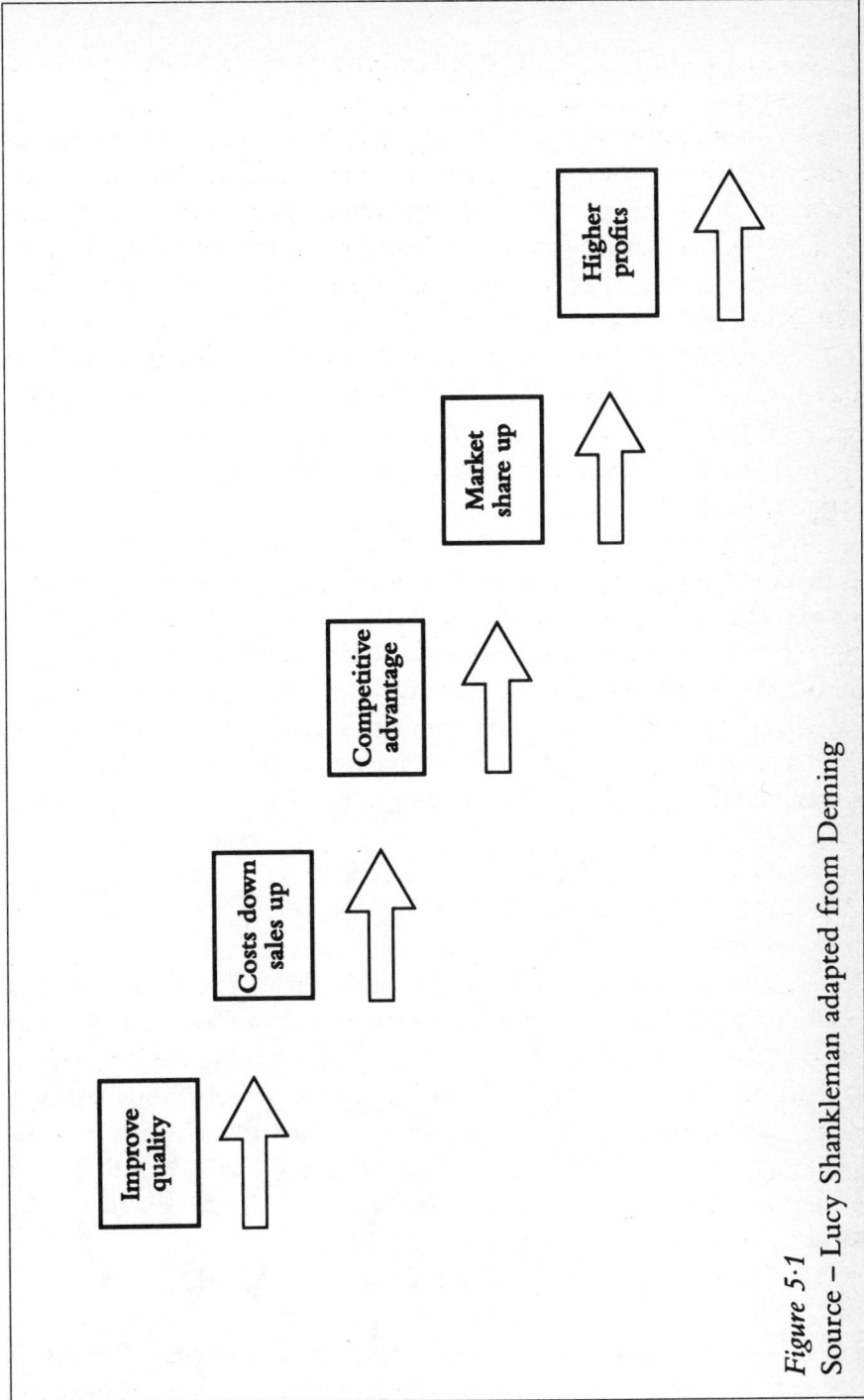

Figure 5·1
Source – Lucy Shankleman adapted from Deming

Improve quality

Costs down sales up

Competitive advantage

Market share up

Higher profits

in from the field staff, sending products to the wrong address, sending out innacurate invoices, giving the wrong discounts, sending out the wrong product and so on – all this in addition to reworks and the non-measurable cost of the disgruntled customer.

POC includes the cost of prevention and appraisal. Crosby summarises the cost of quality as comprising the following:

- Prevention.
- Appraisal.
- Failure.

The first is an acceptable cost, so long as the best method is used. And nothing can better a quality conscious workforce who are continually doing their best to prevent defects occurring and a perceptive management who ensure that the workforce are working within a system which doesn't saddle them with defects beyond their power to prevent. Included in prevention are all the costs of training people in quality procedures and philosophy, of joint activities with suppliers, of preventive maintenance, of studies of process quality, checking drawings and reviewing specifications.

Appraisal is the cost of of conducting tests, inspections and planned evaluations in checking out the suppliers and ensuring that all specifications are in line with the customers' requirements. This includes a study of what the customer said was wanted, how marketing, design and engineering have interpreted this and all the procedures and processes about to be set in motion to meet the requirements. Appraisal should be carried out as close as possible to the point of origin.

Failure costs are those connected with any product or service which does not conform to the customer requirements, such as those we have discussed above. Absolutely everything which fails is involved here, whether it is the output of a machine, a pencil, a voice or a computer.

It is failure which costs the most and which clearly indicates that the price of error is enormous. Crosby recommends the measuring of the failures to bring home the seriousness of the issue. He doesn't mean that there should be a measurement with the type of accuracy needed for the company accounts. If you can measure 80 per cent of the failures, there will be enough to shock everyone into the action they can take and to achieve considerable improvements.

QUALITY ATTITUDES

Treating cost of quality figures as if they were a precise part of the company accounts is to miss the point of the calculations, which is to alert everyone to the need to act within their capacity and authority. The key to success is the creation of a workforce (managers and operators) who are unceasingly aware of the need for quality. Awareness of cost is one of their motivators. If everything done in the company is built on teamwork, trust, and putting the customer first, including the internal customer, with everyone participating and feeling it is their company then the present is likely to be more secure and the future positively rosy.

This has been the experience of Bob Knox, of Stanbridge Precision Turned Parts, whose story I tell in chapter 11. In 1991 he went for the Ford Q1 award and was one of a very few automobile companies to prosper in a recessionary year, even to the point of taking on extra staff. IBC Vehicles were also busy recruiting when so many companies were laying off workers. (See chapter 14.)

And if you do manage to get temporary respite through buying cheaper and inferior supplies, what about the customers who don't complain, but quietly take their business elsewhere, or perhaps not so quietly, telling all their business acquaintances on the way. Various figures are bandied about on this issue, but in general it is reckoned by market researchers that satisfied customers might tell another six or so people about it, but that dissatisfied customers will tell at least another 20.

6. Teaming up with Customers and Suppliers

When I said you always come back to people when you talk about quality, I had employees in mind. There would be no employees, however, without customers. Therefore this chapter looks at the relationships between customers and suppliers, recognising that they are internal to an organisation as well as external.

Customers are the reason behind everything that everybody in a company does. This is not exclusive to companies either, as will be demonstrated in chapter 13 when we look at the work of Braintree District Council. The people who live there and pay for the services in one way or another are regarded as customers. They are to be shown respect and given good service.

FACE TO FACE WITH THE CUSTOMER

Whatever the organisation, the customers are part of the production line or service process. This is even true of the end users or final consumers of a product or service.

When Jan Carlzon, boss of the Scandinavian Air Lines (SAS), revived its fortunes in the early 1980s he inspired people with his vision of an upturned hierarchy. The traditional hierarchy is represented by a triangle with the chief executive at the apex and the masses of front line workers at the base. In between are the various ranks of supervisor and manager. Carlzon turned the triangle upside down and said that he and the management were there to support the front line workers. And they in turn were there to support the topmost part of the upturned triangle – the customers.

The customers were the reason for everything. Their loyalty to SAS depended on the thousands of 'moments of truth' when the front line employees, cabin staff, check-in people, waiters and waitresses, porters, information providers and sweepers were face to face with their public. These employees had the power to make the public feel good about flying with SAS. Top and other senior management had few of these moments of truth. Their job was to provide the front liners with the framework within which they could offer quality service and make the end users feel part of a family.

This is an approach which has spread through many companies. British Airways has had great success with its own customer care programme, where everyone was trained to see the customer as their personal responsibility. No one could say: 'I don't know; it's not my job'. It was up to everyone to know enough to be able to guide people to the information they required. Training was provided to make this possible.

This all makes good sense as well as adding pleasure to doing a job. The joy of life is largely about relationships. If you can have satisfying relationships at work with colleagues and customers, then a large chunk of your waking hours is going to be filled with enjoyment. More times than not you will arrive at work with a sense of anticipation rather than reluctance. There will be some personal fulfilment awaiting you.

I am in the real world and millions of people can echo these sentiments. Unfortunately many more cannot. It is they who do not have the opportunity to provide the quality goods and services which make work worthwhile and customers happy.

QUALITY IMPLICIT IN SUPPLY AND DEMAND

The whole of business is about supply and demand. I have something you want. You have something I want. I supply you with the product or service and you provide me with money in return. If you make no demand there is no exchange. Nothing happens. If what you have requested doesn't materialise or arrives in a form which varies from your request, you will be unhappy and will demand redress or vow never to come to me again. This view doesn't have to be graced with the description 'economics'. It's just plain common sense. Yet how many companies neglect it, eager to get their part of the exchange, but wanting to give as little as possible in return.

Quality is an attitude of mind, which actually believes that you are entitled to what you have asked for, even if your asking is the impersonal picking up of something that takes your fancy in a supermarket.

You could say that providing quality to the customer is an ethical issue. It might even be elevated to a moral issue. This has been done in Mary Kay Cosmetics. Wherever you go in that organisation you will see the golden rule displayed: 'Do to others as you would have them do to you'.

Providing quality is good business too. In fact you can say it is the foundation of business, even if sometimes it has to be enforced by law. Trust, however, is a better route than law enforcement. The best companies are those where self-interest and high principles coincide. The meeting point is quality.

EVERYONE'S GOT A CUSTOMER

In many business activities most of the workers never see the end user. In this sense they never meet the customer and may find it difficult to be motivated by the thought of serving this unknown, invisible ultimate employer. They are toiling in factories, perhaps on quite a small part of the operation and it would take a rare gift of imagination to be able to think 'customer' in those circumstances.

That's where a new piece of 'imagineering' has come in over the last few years. Imagineering is where imagination is used to engineer a new vision and new consequences. You envision where you want to be and then engineer the steps needed to get there. The vision is of a workforce obsessed with the idea of satisfying and even delighting the customer by providing and exceeding expectations.

Nevertheless some practical steps have to be interposed if this vision is to be fulfilled.

The customer/supplier chain concept does just this. Operators don't have to make the leap from their own work straight to the unseen end user. Everyone who does any kind of productive work has someone who needs the result of their labours. That someone is a customer who can be seen, spoken to and negotiated with. Such a customer can complain directly if your work cannot be used or creates difficulties by being shoddy or late. Such customers can also say thank you directly when you have gone out of your way to make life easier, by the way you have provided what they need.

Most of these customers will be internal – the next in line. As Richard Schonberger (1990) puts it they are 'a group of people connected by work flow'. If people in an enterprise recognise the need to pass on the best possible product or service to the next in line then a spirit of teamwork and co-operation can be established across functional barriers. Teams of teams are established. And work becomes worthwhile.

I could be worried at this stage that readers might think I was going over the top, but for one factor which I describe later on in this book. A new way of working or a return to an old one where people were dependent on each other as they ran the life of the village. I've seen it with my own eyes. It makes me optimistic about the future.

THE CUSTOMER CHAIN

Thus we see that in a manufacturing plant there is a whole chain of customers, needing the results of others' work. Materials come in (there the plant is the external customer of a supplier). The Stores Department checks them and stores them in the most appropriate place, to suit their immediate customer, the driver of the fork lift truck. This will be crucial if they are working on a 'just–in–time' basis, as there will be no time to be lost; the fork lift driver's customer will be waiting to take the first steps towards transforming the raw material into the product to be bought by the ultimate customer.

The recipients of the material may be people who transfer the material into a hopper and thence on to a conveyor belt. A good system is essential, and with careful placing by the fork lift driver everything is running smoothly – more satisfied customers. In spite of automation there are still people who have to observe and control some parts of each operation.

In seeking to please their colleagues, people are likely to make each step of the process a quality one. Every one of, say, 20 steps in a process, from raw material to finished product, is treated in this personal way as between members of one team composed of many interlocking teams. What is the result? Twenty infusions of quality which, joined together by the chain of customers produce a final quality product, which will at least satisfy and at most delight the external customer. It is easier to build in quality a step at a time between people who are known to each other, than to engage in mere propaganda, exhorting workers to think of the customer. The ultimate customer is not very real to them, but their colleagues are.

Customer as visible reality

It's a bit like the Christian idea that asks how you can love God whom you can't see if you don't love your brother whom you can? How can you serve up quality to the external customer whom you can't see, if you don't first serve it up to your colleague, next in line, whom you can see?

The customer chain concept turns quality into a personal reality for everyone. It is also a distinct improvement on the old hierarchical approach. Under this the only real customers anyone had were bosses. You worked to provide them with their requirements. Quality was what they didn't shout at you about. It is quite a shift to think of the most important customer as the one who receives the fruit of your labours, whose own work you are helping or hindering.

Henry Neave shows how this has an effect on organisational structure. Vertical reporting lines matter less and horizontal connecting lines matter more. Information and communication increasingly follow these horizontal lines and enable ideas for improvement to flow. The internal customer/supplier concept helps to produce an organic structure, created by relationships which already exist rather than by someone drawing organisation charts to represent formal authority.

THE END CUSTOMER

Ultimately this customer stream (to vary the analogy) flows beyond the company and reaches the people who created the demand and who are going to do the paying. These are the external customers. They may consist of several layers, or form different links of a chain. There may be wholesalers, then retailers, before we get to the final consumer who drives away with the product to enjoy it at home. Even in the home the children may really be the ultimate customers. They will be delighted by the present their parents have bought them. Or they may treat the house to wails of disappointment if the item breaks down the first time it is used.

Increasingly it is being felt, as we saw from Jan Carlzon, that the customer should figure at the top of the company hierarchy, and be regarded as part of the family.

Deming says that the consumer is the most important part of the production line, ranking higher than the supplier, vital though good supplier relationships are. He considers that the consumer is more important than the raw material. It is easier to replace the supplier, even though long-term relationships are preferred, than it is to find a new consumer, or reclaim one you have lost.

THE SUPPLIER CHAIN

The previous paragraph is not belittling the role of the supplier. It is simply emphasising the overriding primacy of the customer. Nonetheless, without a sound relationship with suppliers quality will not be achieved. The supplier is part of the production line, too.

The supplier chain is the customer chain in reverse. Every customer needs a supplier. Every customer needs to be able to communicate to the supplier in an unequivocal way what is required and expected. If the two can co-operate there is some chance that expectations and needs will be met. If each customer in the chain receives from each supplier inputs which meet or exceed expectations then the end user will receive a high quality end product.

Most of these suppliers are inside the company, but there are also external suppliers. If the quality of their input is poor then the whole chain will suffer and the ultimate consumer will have grounds for complaint. In its progress through the chain there will be a cumulative effect. Things will get worse; errors and defects will be compounded as efforts are made to correct and compensate for elements which do not truly fit.

The traditional way of ensuring that the external supplier sent in quality materials was mass inspection, by either a high level of sampling or total inspection. This is costly in time and money and still may not identify everything which is unsatisfactory. Some of the figures quoted for faulty incoming material are disturbing indeed. Steel delivered to automobile manufacturers of which eight per cent had to be rejected is one example.

PART OF THE FAMILY

In recent years many companies have made considerable efforts to make their external suppliers 'part of the family'. Instead of playing one off against another and selecting them on the basis of price tag alone, they enter into alliance with them. They jointly work out what is needed and what standards are to be applied. This is not a soft option. There can still be demanding standards and some tough talking when these are not met. At least, though, the suppliers know where they stand. They do not feel that the sword of Damocles is hanging over their head all the time, so that if a cheaper supplier is found they will be cut off from a significant part of their revenue. In return they make sure they they conform to their customer's requirement, ensure it is fit for use and even able to delight.

Marks and Spencer have had this kind of close relationship with suppliers for years. They are rigorous in their demands, but in exchange the suppliers have a sense of security.

I visited a Northern Foods factory in Grantham, which is almost totally devoted to providing Marks and Spencer with convenience foods. The long arm of Marks and Spencer reaches right into the levels of hygeine required so that the purchasers in the stores can have every confidence that the products are safe. There had to be two changes of protective clothing during my visit, depending on the nature of the operation. It is absolutely essential to keep out harmful bacteria. All these precautions were agreed between the contracting parties. The opportunity for taking short cuts was non-existent. The staff accepted this and there was no sense of being oppressed by a discipline imposed by a powerful customer.

This kind of relationship also enables the contracting supplier to invest in plant and equipment with a sense of confidence. Employment is secure. All stakeholders benefit. Quality lies at the heart of managing for excellence; it affects every part of all companies in the chain and benefits the local community. The customer organisations no doubt drive hard bargains, but their main criterion is not price. It is uniformity and reliability, as required by ever more discriminating end purchasers. This is particularly significant with food where health is at stake.

Stanbridge Precision Turned Parts (chapter 11) is another case in point. In gaining the Ford Q1 award, it accepted the inspection of the Ford engineers who examined everything Stanbridge did, including plans for continuous improvement. If the long arm of Ford reached into the supplier, Stanbridge could also ask questions about what Ford was doing where it affected them. The relationship was co-operative rather than colonial.

PRICE NOT THE PRIME SUPPLIER FACTOR

The fourth of Deming's 14 points concerns sources of supply. He is quite directive about the need to 'end the practice of awarding business on the basis of price tag'. He is all for minimising total cost, but this follows automatically if you buy good materials which live up to their claims. There are no costs of correction or adapting poorly fitting components.

Deming goes as far as recommending a single source for any one product. This builds mutual loyalty and trust, which begets reliability and uniformity. Such long-term relationships keep companies 'on their toes' more effectively than by maintaining an atmosphere of insecurity and uncertainty which will not encourage straight dealing; on the contrary it provides fertile ground for deception and short cuts.

Juran accepts the need for co-operation with suppliers to ensure a good relationship, but prefers to maintain more than one source of supply in order to avoid vulnerability through the failure of one of the suppliers. Even where these gurus vary, their ultimate intent is the same. Certainly neither of them would wish to force the supplier's price down so they could not provide the required quality economically. Thus quality means a more humane way of working than the ruthless drive for low prices which has characterised so much business life.

Deming says 'Price has no meaning without a measure of the quality being purchased'. He considers that American industry and the US Government are being cheated 'by rules which award business to the lowest bidder'. He considers that when purchasing tools and other equipment, organisations should be thinking long term and aiming to minimise net cost per hour or year, not just basing decisions on today's price. It is not only a question of initial cost, but of maintenance and durability.

It is also foolish to keep switching suppliers for temporary price advantage. The fit between suppliers and other elements in the total product inevitably vary between different suppliers. Things are likely to fit less well and rejects may accumulate with frequent switching. Issues such as precise colour match can be significant. Uniformity and reliability are much more likely to be achieved by sticking with a supplier of known capability, who has served well. The overall cost will thus be less than that incurred by chopping and changing all the time for short-term gain, mainly based on initial cost.

Another aspect of the problem of supply is that buyers in many companies have been conditioned to the lowest bid syndrome. Their terms of reference often require that they take this approach. Sometimes the Purchasing Department is not in close enough touch with the needs of the user departments and is operating on different criteria. This is a case of where functional barriers need to be completely broken down. Producing departments are in this case the customers and they look for a quality service from the Purchasing

Department, one which conforms to their requirements, is fit for use and even exceeds expectations. They cannot afford to go for the lowest initial price.

Cost of supplies has to be seen on a holistic basis. What is being purchased has to be seen in the light of its total contribution to the whole process for which it is being used.

The specifications to which a purchasing department works have to make clear all these needs, and the interrelationships of what one supplier provides with other provisions. It is a much more sophisticated process than negotiating on the basis of driving a hard bargain. It is much more in the direction of win–win negotiation, as recommended by Fisher and Ury in *Getting to Yes*.

LONG–TERM RELATIONSHIPS WITH SUPPLIERS

A good long-term relationship means that suppliers understand what the material is being used for. They do not just mechanistically comply with specifications, but understand the subtleties of fit with other elements in the customer's process. It is a sound principle to stay with a supplier who has come to know your business.

Another angle on long-term supplier relationships is the need to have *kaizen* (continuous improvement) within your company matched by a search for continuous improvement by the suppliers, continuous improvement which will mesh with the improvement activity within your company. Ford required a commitment to continuous improvement to be spelt out and accepted by Stanbridge before awarding the Q1 flag of quality. (See chapter 11.)

You would never get this enthusiasm for continuous improvement and the investment in innovation from a supplying company which was in fear of being dropped at any time.

A number of companies who have opted for long-term relationships have also found that the administration is easier, with fewer problems over invoicing and checking.

JOINT PROJECT TEAMS

The most successful way of achieving the integration of the external supplier with a customer company is for them to group their key managers together as a project team. They work out together in some detail what the customer wants to achieve, both at the earliest stages and throughout the design and development work. The designers and engineers from both enterprises serve on this project team along with the sales and purchasing experts, the production specialists and research departments. They all pull together to ensure that something can be produced which enables the customer to make optimum use of what the supplier provides. The fit between the two is worked out jointly. There is partnership.

In addition to the major issues of design and fit, the accompanying features will be mutually agreed. These include tolerances, cleanliness of production and the manner of delivery to a particular part of a specific factory. Nothing is too detailed to be considered. It is because of this need for close harmony that Deming proposes single sourcing. Then the partnership is absolute – there is real knowledge and understanding on both sides.

INTERNAL PARTNERSHIPS

If this concept of partnership between external supplier and customer is important then it surely must be of value within the company. Easier, too, one would have thought, because all parties serve under the same ultimate banner.

The internal politics of a company, however, can be as bitter and divisive as any relationship outside the company. Departments often regard themselves as companies within companies and indeed the financial discipline of being a profit, cost or responsibility centre as well as creating commercial rigour has a downside. It can make departments see things only from their own perspective and not from the angle of serving the company as a whole.

It is clear that if the ultimate customer is to be given quality then internal barriers have to come down and all departments have to be 'singing from the same hymn book'. They will maintain their own perspective as a valid contribution, but they will aim to arrive at the kind of consensus which shows that they really believe that the whole is more important than the parts.

BREAKING DOWN DEPARTMENTAL BARRIERS

This principle is emphasised in the ninth of Deming's 14 points, which aims to break down barriers between departments. It envisages all employees working as a team. They each try to see the problems that their specific activities may create for the others.

This idea has been around for a few years, yet while writing this book I was involved in conversation at a conference, first with a production person and then separately with a sales manager from the same company. Neither of them had a good word to say of the other department. They both accepted continual feuding as being part of the nature of things that would never alter.

Companies which really commit themselves to the total quality approach certainly seem to be less afflicted by inter-departmental warfare. They are trying to see things from a customer perspective and they set in motion procedures to encourage internal working together. Juran particularly recommends the formation of multi-functional project teams to ensure that all perspectives are taken into account in the design, development, creation and delivery of a product or service.

If barriers are not broken down you can have a range of departments each doing a highly competent job, seen on their own, yet their efforts are not contributing to a coherent whole. Each department is optimising its own activity, but is not understanding how to optimise the whole organisation.

COMMUNICATING ACROSS FUNCTIONS

If this cross-functional partnership is going to succeed there must be good communication across the divide, which then disappears. An outstanding example of this is where salespersons are seen as the eyes and ears of the company, not just sellers of goods and services. They meet a lot of people and learn a lot about what is going on. There should be procedures for ensuring that this vital information is caught and used. Relatively junior members of the sales force may often come across information strategically important to the whole company. Training must create awareness of such situations and knowledge of how to ensure the company gets the benefit.

No one department or manager, however senior, has the right to make last-minute alterations without consulting everyone who might be affected. Innovation and entrepreneurship are not the partners of inconsistency and changeability.

Japanese companies are notorious for the time they take in trying to use all information to get internal consensus and impatient Westerners are often frustrated by being kept waiting for an answer to their own business proposals while this debate goes on. Once the debate is over, however, the Japanese move with breathtaking speed, because all the dangers have been foreseen, thought through and overcome. Everyone knows how far ahead they get in straight competition with most Western firms, with far fewer delays due to traditional teething troubles.

WHO IS THE CUSTOMER AND WHO IS THE SUPPLIER

One feature of our consideration of the customer/supplier chain is the ambiguity as to who is a supplier and who is a customer. This arises both internally and externally.

I was recently discussing the growth of agencies which arrange the letting of properties for people, who, for example, have to spend a few years in other countries as part of their career development. They become the customers of the agency who finds a suitable tenant. They become landlords and pay for this service. Once the agency has brought landlord and tenant together, then the tenant is the customer of the landlord and pays for a service – a roof over his or her head. Nonetheless the agency needed people to pass to the landlord and although no money exchange occurred between tenant and agency, yet the tenant asked the agency to supply the service of finding a roof, and so in a sense was a customer. It's all very blurred isn't it?

In all cases some kind of exchange is taking place. Each wants something from the other and is prepared to exchange something, money, product or service for it. When you look at business like this then the chain of suppliers and customers being intimately linked makes sense. It is inherent in the relationship. It is the corollary of human interdependence.

Total quality picks this up because it seeks every possible way of ensuring that customers get what is required or something better. That is why this book on total quality seems to be more about management as a whole than about a separate facet called quality. Because the purpose of a business is to get and keep a customer, and quality is a key route for doing this, we therefore have to discuss all aspects of business management in discussing quality. It becomes a focus which makes us do what we should have been doing anyway to survive or grow.

7. *Working in Teams*

At the beginning of this book I offered a definition of management. It is worth revisiting in the light of our study of the practice and theory of managing for quality, with managing shared by all employees. In a sense every employee is a manager. The definition is:

> *Managing is risking yourself in the mobilising of resources and relationships to add value to the enterprise.*

I mentioned that the word 'relationships' didn't feature in my original definition. Its insertion arose from a meeting with David Cox, ex-managing director of Ind Coope Brewery at Burton on Trent. We were discussing the revolution which he had inspired at the brewery in the mid 1980s. I trotted out my definition. He indicated general approval, but said there was something missing. It was the word 'relationships'.

RELATIONSHIPS

Everything we have considered so far supports this definition. There have been relationships between managers and the shop floor, revolutionised by the passing of the old hierarchies and the need for thinking workers. There have been relationships between outside suppliers and the firm, to work together for common objectives. There have been relationships across internal functions breaking down barriers to create an internal chain of suppliers and customers. You could say that quality is all about people's relationships. Defining quality in terms of customer requirements supposes a human relationship.

INTERLOCKING TEAMS

We now pick up the theme of relationships by viewing employees in their mutual relationships as members of teams. We have seen in the chain concept the idea of the whole company as one big team, passing the result of activity on from one to the next in a co-operative way. Now we consider the way in which each step along the way in a quality organisation is the outcome of team effort, rather than of rugged individualism. This is the feature of total quality crucial to its success in mobilising everyone's energies behind the concept.

David Cox attributes the success of the changes at Burton Brewery to the reorganisation of all functions into interlocking teams. The leader of any one team served as a member of another team concerned with the linking of several processes; the leader of that team in turn served in a team with other interlinking functions. The whole organisation looked something like figure 7.1, reproduced with permission from David Cox's book *Exploiting Change*.

Some of the teams, for example the executive team, were at a higher level than others, but the whole point of the figure is that it does not represent a reporting structure, rather one of relationships. Ideas, plans and information about action flow up, down and across to ensure that everything is integrated with one common purpose.

The team leaders serving on another team were what Rensis Likert called 'linking pins'. Even if sometimes it worked out that one team had more influence than another, because it was concerned with a number of functions, the approach was psychologically different from the normal hierarchy. People felt freer to suggest and propose, whatever their formal level. It was a team, a contrast to the normal organisational chart which portrays relatively isolated individuals calling other individuals to account, issuing orders, making decisions and personally deciding how far to consult others.

Wellins, Byham and Wilson in *Empowered Teams* have similar ideas. Members of self-directed operations or line teams are also members of specialist support teams such as the software team, training team or budget team.

Figure 7·1 The full ICBB organisation structure diagram as at Spring 1988

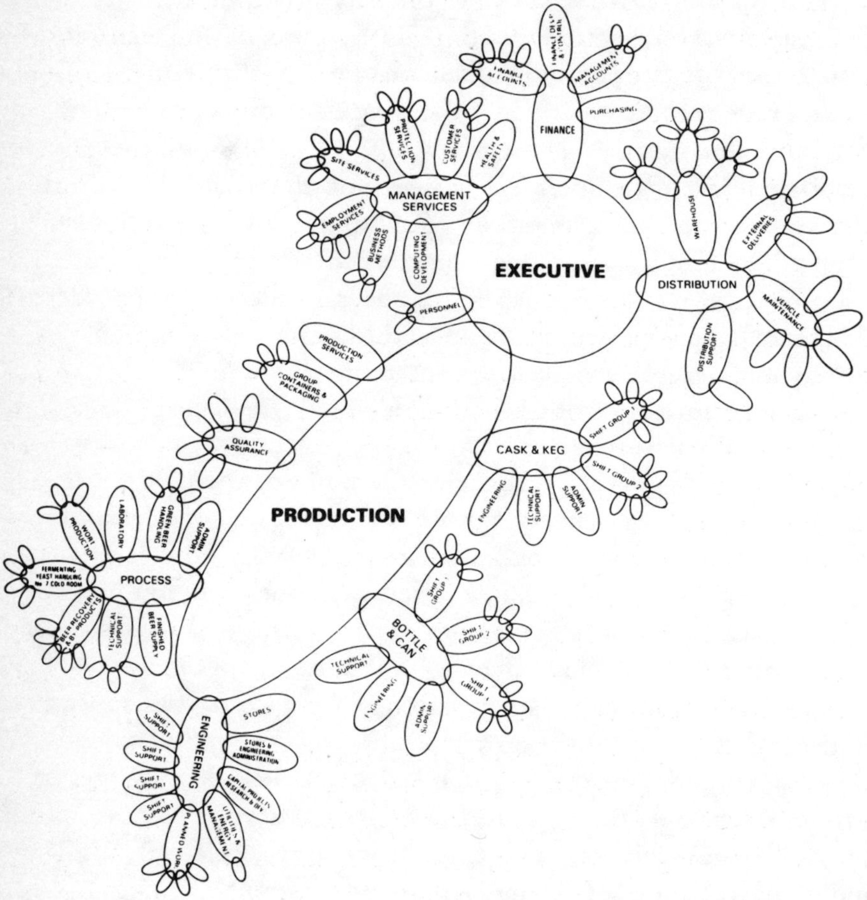

This approach is in line with systems thinking, where everything in a sequence of activity is affected by everything else. Change one aspect and you have to think of all the other aspects of the process which need changing. If every operations team is represented at every other part of the system awareness of the whole system has the opportunity to grow. Tampering with one part of the system without regard to other parts can only create problems.

A related benefit derived from operations or line team members also serving on support teams is that the specialist departments, themselves run on a team basis, are then in touch with the basic producer (line) teams. The operations team member is also able to help line teams understand the support teams' problems. This is one way of implementing the view that 'staff' departments should be consultants to the 'line'.

This is relevant to human resource management departments. It is increasingly recognised that managers have responsibility for developing their 'subordinates' (unacceptable word). The human resource specialist acts as a consultant to the manager, providing coaching and material to enable the manager to fulfil this development function.

Wellins and his colleagues tell of some companies where the training members of operations teams are assisted by also being members of the training teams which provide their operational teams with guidance on available training. In some cases training team representatives will also be involved in the delivery of training within their teams. This certainly ensures that the training is relevant.

The same approach applies to other team representatives. For example the budget team representative on a line team has a special role when budgets are being worked out. This helps the other members of the team to exercise their responsibility, not to abdicate from it.

This approach of line operations team members serving on support teams and bringing back the knowledge and expertise they gain helps to develop the concept of shared leadership, where while there will probably always be team leaders, the distance between them and the rest of the team is an ever diminishing one.

If you accept such a team approach the words 'subordinate' and 'employee' disappear in favour of 'team member' or something more personal and equal. Throughout the world the employees of Mars are called associates.

THE DYNAMICS OF TEAMWORKING

The dynamics of teamworking are entirely different from the standard hierarchy. Everyone has the right to be listened to, even if the experience of leaders may give them added weight, and informal leaders will emerge with persuasive powers. In the end a leader has to decide or take an issue to someone more competent to handle it, but it will not arbitrary or secretive.

And this again *is* the real world. It happened at Burton Brewery and continues years after its establishment. It is the basis of Rothmans, the successes of Nissan and Komatsu in County Durham, Bosch in Cardiff, Toshiba in Plymouth, Holloway Prison in London and Sony in Bridgend. It is universally successful in Japan, but it cannot be attributed merely to a more collective type of culture, because wherever Japanese firms set up in other countries, as in the UK, it works just as well.

Human beings are gregarious and where this is given scope, people rise to the opportunity to fulfil their inner needs in the world of work. In Maslow's hierarchy of needs you don't get to self-actualisation without first experiencing the esteem of others and the sense of belonging.

It can be argued that self-actualisation is not the apex, that it depends on the participation of others. As Martin Buber has shown, there is no 'I' without a 'thou'. George Mead and others of the 'symbolic interactionist' school of thought have demonstrated how the essential 'I' is constructed out of millions of interactions with others. Each day as we interact with others we are slightly changed. I am still I, but an enriched I if I truly allow other influences into my life.

THE PROOF OF THE PUDDING

The proof of the pudding is in the eating. Teamworking was the key to success in every company I visited where total quality was the main concern. When Bedford Commercial Vehicles became IBC Vehicles, the 1,250 employees were organised into 130 teams as outlined in chapter 14. The press shop, body and paint, and final assembly all worked in teams of about 12 people and the administrative support teams were a bit larger. Team leaders were appointed on the basis of ability to weld the groups together and a free flow of ideas was encouraged. After ten years of losses everyone knew their jobs were on the line. They needed to ensure that their teams worked, just to survive.

They learned willingly to monitor their own work. They learned statistical process control, so that the information boards were meaningful to them. They put up their own results in a clear manner. Daily meetings became a feature to create the kind of harmony that would make for a successful day.

Within one year there was a small profit. This reversal of ten years of failure must be partly due to the new way of working.

I was particularly impressed at Nissan Motor Manufacturing in County Durham at the way in which no one seemed in a particular hurry to leave at five o'clock in the afternoon. The department where I was at that time seemed to want to clear up outstanding matters, so that they could start with a clear run in the morning. There was none of the traditional stampede for the door. Doug Lorraine, responsible for training, suggested that a sense of working for the team involved everyone supporting everyone else. This was particularly noticeable at eight o'clock every morning. For about ten minutes, no one appeared to be doing any work. They were all at their team meetings. That was work and got the day started well.

An interesting by-product of these Nissan meetings was that people hardly ever arrived late. That would let the team down and make the latecomer open to peer criticism. That wasn't the purpose, but it illustrates the power of teamworking. It achieves what exhortations from foremen and even pay docking never could.

SELF-DIRECTED WORK TEAMS

The key feature of the teams set up in pursuance of quality is that they are self-managing – self-directed. This doesn't mean that they are leaderless – far from it – but the role of leaders is to elicit their talent and weave together their ideas and energies to achieve what mere orders never could.

The Tom Peters video *Leadership Alliance* illustrates self-managed teams at work. The firm is Johnsonville Foods, a Wisconsin sausage company. Teams of about eight people have their own budgets and authority to work out best how to do their jobs. They even recruit new members of the team, choosing those with qualities favourable to co-operation. The subtleties of team dynamics have to be maintained in spite of personnel changes.

Wellins, Byham and Wilson offer an excellent definition of self directed teams in their book, *Empowered Teams*:

> *Self-directed work teams are small groups of people empowered to manage themselves and the work they do on a day to day basis. They are different from other types of teams or 'teamwork' you may be using in your organisation, in that self-directed teams are formal, permanent organisational structures or units that perform and manage work. Typically members of self-directed work teams not only handle their job responsibilities, but also plan and schedule their work, make production related decisions, take action to solve problems and share leadership responsibilities.*

Such teams are based on the premise that those closest to a job know best how it should be done and are most likely to have ideas on improving performance. There is no better way of securing worker participation in organisational objectives and a sense of owning the work. The achievements of a self-directed work team are likely to jell with those of the whole company. There are checks and balances in the diversity always found in any group. There will be disagreements and variations of perspective, but these are just what you need to ensure that no one voice has all the say, unchecked by alternative possibilities.

THE DIFFERENCE FROM OTHER TEAMS

The distinction between project teams, football teams, quality circles and self-directed work teams is considerable. The normal team pulls together for a common purpose but does not by definition have the shared self-governance of the kind of team we are talking about.

Most of the other teams are of a temporary nature or come together from time to time to perform a particular operation or play a specific game. Take a sports team, say a football team: they are together only during the practices and at the actual match. The self-directed work team is together the whole of its working days for as many shifts as it works in a week, a month and a year. It is responsible for the whole of a segment of the firm's operations. It delivers a completed item or set of items, product or service, to its customer, the next in line or the external customer.

Though at different levels of competence and expertise, they work together daily solving the problems which arise, finding opportunities for continuous improvement, which they carry out where feasible, or alternatively propose to those who can. Particularly significant is the fact that within wider pre-set parameters they plan and control their activities. They do their own scheduling and act in a way contrary to the Taylor division of people into thinkers and workers. They are all thinkers and they are all workers.

One of the outstanding features of the self-managed team is the way in which people learn to do a number of jobs, so that the most effective team is completely multi-skilled. Everyone can perform all the operations. This means that if anyone is unavoidably absent, the show goes on. There is no hold up while a spare person with a particular skill is found to fill the gap.

I saw examples of this at Rothmans (see chapter 12). Two team members went off with the team leader to have discussions about faulty material with a supplier of aluminium foil. The rest of the team covered for them and the work went on. This enables everyone to have a more interesting job, both because there is more variety in what they normally do and because of the opportunity it affords to participate in specific managerial roles. There is no question of a team leader saying: 'You get on with your work and leave me to get on with the managing'.

NEW UNION ATTITUDES

The self-directed team approach also means that the traditional divide between management and 'labour' is eroded. This sometimes causes tension initially, particularly where old style trade unions fear an erosion of their power. They used to claim to be the channel of communication between the workers and management on anything which could remotely be called policy.

There are signs that this attitude is changing. Unions are becoming increasingly interested in pressurising management to pay more attention to the training and development of staff. There is less sole concentration on an annual round of basic wage bargaining and a recognition that many other issues affect worker well-being. There are an increasing number of single union agreements, or where there are several unions, they will often agree to speak to management with one voice. Their members would not forgive them if opportunities to have a plant established in their location were lost through union politics. Progress is sometimes slow, but in my opinion a sense of reality is creeping into union activity. Bill Jordan's words quoted in chapter 20 illustrate this.

IBC Vehicles is an illustration of a company which would not have survived if the union had been intransigent. Instead it recognised the logic of survival and agreed to a non–confrontational approach, which has served everyone well. (See chapter 14.)

Self-directed teamworking is real participation, whereas some of the institutional type of participatory arrangements are more cosmetic than real. The ordinary worker does not get involved in a wider range of responsibility. Sometimes it is a matter of union officials having worker seats on the board or on a second tier of the board. This is proxy participation. It makes little difference to the quality of daily work life. It does little to enhance the self-respect and skill range of the individual worker. Being a responsible member of a self-managing team, however, does. This is direct participation.

Some senior managers who read these words may be doubtful

whether such an approach is feasible in their companies. Perhaps this is the opportunity to display managerial courage, to show belief in staff and skill in advocacy. Self-fulfilling prophecies can be very powerful and if managers show confidence that staff can accept the responsibilities, then in time there is every hope that they will. It does mean a total change from the old 'us and them' attitude. It means persisting in the belief that the new approach can work and resisting the temptation to feel that you are the fount of all wisdom who must always tell others what to do.

FROM INDIVIDUAL TO COLLECTIVE WORKING

Changes in the relationships between management and unions have been signalled in human resource literature as a move from the collective approach to a more individual one (Storey 1989). This reflects the move from a total concentration on collective bargaining. Collective bargaining had egalitarian overtones; it sought to ensure that all the members were treated on a fair basis.

Now individual diversity is being recognised and there is a move toward a recognition of difference so long as the base line is equitable. Also, with growing decentralisation, there is increasing acceptance of the principle of subsidiarity, where everything in business life is handled at the most local level possible. Individuals are counting for more in their own right and are less influenced by unions which in the past claimed the right to speak for them. This is what is meant by human resource writers who speak of the move to a more individual climate in personnel issues, by which they here mean industrial relations issues.

As the individual becomes more liberated, however, there grows a move toward a new form of collectivism in which the individual gains in power, influence and opportunity to contribute, by co-operation and joint activity with colleagues. In that sense I find myself at variance with those who say we have now moved into the era of individual primacy in human resource management. We are in fact on the verge of the new collective era, where people realise the fullness of their individualism by a varied range of joint activity. That way the individual *and* the group win and there need be no conflict between the two concepts.

Of course we are not there yet. The human resource or personnel world is ringing with discussions of performance management, by which (as we saw in chapter 5) is meant a range of ways of rewarding individual achievement, by which people stand out as superior to their fellows, and are rewarded with incentive payments and individual bonuses. We saw how Deming attacks these approaches, regarding them as divisive and destructive of team cohesion. *The Economist* (18.1.92) commented that some see Performance Related Pay (PRP) as 'antithetical to teamwork'.

In place of the rat race

Once you recognise the cohesion of the team and the dependence of every member on all the others, then it is less than fair to pick on some as producing superior performance. They are all 'members one of another' and achieve most by recognising this old biblical concept in the secular world. This doesn't mean a dull uniformity where the unique features of the individual are no longer appreciated. Rather the reverse, when a team says: 'Oh, Fiona can handle that; she's really good at it.'

Of course some will emerge as informal leaders and will coach and counsel their colleagues, thus making life easier for everyone. Coaching and counselling and enabling others to perform more effectively, as Colin O'Neill pointed out at Rothmans (see chapter 12), is the key activity of managing. Wellins and his colleagues report how Beckon, Dickinson and Co. of North Carolina found that when they moved from the traditional supervisory model, the new style team leaders spent 60 per cent of their time in coaching and training, compared with 10 per cent for the previous traditional supervisors.

Some members of the teams with such capacities will tend to go on to formal team leadership themselves. Rothmans makes a point of ensuring that such people receive the training which enables them to apply for the position of team leader when one becomes vacant.

Such team leaders are first among equals. With the hierarchy becoming flatter and middle management having fewer levels, the rat race and ceaseless anxiety about promotion has to diminish.

People have to find their motivation in more interesting work and membership of the working group. It really does mean a transformation of working life.

QUALITY CIRCLES

Quality circles should not be confused with self-directed teams. They were defined by David Hutchins in 1980 on the basis of work by Kaoru Ishikawa and Jeff Beardsley as:

> *A small group of between three and twelve people who do the same or similar work, voluntarily meeting together regularly for about an hour a week in paid time, usually under the leadership of their own supervisor, and trained to identify, analyse and solve some of the problems in their work, presenting solutions to management, and, where possible, implementing the solutions themselves.*

This definition was officially adopted as a standard in the UK by the National Society for Quality Circles (NSQC).

The original idea was that quality circles should be work group based, rather than cross-functional. People should work together on their own areas where they really are the experts. They have been successful in Japan, where they have fitted into the structure of total quality as a whole. Where, as often in the West, they have been seen as quick fixes and unrelated to a total quality programme, they have often fizzled out.

Another factor is that quality circles need to differentiate between special causes of variation and systemic ones. The latter are of more general contribution to improvement, so long as they are not just interfering with something already in statistical control and management will pay serious attention to their recommendations.

In one sense quality circles are extra to the daily work, though closely related to it. They address specific problems and not the whole activity of a work team. In this they vary from the self-directed work team which is totally involved in the whole job. This obviously has value in securing special attention for a specific problem, but is not so deeply embedded in day-to-day work as the self-directed work team.

Quality circles depend very much on the enthusiasm of a few members and if the membership changes substantially they often fade away. This is a pity because they can make a valuable contribution, though they are not the major part of total quality as they have often been perceived. They should spring out of the wider concept as one of a number of mechanisms and techniques for the creation and maintenance of quality.

When Stanbridge Precision Turned Parts (see chapter 11) were applying for the Ford Q1 quality award, they had to provide evidence that they were involved in the quality circle kind of activity. They initiated improvement teams as their version of the quality circle and these run side by side with the ordinary working teams.

WORK LAYOUT

A significant factor in the effectiveness of teamworking in the manufacturing world is the way in which the production facility is laid out. The Western world probably first became aware of this when the press began to report what was going on at Kalmar in Sweden, where Volvo had introduced a totally new way of working.

They moved away from the traditional assembly line where workers performed in endless repetition a few simple operations as the vehicle or other product passed slowly by them. Volvo built a new plant in which the key factor was ferrying around the cars on mechanical carriers to various teams of workers, who would be responsible for a complete aspect of the finished product. They reduced costs by 25 per cent compared with conventional plants and defects were down by 90 per cent.

They have since gone further and the story has been told of how, as a press headline puts it: 'Volvo's new assembly plant has no assembly line'. In place of the assembly line the plant at Uddevalla is based on six workshops which surround a central parts warehouse. The teams in each of the workshops build whole cars. This goes a long way towards meeting Deming's appeal for the restoration pride of workmanship. Such pride is collective as well as individual.

In a smaller way the arrangements at Rothmans are of production equipment surrounding the central facilities, which I have dubbed 'bungalows' (see chapter 12). The physical layout facilitates the team approach. It makes it almost inevitable.

One of the challenges we have to respond to is how to achieve similar improvement to work layout to encourage teamworking in the support facilities and administrative functions.

THE NEED FOR FLEXIBILITY

Another significant contribution from the self-directed team is in meeting the need for flexible production. Stan Davis introduced the term 'mass customisation', where the use of computers enables mass production to cope with highly individualised items. The flick of a few computer keys and the equipment could adjust, for example, from small garments to outsize ones.

A flexible workforce organised in teams which are multi-skilled is obviously more able to respond to the frequent adaptations required by such a process. A mind is required which can cope with frequent changes. The mass assembly line approach had that type of flexibility scrubbed out of it. It was seen as a positive disadvantage. Not so any longer when discriminating customers define quality in terms of ability to meet their specific and often non-standard needs.

As mass customisation gathers momentum, the number of changes to meet customer demand each day will grow. Quality is about responsiveness to customer need and the flexible, multi-skilled, self-directing team is the best organisational form for providing it. People who share in managing their own activities don't need to be told all the time what to do. Thus the frequent adaptations come easily to them and the customer is satisfied. Quality prevails.

COMPETENCIES FOR TEAMWORK

When teams are choosing replacements for people who have moved on, or when any team vacancy is being filled, they need to know which knowledge, skills, attitudes and aptitudes they should be looking for. The catch-all word nowadays is competencies.

There is much debate as to whether personal traits should be included, but in teamwork they are very important. They can be developed, unless someone has a disposition totally at variance with them. Competence theorists would also say that traits can be related to behaviours which can be learned. We enter an area of controversy here, but it is true that we do need what Deming calls operational definitions. They enable us to describe what a suitable team worker will do in various situations.

When selecting new team members many organisations involve the whole team in group discussions and simulations so that there is some opportunity for prospective members to reveal something of themselves in the interpersonal situations which are the essence of team life.

EMPATHY

Whatever it might mean in terms of actual behaviours, I would say that a prime capacity is empathy. This is different from sympathy. Sympathy means feeling at one with another person and in harmony with what he or she is going through. It is a word usually used in connection with some kind of suffering or a cause that is being fought for.

Empathy on the other hand does not imply any agreement, any feeling of unity with or liking for the subject of it. It simply means that you have the ability to stand in the shoes of the other person and imagine what it must feel like to be them. You can then shape your course appropriately and deal with problems with a likelihood of solving them.

If, in the days leading up to World War Two, statesmen had been able to empathise with Hitler, while being totally out of sympathy with his objectives, they might have better understood what to do at an earlier stage, before he had acquired the power to be the menace he became. They would have understood what motivated him, how he could play on the fears of other people. However much they loathed his approach they would have been equipped to handle him. They would not have been surprised or fallen for promises he had no intention of keeping.

The advantage of a real team is that not everyone will have equal amounts of empathy in their make up, but between them they will be able to fathom out the motivation of people with whom they have to deal. Different members of the team may understand different categories of people. There will be a wealth of human understanding which can be utilised for the meeting of problems, which nearly always have a human component.

It is also important for the members of a team to be able to stand in each other's shoes and understand the point of view of others even where they do not share it.

Behaviours which manifest the empathetic quality will include willingness to listen to the ideas of others, to reserve judgment until they have heard the other person out. How can they stand in the other person's shoes unless they do this?

In discussions the empathetic person will be able to offer help, suggestions, advice and ideas of such a character and in such a way that they are likely to be accepted. Similarly they will be more likely to know when to offer help, even though it has not been asked for. When someone offers suggestions they will understand his or her viewpoint and be able to assess the value of the ideas better.

There is a wide range of individual behavioural competencies involved in the single word empathy, but if once it is grasped and its related behaviours learned, it is probably the most crucial of all.

Quality has been the main theme of this chapter. It is about working methods, competencies and relationships which enable a team to provide customers, internal and external, with their unique requirements.

8. Service and Support Quality

Discussion of quality tends to take its cue from manufacturing. This chapter will concentrate on service activity. The principles of quality are largely common to both services and manufacturing as we shall see, though some differences will become apparent.

Measuring quality is more difficult in the service area than in manufacturing. The evidence is likely to be anecdotal rather than based upon scientific measurement. You can measure the acidity of a sample of food; but it is less easy to measure the acidity of a customer's complaint about a store assistant's attitude.

The number of complaints can be catalogued and, more to the point, how rapidly they were dealt with to recapture lost reputation. Writing in the *Financial Times* (10 January 1992), Christopher Lorenz refers to Richard Whitley's book, *The Customer Driven Company*. A plea is made for the adoption of 'measurement and research techniques which are available to transform many intangible aspects of a service into tangibles'. This involves measuring every possible customer and employee attitude and acting on the results.

QUALITY RESPONSE TO DISASTER

Nonetheless, there is nothing to better prompt action on the spot by the one who is face to face with the public. A serious complaint can sometimes be turned into a benefit. Simon Gulliford of Ashridge Management College tells the story of a holiday he and his family had when he was a boy. They stayed at a small hotel in Bournemouth. Dinner was a special occasion. Then the waiter spilt the custard all over father's best suit. Hardly quality service!

Without hesitation, however, the manager fixed father up with a new suit from the best tailor in town, and he had the soiled one properly cleaned. It was all done really fast; the Gullifords were treated like royalty for the rest of their stay.

The manager could have dithered and tried to escape with the minimum correction cost and profuse apologies. At worst he might have blamed the waiter or even tried to make out it was all Mr Gulliford's fault. Instead he made full and quick restitution with a courtesy and concern that created a spirit of friendship. The result was that for years the Gulliford family came to this same hotel at Bournemouth for their holidays. One costly mistake, put right in a costly, but unreserved manner and that manager secured the long-term loyalty of a customer. It recouped the cost many times over.

FACE TO FACE WITH THE CUSTOMER

Failure to provide quality is even more obvious in service industries and support functions than in manufacturing, because the provider is usually in the customer's presence.

As Jan Carlzon has described it, many more of the providers of service experience those 'moments of truth' when they are face to face with the customer. Many more people are now employed in the service industries than in manufacturing, even though manufacturing is still the foundation of prosperity.

We have all experienced examples of bad quality service. I hope too we can remember good service, though with human perversity we are more likely to remember the bad. Or is it perverse? We are paying; so we have a right to expect good service. Sometimes, however, we get that extra 'bit' that really adds to the pleasure. Deming's idea of delighting the customer!

A PERSONAL EXPERIENCE OF DISCRETION NOT EXERCISED

I think back over my own experiences. No doubt you can do the same. I think of an Electricity Board which claimed their strictly legal right of charging me for reading my meter (I had been unable to make arrangements for anyone to be present when they wanted to read it). Eventually they found me at home and read the meter; this was followed by a bill for £9.50. Their estimated readings had in any case been in excess of the actual.

I told them that I had no intention of paying, that they had discretion to remit it and that it would make for good customer relationships to do so. For several bills there was no reponse; the charge still appeared and I deducted it when paying. I wrote again and received a curt reply informing me that the charge would continue to appear on my bill until I paid it.

At that point I wrote to tell them I was writing a book on total quality. If they didn't respond positively I would reproduce their curt letter in my book. I never did get a reply, but I did get a credit note cancelling the £9.50, although without a covering letter. Still they did cancel it, so I haven't reproduced the letter. If they had taken the Bournemouth hotel approach I might even have been telling a story which commended them. As it was they ungraciously gave into my insistence.

Why bother to tell the story? Because there is a lesson to be learnt from it. It is about giving quite junior people discretion – empowerment. I assume that there are precise procedures for dealing with fruitless calls to read meters. After a certain number of calls and non-responses, make sure that customers stay in for the meter man. Threaten them with a kind of fine and when at last the meter gets read impose the fine.

Presumably a junior person applied the rule. When I wrote on several occasions another person or persons ignored my letter. Eventually a more senior person signed a letter putting me in my place. I was just a faceless nuisance.

Who was to blame? Was it a special cause where the individual was the sole cause? Or was it systemically caused, because management hadn't given discretion to people and trained them for it? It would not have taken a very senior person to see that it might have been wise to exercise discretion and cancel the charge. This is how a quality relationship is built up. But in Deming terms you have to drive out fear if junior people are going to feel comfortable about making a liberal interpretation of the rules.

OTHER EXAMPLES GOOD AND BAD

I can tell a recent story about a good response. I paid twice by mistake for some attention to my heating system. Back on Christmas Eve came the cheque with a little note: 'I am so glad you appreciated the work I did on your heating. But there is really no need to show it by paying twice.' A little humour goes a long way.

Then on the other side there are some check-in people at the supermarket who ignore your presence as they deal with your goods and talk to their neighbours at the next desk. I believe this is improving. I suspect someone has arranged for it to be covered in employee training.

I think of the motor repair specialist who couldn't solve the mystery of the noisy exhaust system he had sold me, but who took it all to pieces and put it together again without charge, although he could have argued that it was out of warranty. I always go there now. He even remembered my name when he met me after an absence of some months. Those are the little things that make a customer feel good.

I think back to a few years ago when motorway service stations were the last places one would have chosen to eat. The service was often surly and the food inevitably poor. Yet apparently the service message is getting through and great improvements have occurred. The food is better due to systemic decisions, but the attitude must have been the subject of training.

I'm sure we all can tell stories good and bad about restaurants where you can't attract attention to pay your bill. This must be a custom loser, when people are waiting to be seated.

A GOOD ELECTRICITY STORY

I will now tell a good story about an Electricity Board retail shop, to make amends for the bad one. My washing machine was leaking badly. I could have bought a new one from the shop, but it would have taken nearly a week because it had to come from a central store. The last day for ordering for Tuesday delivery was Friday. This was Friday but I was expecting a call from the Hoover service man the next day to see if it was worthwhile repairing my old machine. Therefore, if it couldn't be repaired and I wanted a new one I would have to order on Saturday and wait till Thursday.

The sales lady came up with an excellent solution. I could order a new washing machine there and then, and if the Hoover man was able to repair my machine I could ring up and cancel the order. That is exactly what I did, but because of the initiative shown I have a good feeling about the shop and will no doubt return.

I have just one reservation left. Why does it have to take so long to get the equipment out of the central store? Is this for the convenience of the Electricity Company or of the customer? Does the customer exist for the supplier or the supplier for the customer? Nevertheless, I do have a soft spot for the lady who used her initiative.

WHO IS RESPONSIBLE FOR BAD QUALITY SERVICE?

The examples we have been talking about have tended to concern the end user's experience. They have been about how you and I as purchasers of services and goods from stores and public utilities, perceive the quality of the service we get. A lot of the examples illustrate the way people treat us, what kind of attitude they display and how they use their initiative. They have certainly not involved actions that can easily be measured.

It would be difficult to create a statistical process control chart about discourteous behaviour. First it is subjective in its definition, though you could say that what the customer perceives as discourteous is discourteous. Second it is a case where no variation is acceptable. There's just no room for treating customers with rudeness or indifference. Does this mean that every case of discourteous behaviour is the responsibility of the person who displays it? Or can it be the fault of the system, which is the responsibility of management? The principle that tends to apply in manufacturing is that less than 20 per cent of the problems are due to the worker; more than 80 per cent are the responsibility of management. Management are the only people with the authority to change the framework within which workers operate. Does this apply in services?

If people are discourteous are management truly exempt from responsibility? Who recruited these discourteous people? Who put them into a straitjacket of inflexible procedures supported by fear, so that they cannot use initiative? Management. Who failed to give them good induction training and subsequently gave them little opportunity to grow in understanding and skill? Who presumed that they could be used as 'unskilled labour', who neither need nor can use training? Management. Who failed to watch closely enough what was going on, so that they could encourage more satisfactory and satisfying attitudes? Management. So perhaps it *is* a case of the 80/20 rule again.

Who represents quality to the customer?

Where the customer is face to face with the provider of a service in a store, bank, post office, ticket office, or on the phone to a public utility or government department, it is that front line person who is perceived as the bearer of quality or the one who fails to give it. So that if quality is to be defined in the terms of the customer, there is after all a difference between responsibility for quality in the manufacturing and that in the service field.

Perhaps as far as the customer is concerned it is the shop assistant or ticket person who is responsible. The customer rarely sees the manager and will hardly ask the question: 'Is this a systemic problem, which management should address?' Just now and again some people might ask whether a shop assistant, who is obviously very junior, is receiving the right training, but generally it is the assistant who will be blamed. We have to accept this if customers are the definers of quality.

PRINCIPLE OF VARIATION IN SERVICES

What about the idea we discussed in chapter 3, however, that eventually you get the work of production into statistical control. It is stable. The variations are predictable and will not be changed by personal effort; only a change of system will do that. What Deming calls common causes are now responsible for these variations. They may lie within tolerances acceptable to the customer; and in that case the aim is to get them to new levels of excellence and to go beyond current levels of customer expectation. Or it may be that a policy is being followed or equipment used which creates situations unacceptable to the customer. In either case the action lies with management and changes in the system. The operator can't do this or improve the situation by better personal service; the framework has to be changed.

These principles also apply to services. There are still two kinds of variation in the process – those due to special and unusual circumstances and others due to the system. The system may need changing either to exceed current customer expectations and enhance competitive edge; or to deal with a fault of design or policy.

However in the service area it is less easy to distinguish the various categories. In the *Financial Times* article mentioned above, Christopher Lorenz cites various examples of unsatisfactory service he has received from companies generally renowned for quality in the airline, hotel and mail courier businesses. He tells of being billed in error for services, followed by threatening letters from the Paris office in French and no acknowledgement of his protestations. He goes on to talk of food defects in certain hotel chains and related airlines and says they were so widespread that they could not arise from human error but from 'some sort of system fault'. All the efforts of airline staff to make you happy will be wasted if you have to line up for hours at inadequate ticket desks or if when you get on board there is not enough leg room. Again says Lorenz, 'systems faults' must be responsible.

Lorenz refers again to Richard Whitley's book and comments that it is not enough to get thousands of staff to behave impeccably in their moments of truth; 'product and service quality are intertwined in an intimate fashion'. 'Every aspect of the product and service must be designed, produced and delivered correctly.' This is improving the system to meet faults. Lorenz also emphasises the fact that, 'last year's excellent service may become tomorrow's also ran'. In other words the other kind of system attention which seeks to exceed the expectations of the customer is necessary if you are to have competitive edge.

ZERO DEFECTS IN SERVING THE CUSTOMER

All this being granted, how far can the concept of the process being in statistical control be relevant to face-to-face service to the customer? Can there be variations in relation to discourteous behaviour? Can you say our discourtesy level is predictable and stable. Now we'll hand over to our system experts to see if they can find new and lower levels of discourtesy, where our front line staff are only half as rude. Won't the customers be pleased? Surely on issues of service there must often be not only the search for zero defects, but a recognition that nothing less than the most rigorous definition of zero defects is good enough.

Similarly there is no room for variations in those areas of public service where safety is a prime consideration. You can't talk about the process being in statistical control when you are dealing with people's life and limb. One death is one too many. Only military generals can talk in that way on the field of battle, when they calculate acceptable casualty levels. But in normal peacetime life, zero defects of the most rigorous nature alone will do. We have already mentioned the organisation which aimed to halve serious accidents in the following year. Did they plan to have some?

ROSANDER – SERVICE QUALITY GURU

I had reached this stage in my thinking when I remembered I had a book on my shelves entitled *The Quest for Quality in Services*, by A.C.Rosander. He is a veteran in the field of quality, with a statistical background like Deming and Juran. I pulled it off the shelf and sure enough all the points I had been discovering for myself were dealt with at length. Like Deming in *Out of the Crisis* he is somewhat discursive, but his headings make it easy to find your way around. It is a standard text on quality in the service context.

Deming includes a whole chapter on service organisations and quality in *Out of the Crisis*. He recognises the differences between services and production, particularly the fact that in the service industries many more employees have direct contact with 'masses of people'. He also mentions the large volume of transactions; the vast amount of paper used; the enormous load of processing; great numbers of small money exchanges; all linked with great numbers of small items to be handled. This all results in a tremendous opportunity for making mistakes.

Deming still emphasises the need for management to create the right conditions for people to reduce the number of errors and to increase the pleasure of the customer. He lays great stress on care in hiring and training, not only of the people directly engaged in selling, but of all those who have contact with the public. He cites the way in which a Japanese company gives special training to the person who travels in the lift (or elevator) with the customers. Two months' training is given in order to prepare her to answer questions by the travellers, which may cover a range of issues about the company and its products. The elevator lady is a prime information source.

Rosander is quite specific on the differences between the production and services categories. He complains that concentration on the quality of products has pushed quality of services into the background. Yet as we have seen, the first thing most people think of in relation to quality is some experience with shopping, travelling or public utilities, in which the product itself may play only a small part. The Juran Institute is now giving seminars devoted to quality in the services area.

Rosander makes the point that the manufacturing company buys materials to make a product. The service organisation buys materials to provide a service. The latter will often be judged on the way in which it can bring together a number of products and intangible benefits to provide a total package. Quality provision means that this is done with maximum flexibility to meet the customer's varied needs and not the convenience of the supplier, who may try to restrict the number of options.

In general it is more difficult to measure services than products. Services have the following characteristics:

- They cannot be stored.
- They cannot be inspected or examined – they largely depend on words and expressions during an interaction.
- They cannot be determined beforehand – they consist largely of responses in the situation.
- They do not have a lifetime – they happen there and then in that moment of truth. They depend on the attitude of the person rendering the service at the time. That person is often one of the lowest paid and most junior of the staff.

A GALLUP POLL ON SERVICE QUALITY

A Gallup Poll carried out in the US in 1985 questioned over 1,000 people about quality of services in banking, insurance, government, hospitals, airlines and auto repairs. Employee attitude, behaviour or competence were cited by 67 per cent as the main quality factor; 81 per cent of the reasons for specifically poor quality lay in this same area. This means that the front line person, who is not the developer of the system, is held responsible by the customer for poor quality service. This supports the perception that was dawning on me before I remembered Rosander, that in services the front line operator does have to accept responsibility, though management in the background have to be held to account for not training them better.

The Gallup Poll highlighted the factors which constitute quality service. Under behaviour were included: acting promptly, listening carefully, making clear explanations, getting on with people and showing ability to do the job. Adjectives describing good attitudes included: courteous, friendly, kind, alert, concerned and responsible. There was also concern that the server should appear clean and tidy and dress appropriately.

WILL NINETY PER CENT GOOD BEHAVIOUR DO?

It is obvious that merely being in statistical control of service quality is unacceptable. Ninety per cent courtesy will not do, nor will 90 per cent clean or 90 per cent getting on with people. The system and the individual work together and continuous improvement is not something which can be delegated to management to achieve by action on the system. The individual is responsible, though management can help this to be understood and lived by. Ultimately management are responsible – they do the recruiting and establish the working ambience.

These days, one often meets the tendency of service workers to blame the computer. 'It's the computer you see.' We are less likely to be fooled by that excuse now. I am writing this on a powerful computer. My grandchildren are adept at computers. We know that the computer only acts in accordance with what people tell it to do.

In some parts of the services sector such as transportation and health, the cost of poor quality decisions can be fatal. A faulty computer can lead to an air accident or a train crash. Someone has the responsibility for monitoring such possibilities. Management can establish better systems which make it less likely that such errors will occur, but at the end of the day the person charged with doing the work has to accept responsibility. Zero defects and no variation is the only possible standard.

MARKET RESEARCH

Can service quality be measured? A lot of it is certainly anecdotal. You can't measure it in the same way as temperature, acidity, moisture content and so on. Perhaps there is a similarity between number of rejects and number of complaints, except that the physical state of a defective product is measured and can be placed in a specific category. It is more difficult to categorise complaints with precision.

However if quality is about customer perception, skilfully conducted market research can be utilised to find out what the customer is thinking. This will give some clear indications of what can be done. Rosander suggests making regular surveys of all customers, including lost ones. It is not enough to follow up only complaints if you want to have a balanced picture on which you can base sound decisions for the future. A body of accurate knowledge needs to be built up, as Lorenz and Whitley advocate.

Such customer surveys need to be carried out professionally by a reputable market survey firm, which can identify a reasonable sample and ask questions which produce useful answers, which are designed not to influence the respondent, perhaps unwittingly, to secure the answers it would like to hear.

What can be measured?

A number of service elements can be measured. Wherever they can they should be, at least on a sample basis, with sufficient frequency to know the broad direction, before the complaints start rolling in. Errors in typing and completing forms and invoices create an enormous amount of work in their correction, particularly if they get as far as the customer, who may be so disgusted as to take his or her business elsewhere.

None of these measures should be used to apportion blame, but to direct training emphasis. If someone is untrainable that will emerge later and is a different issue. You will never get people to improve by making criminals of them; the object must be to help them to achieve success, with belief in them for as long as possible.

When it comes to measuring attributes like honesty, reliability and helpfulness it is a matter of observation, of getting to know people. This is part of the managerial or team leader role. Accurate observation is a characteristic of the self-directed work team. Peer pressure is a wonderful educator. The fact that it cannot be quantified (John is honest at a scale of 7 out of 10, Janet is rude at a scale of 6 out of 10), does not make the observation any less accurate. Life would be impossible if this were not so.

SERVICE IN MANUFACTURING

In this chapter we have been making distinctions between services and manufacturing. We have to bear in mind, however, that direct factory production is only part of the work of a manufacturing plant. There are a whole range of support functions, such as budgeting, accounting, purchasing, personnel, administration, storekeeping, transportation, packaging and despatch. Without these the manufactured goods would never be completed or reach their destination. Therefore quality of service must be included in what goes on at a manufacturing plant.

The measuring and observing we have discussed above has to be carried out for those services which make manufacturing possible. These also have a great bearing on the timeliness with which the goods reach the customer, and the condition in which they arrive and, indeed, whether they arrive at all. In 'just–in–time' systems this is critical, though the system is designed to make it easier. In addition to the tangible products there are many intangible facets which accompany the goods; without these the service is unlikely to meet, and certainly not exceed, the expectations of the customer.

It is important that at the manufacturing plant the control of quality for the intangibles is not neglected, just because it is on a different basis in many respects from the quality considerations for manufactured products.

Because quality in the factory has been associated with engineering we tend to think that its methods provide the only way to measure quality. If we stay with our initial definitions of quality we will see that this is not so. 'Fitness for use', 'meeting or exceeding the expectations of the customer', such definitions put the meaning and implementation of quality firmly in the customer's terms. In service and support areas in particular the customer will express quality experiences in narrative terms which can provide unambiguous lessons as a guide for the future.

9. *Techniques for Quality*

One aspect of the quality movement that impresses me is the way in which operations staff have absorbed the principles of statistics in order to control their own work, particularly when working in self-directed teams. It is certainly a revolution in business life when it is considered important for everybody in a plant to have the opportunity to be trained in basic statistics.

This chapter will outline briefly some of the main tools by which workers or associates can record and monitor what is going on and take remedial action when required. In doing so we shall get a better idea of the principles of variation which were set out (without too much statistical detail) in chapter 3.

I am particularly grateful to Henry Neave for the clear way in which he explains statistical charts in his book *The Deming Dimension*. Material produced by Alex Knight and Kathryn Leishman at Ashridge Management College has also been helpful.

THE STATISTICAL PROCESS CHART

The key statistical tool is the process control chart, developed in the thirties by Walter A. Shewhart (who was Deming's mentor). It provides a visual image of what is happening. At Stanbridge visual display units present the situation in relation to any machine so that special problems can be highlighted.

Before we look at the process control chart we consider briefly the run chart. Although this is the basis of the process control chart, it would not give sufficient information to be really useful. It simply

Figure 9.1 Run chart

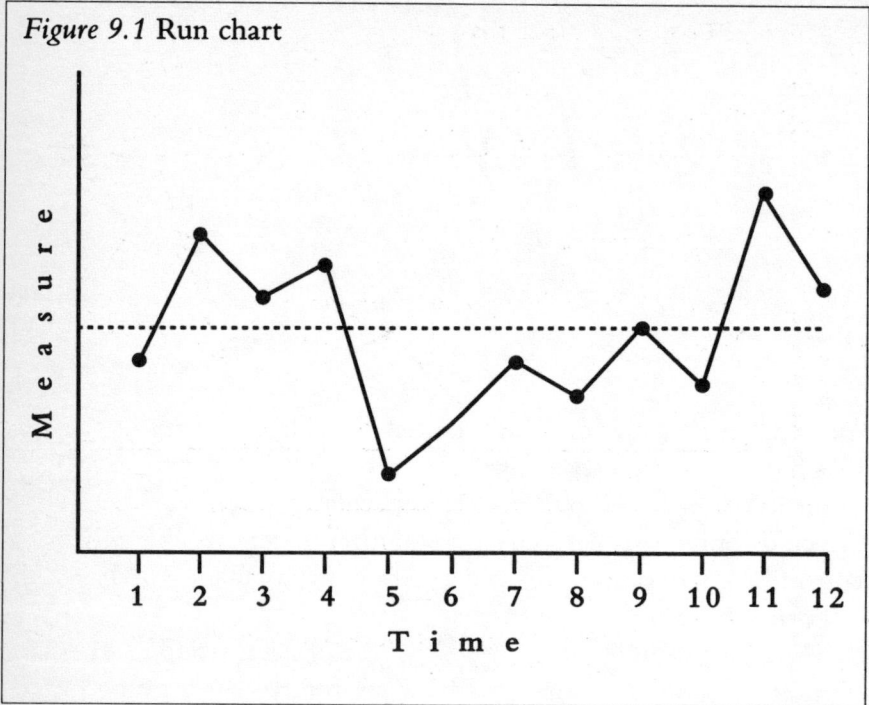

plots samples, at intervals of time, of what the process is producing, whatever it might be. It might relate to the time customers waited in line before being seated at table in a restaurant; how long it took before the drinks order or meal order was taken and so on. This kind of information would have to be specially charted and would normally be part of a survey. With manufacturing processes and many distribution activities the information would be produced automatically. It would look like figure 9.1.

However, this does not tell us enough. It does not indicate whether these ups and downs are serious or not, although we might guess that numbers 5 and 11 need watching. We need the plotting to be compared against something. Here is an example of a process control chart. (Figure 9.2.)

You can see at a glance that superimposed on the run chart are two lines called the upper and lower control limits. These limits are drawn in such a way that a measurement would only be outside the limit once in a thousand times if the sources of variation are merely

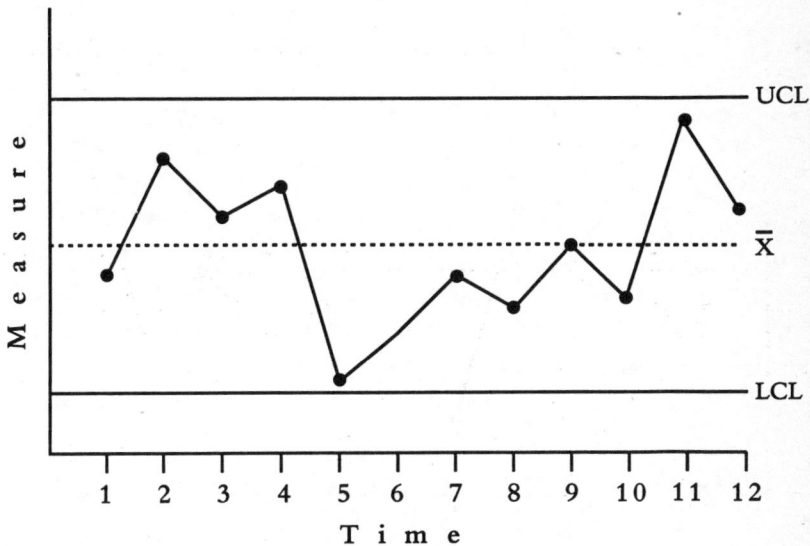

Figure 9.2 Process control chart

UCL = Upper Control Limit
LCL = Lower Control Limit

random fluctuations. So if the limits are breached it is most likely that some special cause, something that is not a random fluctuation is happening. The random fluctuations within the limits are inevitable, though a change to the system might reduce them. As we saw in chapter 3 this would be the responsibility of management.

To make the variations more meaningful and to make the pattern clear, a mean line is charted mid-way between the two limits. When the variations move up and down in a fairly regular manner yet stay within the limits the process is said to be within statistical control (that is stable). This is the position in figure 9.2.; even points 5 and 11 are within the limits, so that any action taken to deal with them would be 'tampering'.

(There are two kinds of control chart. One is called the $\overline{X}$ chart; it measures the mean of each sample and reveals any tendency for drift. The other, the $\overline{R}$ chart, measures the range of each sample, the largest measurement minus the smallest. It reveals the the tendency of the process to behave more or less randomly. For our purpose here, which is simply to get a broad idea, we will not worry unduly about the distinction.)

However now look at a different chart in figure 9.3; something is happening. It is in statistical control but it seems to be hovering near the lower limit. As long as it is within limits, however, we will not intervene. If we 'tamper' we shall establish new limits and new means and in time will have corrupted the whole process.

Bill Scherkenbach tells how a machine at Ford Motor Company for turning out transmission shafts was fitted with an automatic compensating device to change the setting whenever the shaft diameter was deemed too large or too small. When as an experiment the compensating device was turned off the variation was in fact reduced. The compensating device did not take account of the fact that the process was already in control. Its ups and downs represented the lowest variability of which it was capable under the present system. Every time compensation took place it was in fact

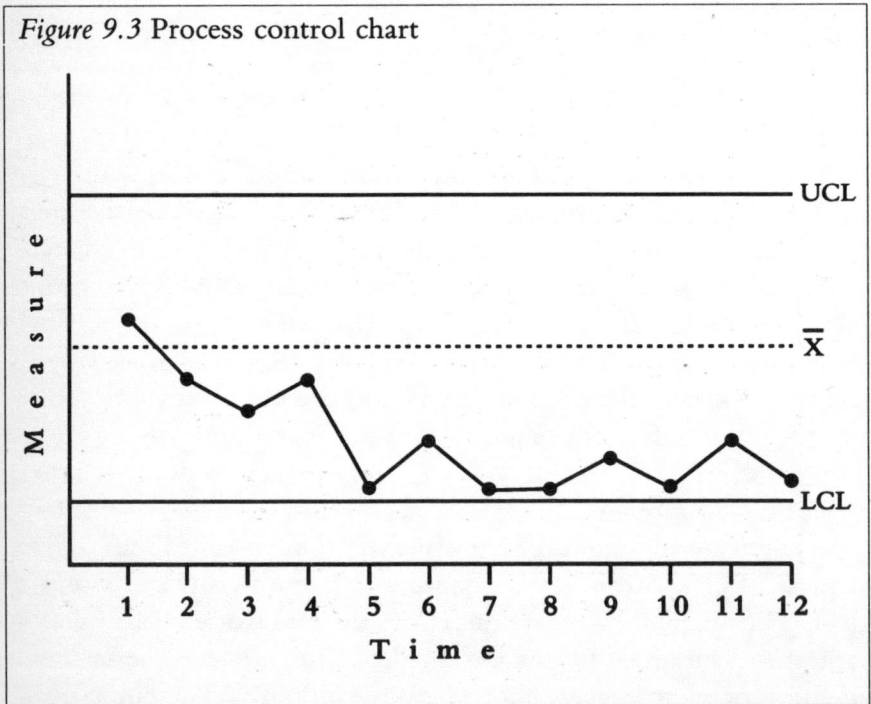

Figure 9.3 Process control chart

changing the mean and the limits and creating extra variability from the original limits. There were no special causes. To reduce the variability would require a change to the system, to address what Deming calls 'common causes'.

The variations which occur while process performance is in statistical control or stable are the result of a multitude of small random fluctuations. To get these to zero is impossible given the nature of matter, a concept we are understanding better with the advent of chaos theory. Even Crosby is not referring to these when he speaks of zero defects, though the smaller these can be made by improving the system the more likely you are to delight the customer.

Figure 9.4, however, is a cause for concern. The process is not in statistical control. $\overline{X}$ has shot right over the upper limit. Some special cause may be at work, an irregular cause of variation. This does call for attention, for if not dealt with some serious loss of

Figure 9.4 Process control chart

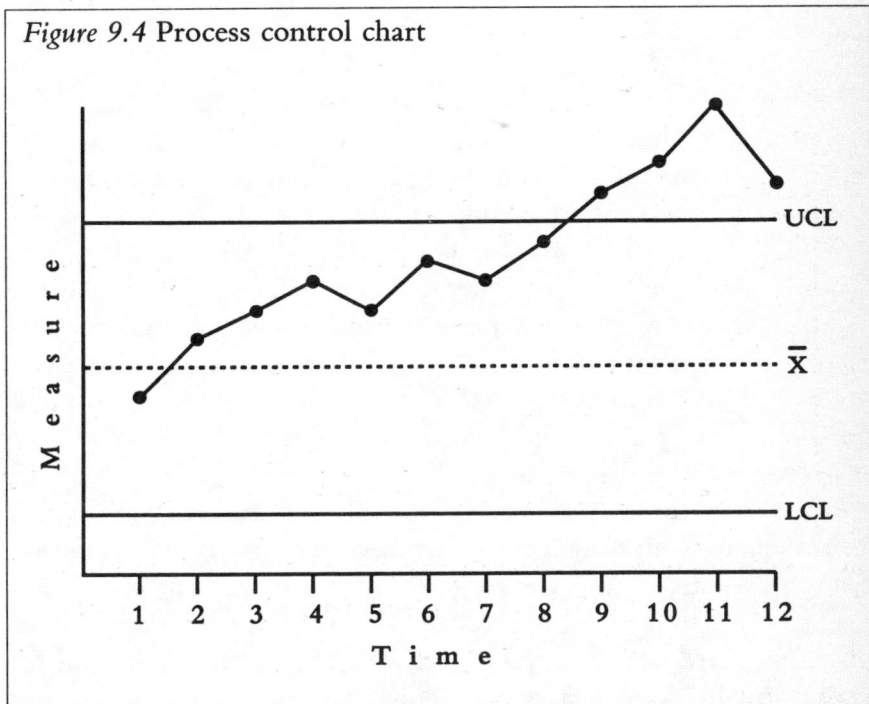

Figure 9.5 Process control chart

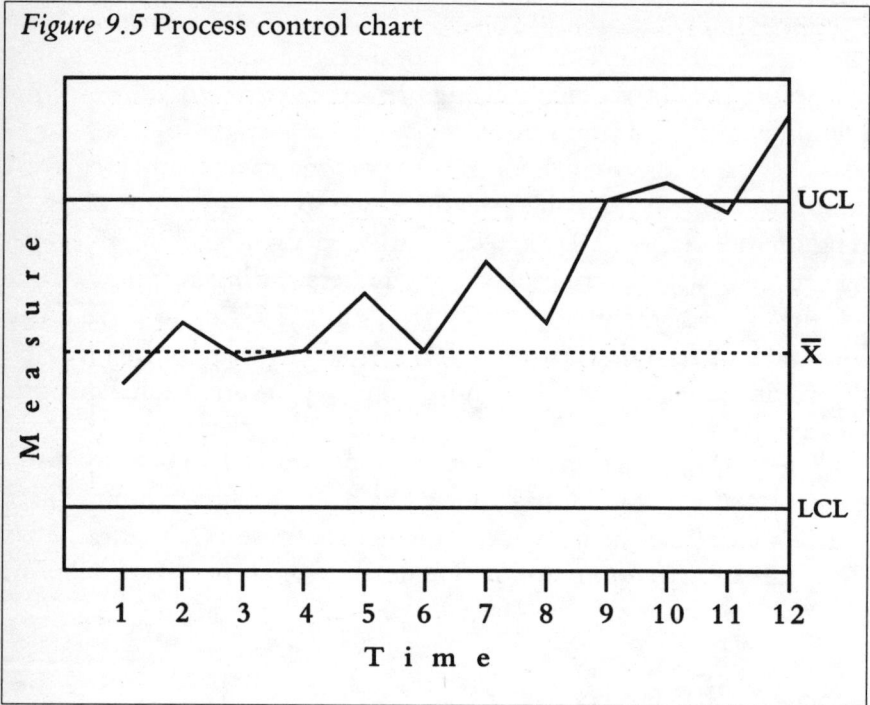

quality might occur. It could mean a variety of things. That is what the team must find out. It could mean a change in machine setting, an employee unfamiliar with the specification, or the introduction of material from a different supplier.

Figure 9.5 (also $\overline{X}$) could indicate three different operators who set up the machine and operate at different levels. Figure 9.6 ($\overline{R}$) could be a case of an inexperienced worker who eventually learns the job and gets into control.

In each of the cases 9.4 to 9.6 action has to be considered. The purpose of the public display of the charts near the machine is so that the trained workers, especially if they are members of a self-directed work team, can themselves deal with some of the special causes. They cannot change the system, address the common causes, though they may well have suggestions to management on the best way to do that. The process control chart simply provides a quick visual way of answering the question 'Is this process behaving the way it usually does, or has something changed?'

Figure 9.6 Process control chart

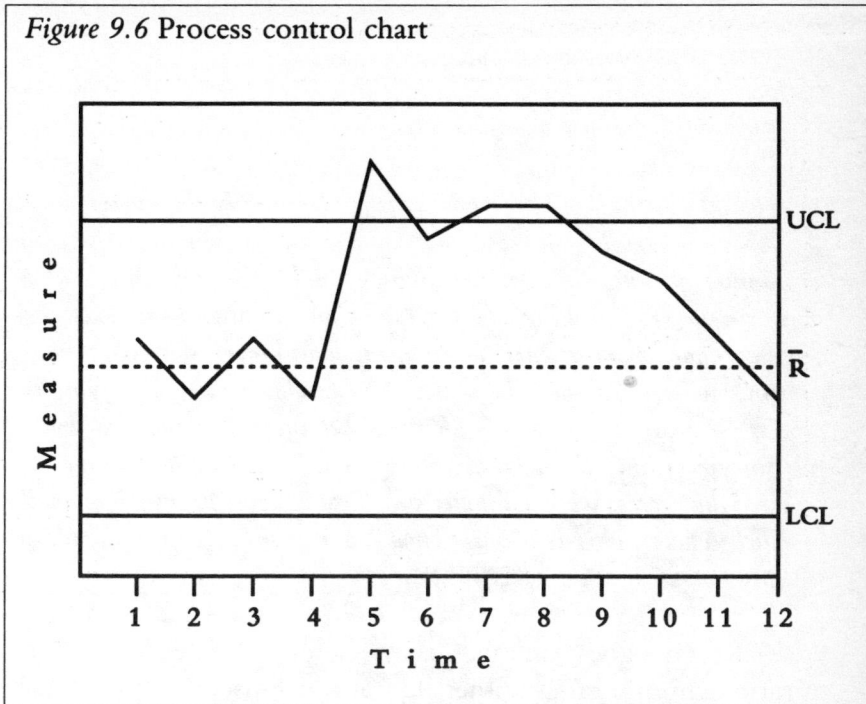

EXAMPLES OF PROCESS CONTROL CHART USAGE

Most repetitive processes can be tracked by these charts. The aim may be to check on the size of a part being machined, labour time used to produce a part, speed and accuracy of information processing, (say in a bank), checking on a telephone ordering system, late departures in airlines and railways, lost baggage, overbooking and underbooking in airlines. In the case of some personalised services an out-of-control chart may reveal that something has changed in the environment and the service needs to adjust to this.

Alex Knight in an Ashridge programme note makes some useful observations on how to interpret a process control chart:

Just because a process is 'in control' it does not necessarily mean it is within tolerances or up to the standard of the customer's expectations. Being 'in control' is a characteristic of the process, whereas the

113

'tolerances' of specification are a characteristic of the design.

If the design tolerances, specifications or customer's expectations are too high then a particular process may be physically incapable of meeting the requirement 100 per cent of the time, even if the process is statistically under control. No amount of objective setting or incentive schemes will improve the situation until the process is fundamentally improved.

As an example, suppose that in a bank the manager sets the maximum queuing time to two minutes and the process control chart shows an upper control limit (UCL) to be two minutes 45 seconds, then it is clear that some customers will have to wait longer than two minutes and improvement can only be achieved by fundamentally modifying the process. Rewarding the tellers for the times they meet the two-minute rule and punishing them for exceeding it can only be destructive. Of course if the process were not under statistical control, the problem would be much worse. This is because even more of the customers would be waiting longer than the specified time.

Alex Knight goes on to comment on the need to make specifications meaningful, neither tighter nor looser than is actually needed. This is a system problem, but in handling it we need to bear in mind the telephone clerk with two minutes per telephone enquiry.

There are a number of other tools used, especially by self-directed work teams and quality circles, in addition to the control chart. I set out below a brief description of some of them.

CAUSE AND EFFECT DIAGRAM

This is most frequently called the fishbone diagram, though sometimes the Ishikawa diagram, after the man who developed it, Kaoru Ishikawa. These diagrams (see Figure 9.7) are used in problem-solving sessions as a means of trying to identify the most likely causes of the problem and trying to decide which possibility to investigate first.

The head of the fish is the effect which is undesirable, the cause of which is being searched for. One then works back along the 'spine' and upward and downward along subsidiary bones. These are usually labelled people, money, materials, machines or whatever

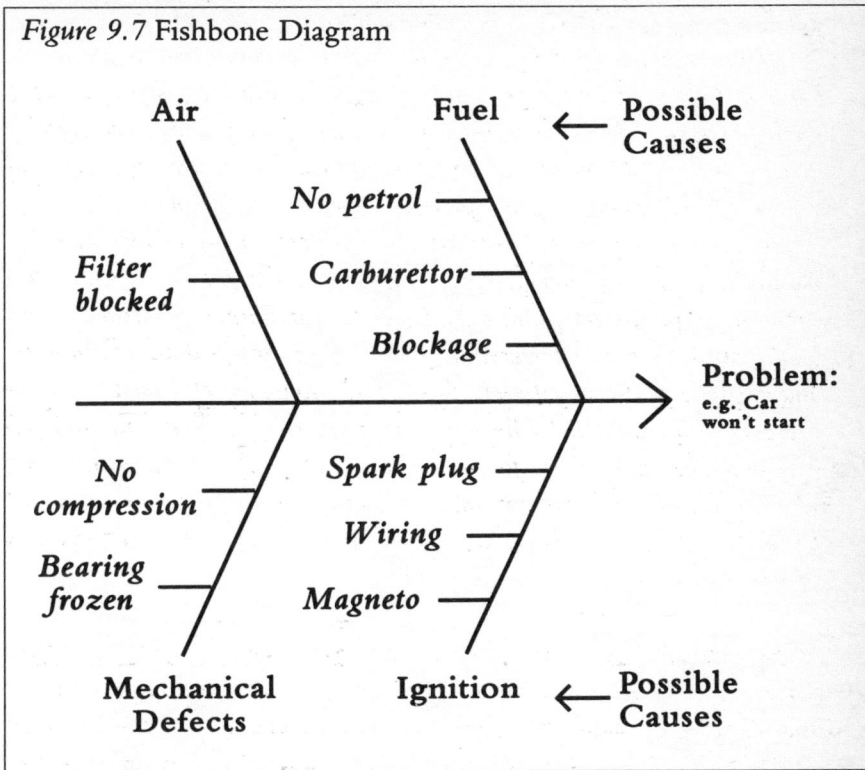

Figure 9.7 Fishbone Diagram

is appropriate to the area under consideration. Further bones lead off the subsidiary ones within the limits of space. The fishbone diagram gets discussion going, with a focused approach to searching for the cause of the problem. It points out where extra data is needed and keeps the discussion on course.

FLOW DIAGRAMS

Flow diagrams are familiar to those who work with computers. They encourage systems thinking with all the interdependent links being shown by the connecting arrows. Flow diagrams can be used to display what *should be* happening, with an alternative showing what is *actually* happening. Figure 9.8 illustrates the skeleton of a flowchart, which as the description suggests, shows the flow of the action.

Figure 9.8 'Getting up in the morning' (abbreviated)

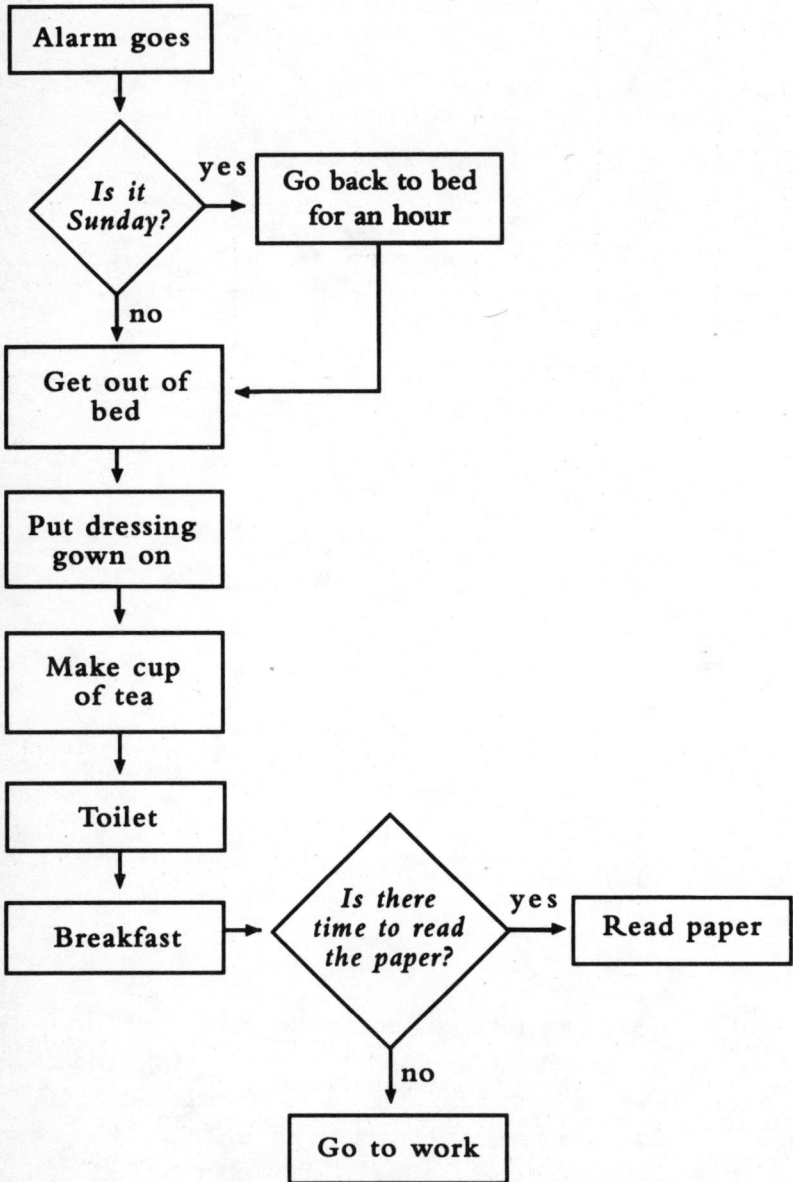

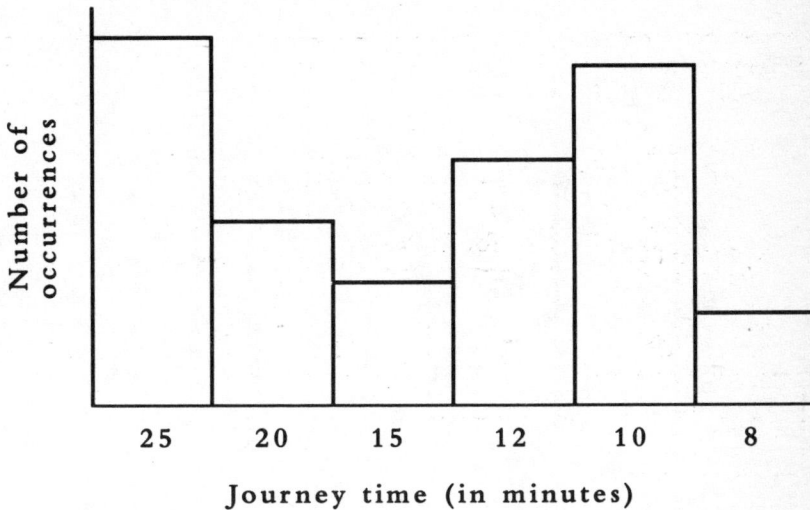

Figure 9.9 Histogram

Number of occurrences

Journey time (in minutes)

25   20   15   12   10   8

HISTOGRAMS

Illustrated in figure 9.9, these measure how frequently something happens, whether it is time taken over a journey at different times of the week or the number of sales at different times of the year. Joining the tops of the columns produces a graph which can show trends.

PARETO DIAGRAMS

Looking a bit like histograms, these put the results of investigating an issue into some kind of priority order (see Figure 9.10). They are likely to reveal that 80 per cent of the problems come from 20 per cent of the causes, a principle to which Pareto gave his name.

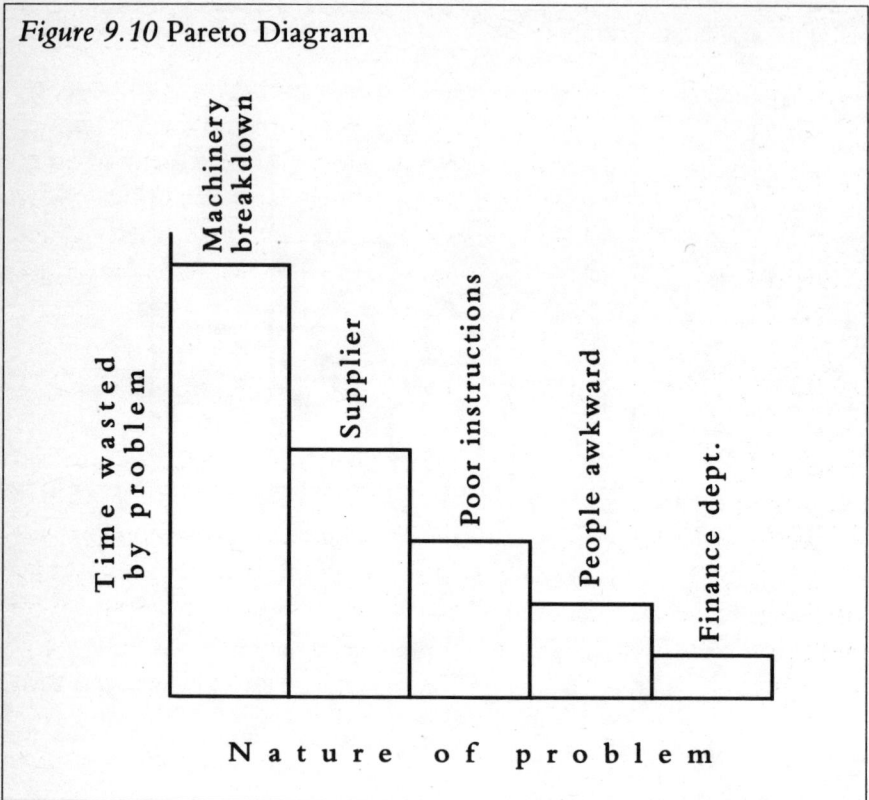

Figure 9.10 Pareto Diagram

SCATTER DIAGRAMS

These are a method of charting the relationship between two variables (see Figure 9.11). They might be used to plot the relationship between the extent of a worker's training and the number of defects, between light levels and computer errors or between moisture content and durability. Figure 9.11 illustrates this.

THE VALUE OF THE TECHNIQUES

This chapter has been concerned to give just a taster of the techniques of controlling work and solving problems, as used in the pursuit of

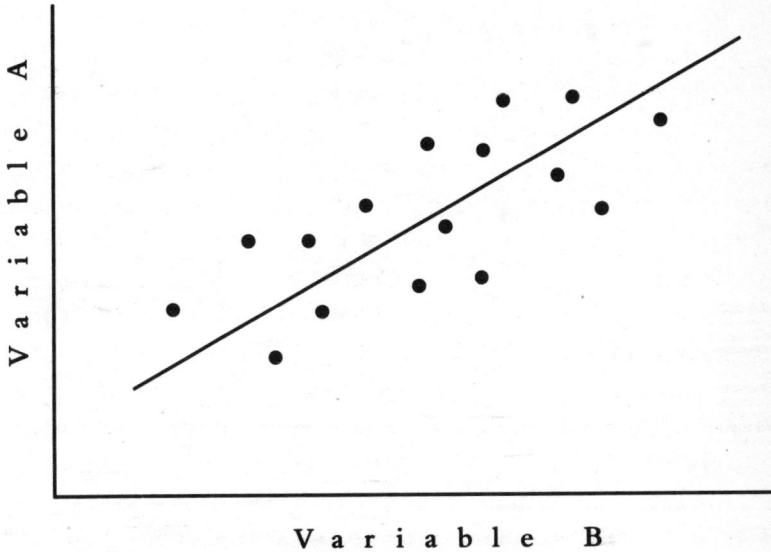

Figure 9.11 Scatter Diagrams

quality, by self-directed work teams and similar working groups.

They are simple enough to use. They do not require a degree in statistics, but they add to the likelihood of results being uniform, which is the key to quality in the customer's terms.

Another significant feature is the amount of interest they generate. No longer do workers just come to work and do as they are told. They have a role to play, an opportunity to be part of a team which wrestles with problems. The popularity of puzzles of one kind and another shows that people appreciate something to tease their brains. And if they get some of that at work it means that they will actually enjoy the job. Thus the use of these techniques is motivational. It was therefore necessary to say something about them from this motivational perspective as well as from the operational point of view. I hope enough has been said just to give the flavour of the new way of working.

10. BS5750 – Sound Procedures

No book on total quality published in the UK would be complete without some information about the BS5750 series, the standard of the British Standards Institute, which is virtually identical with the international standard series ISO9000 and the European standard series EN29000.

Increasingly accreditation under this standard is being insisted upon as a condition of being accepted as a supplier by many of the most reputable firms. We need to be clear about what it offers and what it does not. It does not accredit companies as total quality firms, but it does mean that procedures are followed in a firm which gives a framework which facilitates the introduction of total quality management (TQM).

A colleague at Ashridge, Rod Boyle, has helped me with this chapter and he makes it clear that

> *BS5750 is not a product specification standard, but a management standard system, relating to HOW quality is provided. It provides a framework of procedures with which to achieve quality, but it is a means to an end and should not be seen as anything more. It is geared to the achievement of quality of production, not the production of quality.*

ITS ORIGINS

BS5750 was first published in 1979 as the quality assurance standard intended to cover manufacturing industries, especially engineering. It was revised in 1987 and harmonised with the ISO9000 and

EN29000 series standards and is now applicable to a diversity of industries, so that a company accredited under BS5750 is automatically accredited under ISO9000 series and hence recognised internationally as meeting quality standards.

Its principles

The guiding principle of the standard is the same as that of total quality in general. Goods and services are produced *right first time*, with everybody in the organisation having a part to play. The entire organisation is expected to be committed to quality as defined in the procedures.

The Employment Department has issued a booklet: *Total Quality Management and BS5750 – the links explained* (published by the former Training Agency, undated, but obtainable from the Department at Moorfoot in Sheffield). This defines quality in the BS5750 sense as

> *Fitness for purpose and safe in use. Quite simply, it is the service provided or product designed and constructed to satisfy the customers' needs.*

This requires sensitivity to reality and to the needs of the marketplace. It does not aim for perfection, but simply for all goods and services consistently to meet an agreed standard.

Tolerances determined by the customers are acceptable. They need only be tight enough to meet the customers' needs. BS5750 doesn't go beyond into Deming-Land and talk about exceeding the customers' expectations. If there are any legal requirements to be met, of course, there is no tolerance there.

BS5750 claims, according to the Employment Department paper, to be a common-sense approach which gets you to set down the following points on paper in an organised way:

- What you do.
- Justification of what you do.
- Evidence that you do what you say.
- A record of what you did.

BS5750 requires all aspects of an organisation's operations to be covered: the inputs, what is done with these inputs and the resulting outputs. Its aim is certainly not the mere counting of failures and defects as in traditional quality control and the inspectorial approach, which as we have said bolts the stable door after the horse has fled. It starts with a clear description of what the customer needs and finishes with a description of how those needs are met.

It covers by implication all the facets of business activity, the procedures relating to the whole supplier/customer chain within the organisation, and, indeed, all activity from initial supplier to end consumer:

- Design and product development.
- Procurement of materials and components.
- Process, programme or project planning and development.
- Actual production.
- Such inspection, testing and examination as is still required.
- Packing and storage.
- Sales and distribution.
- Installation and operation in customers premises.
- Technical assistance and maintenance.
- Disposal after use, where applicable.
- Marketing and market research

THE STRUCTURE OF BS5750

There are three parts to BS5750. Organisations have to meet the one which is appropriate to their activity. There is an additional two-sectioned part O which gives guidance on choosing the appropriate part to go for and how it fits in with overall quality management. The details of the three parts may be summarised as follows:

Part 1
This is the most comprehensive award and is appropriate where the standards are specifically expressed by the customer. It covers managerial responsibility, the quality system, contract review, design control, document control, purchasing, process control,

inspection, testing, measuring and related equipment, control of non-conforming products and services, corrective action, handling, storage, packaging and delivering, quality records, training, servicing and statistical techniques.

Part 2
This is concerned with quality assurance in production and installation; it does not cover design control and servicing.

Part 3
This is the most limited of the series of standards and is concerned only with quality assurance at final assurance and test stage. It is the furthest of the series from total quality management, but it is saying that if you have not gone the whole way to building quality in as you go along, then at least your final inspection will take place in an ordered and reliable manner. It is a case of 'half a loaf is better than none'. Those who start by getting part 3 accreditation may go on to the fuller accreditation.

It is clear from the above that when an organisation says it has BS5750 accreditation, it needs to be asked how far it has been taken. Often external customers will express a view as a condition of a contract.

BENEFITS OF BS5750

It gives a minimum language with which suppliers and customers can communicate. Suppliers can use it to demonstrate that they have in place a quality assurance system which protects and preserves product quality. This goes some way to producing co-operation between supplier and customer, but not in itself as far as chapter 6 of this book proposes, where supplier and customer enter into a close alliance, so that they are members of one family. Nevertheless, it could lead in that direction.

Following the procedures will lead to many of the benefits of total quality management in terms of reducing rework, retraining and corrective action and lost orders. Many regard BS5750 as a good starting point on the route to total quality management.

LIMITATIONS OF STANDARDS

As this book has made quite clear the goal of total quality management is one that never can be reached. It is an endless journey. There is always a better way. Continuous improvement is of the essence. It is not surprising then that there is no BS, EN, or ISO standard for total quality. It would be difficult to establish a standard for a mindset, for commitment, for empowerment, for *kaizen*, for leadership, for teamwork, collaboration, pride in work, creative thinking by all, and moreover a standard which takes on board all of these and others simultaneously.

The formal standards therefore go as far as they can in this direction, but in the nature of things are bound to be more mechanistic than would be the case if the full quality revolution had taken place. Because they restrict themselves to what they can realistically contribute to, BS5750 and the other standards have to deal with procedures and things which can be documented. There is therefore the danger that it may be applied bureaucratically, without the engagement of hearts and minds. People may then feel that as they have BS5750 they are all right; they are a quality organisation. They may mistake the form for the substance.

I don't think we can blame BS5750 for this, but we need to be aware of the limitations. It's a bit like the whole question of law. How wonderful it would be if everyone did the right thing from the heart because they wanted to. However, we live in the real world.

What BS5750 and the other standards instil as a procedural code, total quality management inspires as a way of life and thought. BS5750 has standards of what is desirable; total quality is a strategy for doing things right. BS5750 focuses on the actual product or service with some recognition of the steps to be taken; total quality follows through in depth all the company-wide steps which lead to the offering of a product or service to the external customers or end consumers. BS5750 offers processes; total quality a management way of life and philosophy.

BS5750 doesn't really cover continuous improvement, except by implication, and it requires no specific commitment to employee involvement, which we have seen is central to total quality. The goal of BS5750 is to pass the test and get the award. The goal of total quality is never to let up in the search for doing things better and better and better and . . . that is, continuous improvement.

BS5750 in a company can be quite low key, run by a few experts as a procedure to which people are instructed to work. There is no inherent ownership by everybody. There is no emblazonment of it throughout the company. It does what it has to do. It is a worthy step along the road, but it should not be seen as a destination. To be fair it makes no other claims for itself. No more than any law or code reckons to be a transforming power in the lives of people or organisations.

Getting BS5750 accreditation

The British Standards Institute can be approached by any organisation intending to get accreditation. Its address is:

BSI Quality Assurance
Business Development
P.O. Box 375
Milton Keynes
MK14 6LL

The pursuance of registration by an organisation will probably require help from a consultancy, experienced in the area, to set up the procedures. I would recommend that a consultant be appointed who has the wider vision of total quality and both recognises the value of BS5750 and can see beyond it to the fuller purpose. Any consultants who are totally absorbed in the procedures, rather than seeing them as stepping stones to greater things, will not be to the ultimate benefit of the organisation. Having said that, they do need to be adept at the procedures.

Before the final application takes place there are accredited bodies, including BSI QA themselves and Lloyds Register QA, who will make an initial assessment and indicate weaknesses which need to be corrected before the final audit.

Once having been accredited, there are twice-yearly audits in order to retain the award. Failure in these means losing it.

ASSESSING BS5750

I suppose one could sum up a reasonable attitude to BS5750 by saying: 'Just because you want to hitch your wagon to a star, there is no reason why you should not drive it efficiently on the earth.' The standard is already making a major contribution to improving quality. It is also required as a qualification for business by many customers. Just because you are convinced that you want to go much, much further is no reason for ignoring it.

Be aware the standard's limitations, exceed it by all means, but use it on its own terms for what it is. If it tends itself to be short term, it does not prevent you from being long term in your perspective. If it does not attempt to cover all the wider issues of a totally committed workforce, it may nevertheless be used to give them some of the tools with which to check their own work. BS5750 is no more the whole of total quality than statistical process control is. We must use everything which will help, but with our eyes open and a vision which is inexhaustible.

11. Stanbridge gets the Q1 award

This chapter is the first of a number which will illustrate the principles we have been studying. We shall see them in action within organisations, starting with Stanbridge Precision Turned Parts in Luton UK.

GROWING THE COMPANY

The story of Stanbridge Precision Turned Parts illustrates what a small company can do in establishing primacy through quality.

The first time I met Bob Knox, managing director of the company, he had been told there was only one way forward and that was to grow. He didn't particularly want the company to grow. After the hard graft of the early years, he was now able to lead something like a normal life, with time for family and golf.

However he had decided to develop the company so as to gain the Ford Q1 award, a prestigious accolade which could be obtained only by following the most stringent quality procedures. It carried with it the right to fly the Q1 flag and was respected by everyone in the automobile business.

My immediate reaction was to assume that Bob had, by default, made his decision and was now committed to growth. I envisaged his weekends spent working and his return to a life of business pressure such as he had left behind. However, when 18 months later, I attended the ceremony at which the parliamentary private secretary to the Prime Minister unfurled the flag of quality, I realised that total quality in fact reduces the pressures on management and shares responsibility more evenly throughout the company.

It certainly increased the prosperity of this company and its 66 employees, six of whom were new recruits, taken on in a recession, to be trained ready for an expected upturn. Among some 70 companies making components for the larger motor manufacturers, Stanbridge was one of only a handful who were weathering the 1991 recession without alarm and despondency. A reputation for quality was the key to this.

INTRODUCING STANBRIDGE

Stanbridge Precision Turned Parts make the small parts which are essential to automobile manufacture, for example the small turned parts associated with a carburettor. If the quality is not maintained you'll either get too much or too little petrol coming through – the resultant mechanical breakdown throwing any manufacturing deficiencies into stark relief. Too much of that would mean disaster for Stanbridge.

Bob Knox is a friendly sort of man who works very closely with all his staff; he knows remoteness won't get results. Bob heads a small management team. He personally attends to the sales and to growing international business. The company is already in the USA (east and west coast), France, Brazil, India, Australia, New Zealand and Holland. The company's turnover in 1990 was £3 million.

Achieving the Q1 award is dependent upon ensuring that all employees understand statistical process control and problem-solving techniques. A full-time training officer must be appointed, a training area set aside, and improvement groups established. Before a contract is signed to supply a customer, the firm has to foresee the things which could go wrong in terms of quality and agree the actions that will be taken should they arise. Clear standards of what is meant by quality have to be agreed.

THE Q1 SYSTEM

Q1 is different from BS5750. BS5750 makes a good springboard for attaining Q1 standards, but Q1 goes well beyond procedural documentation, to focus on attitudes and results.

The Q1 award is made to suppliers by Ford for consistency of quality in parts supplied. Proven commitment to improve the quality of these parts is also required. There is no ceiling to what is meant by improvement. A never-ending journey is implied. You never arrive at perfect quality. Ford Quality Assurance Engineers have to be satisfied that the process of continuous improvement is built into the culture. It has to be evident that all employees check for themselves what they are producing, swiftly rectifying errors and eliminating them at source, thus dealing effectively with rejects and defects.

UNDERSTANDING/COMMITMENT/QUALITY PLANNING

Stanbridge management had to accomplish the following:

- Attend specific seminars on statistical methodologies.
- Communicate a commitment to quality to the rest of the employees and provide evidence that a plan had been developed to guide this effort.
- Ensure that defect prevention and continuous improvement were understood and provide evidence that these principles were high priority management issues.
- Ensure that the management team understood the concepts of variability, statistical control, capability and over-control.
- Provide evidence that there was an attempt to understand quality in customer terms and to obtain customer feedback (including visits to customer facilities and investigating the cause of returned products).
- Implement a disciplined approach to quality planning, as found in the Ford Quality Planning Guidelines.

Training

- Provide training in statistical methodology to all employees.
- Ensure a qualified statistical specialist was continually available as a training resource.
- Prepare training manuals or guidelines on statistical techniques and make them available to all staff.
- Make available training in advanced statistical techniques.

Management controls/implementation

- Have a strategy for pursuing continuous improvement and implementing quality planning and statistical process controls.
- Support the strategy by actions such as preventive maintenance of equipment, statistical activity to prevent defects and reduce variations, employee involvement groups (or quality circles) and monitoring quality costs?
- Encourage a participative management style.
- Monitor training progress and its effectiveness.

Management have to give assurance that better ways of monitoring the improvement statistics are being continuously developed. They are also asked to provide examples of how managers use statistical thinking to manage the operations.

A very important question concerns the way in which the customer chain concept is actively promoted, because as we saw in chapter 6 this ensures that everyone recognises visible customers.

Response to quality concerns

A further category in the Ford review of its suppliers' relates to 'response to quality concerns'. What happens when products are returned, and when customer warranty or field service issues arise? Are such problems turned into opportunities?

The Ford review also deals with suppliers monitoring how their product is used at Ford plants, so that there is a two-way involvement.

THE RESPONSE OF STANBRIDGE MANAGEMENT

Stanbridge management gave impressive evidence of the action they had taken. Training shines through every line. Training courses and seminars attended are specified; the use of outside consultants is described, together with cross-functional teams.

Stanbridge had to provide qualitative evidence that this learning was taking place as an integral part of the job, as well as setting out a wide range of training activities including 'off the job' statistical training. Team building training, machine operating and machine setting in the new context were included.

Such training makes employees marketable outside, but the potential for losing staff is offset, to a certain extent, by the *esprit de corps* that quality builds up. It provides a reward in its own right and creates reluctance to move on to an 'unknown quantity'. (Some employees did feel, however, that the very pressures caused by success made it difficult to maintain the training momentum.)

QUALITY SYSTEM SURVEY REPORT

Before the Q1 award is made, a fuller report is signed by the Ford quality engineer awarding marks for a series of aspects of the whole process.

Planning for quality
This involves clear organisational arrangements for planning quality into the products and reaching agreement with the customer on what defines quality; methods of reviewing design and process changes, updating of operating instructions and analysing faults are also evaluated.

Statistical methods
Control charts and process logs, together with operator and supervisor behaviour, are checked out in relation to statistical

methods employed; continual improvement methods are expected, not least that there are arrangements for those who supply the supplier to be brought into the chain of quality.

Documentation

The documentation for auditing, quality-related functions, monitoring and all other aspects of production is checked for clarity and soundness.

Testing and measurement

Measurement is crucial in the quality process; it is therefore essential to have the appropriate instruments and procedures, together with a ready understanding of them by everyone. Great emphasis is placed on being able to ensure that faulty and sound products do not get mixed. This is being practical, although the ultimate aim is to ensure there are no faulty products.

Customer

All members of the organisation are required to understand the precise requirements of the customer and to exercise a disciplined approach to problems which may arise.

General

Records of tests, rework documentation and packing arrangements which will preserve quality are examined. Environmental standards, such as cleanliness of paintwork and surroundings, housekeeping and working conditions are also assessed to see if they are such as to encourage quality working, on the grounds that non-quality surroundings are not conducive to quality working.

Although Stanbridge got its award, it was not an accolade for perfection. There remained, on the award documentation, a list of things to be done, under the heading 'Areas of guidance for improvement'. Total quality is a never-ending journey, with mileposts along the route to encourage the traveller to continue.

One of the areas noted as needing improvement concerned the fact that the managing director needs to delegate more, so that delays in meeting orders do not occur in his absence. This was seen as a quality issue.

QUALITY IMPROVEMENT TEAMS

All too often, people think of total quality as meaning mainly the running of quality circles. This is only one element of the process. To gain Q1, Stanbridge had to make their quality circles more effective. They restarted them as quality improvement teams, and ensured that lack of training which stalled an earlier attempt was no longer an issue.

Q1 involves continual self-assessment and continual evaluation of the process as well as the outcomes. Q1 looks for a culture change, and because the improvement sought is never-ending, the goal-posts are constantly shifting; everyone has to adapt constantly.

One of the strategies used in helping the improvement teams to function effectively is to bring in an outside consultant to contribute some discipline to the process. The discipline includes encouragement to 'Congratulate your team on a job well done'.

Self-monitoring and self-knowledge are essential to the quality programme at Stanbridge. It is not enough to rely on the statistical process control facilitator. Everyone must take responsibility for their own work, both individually and jointly as team members. This is implicit in a Team Oriented Problem Solving (TOPS) system which is used by the Stanbridge quality improvement teams. Everyone was issued with a training manual and was expected to understand it.

PARTNERSHIP BETWEEN SUPPLIER AND MANUFACTURER

The quality manager would once have been described as the quality controller, but now everyone is a quality controller. When quotations are being made to customers, there is an advanced planning quality team who, as a team, look at the specifications and capabilities of the machines employed to make the part. This enables them to make a feasibility and capability statement to send with the quotation. If the machine is not capable of operating at the required tolerance, this is openly stated and the customer is invited to consider whether the tolerance is too high. It is a joint decision between Stanbridge, the supplier, and the customer.

This partnership between supplier and customer is fundamental to the success of total quality. Thus it is not merely a matter of the main manufacturer having a well-trained workforce, but of all its suppliers, such as Stanbridge in relation to Ford, being similarly well trained.

An attitude survey of customers – the various automobile companies Stanbridge supplies – was taken. It included those who were the most likely to complain, so that the strengths and weaknesses of Stanbridge could become apparent. Quality customer care is a matter of growing in empathy so that you stand in the customers' shoes and share their expectations.

QUALITY MEANS EVERYTHING

Total quality is what it says, total. At Stanbridge it is not just the components which have to have quality built in, but quality exists in relation to every aspect of the business.

Stanbridge really do follow the working environment aspects of the Q1 document. They do paint the surroundings, because first impressions and tidy areas help to keep the staff working up to standard. The paint brush has moved on to the goods van which promotes the image of Stanbridge when it moves around the Luton area on its delivery schedule.

The Q1 teams cover the whole organisation and all employees are fully involved. There were difficulties at the beginning of the programme; the main one was the fact that the prospect of change itself was rather unnerving. However the obvious benefits to the viability of the company eventually won people over. The operations manager feels that total quality has ultimately consolidated the best of Stanbridge's past and enhanced the family spirit. The managing director did his utmost to convey to people how vital they were to the success of the business.

OPTIMISM

Bob Knox is optimistic about future business. Stanbridge expect their international connections to grow. They have gained a large contract from a European firm because their manufacturing is cheaper and there are only two others in the UK who can compete with them.

A LEARNING CULTURE

The company is not resting on its laurels. Q1 is a beginning not an end. Stanbridge recognise that they always have to be aware of their competitors and the developments taking place in technology. They make it their business to have a learning attitude, listening to the market-place, and watching out for technological development some of which could threaten them if they did not maintain awareness.

I found Stanbridge to have a learning culture in every respect. There is training to enable everyone to be part of the quality crusade in practical ways. There is development activity to help everyone in the organisation, and thereby enable the organisation as a whole to grow. There is the power of continuous improvement in which learning to do things better never ceases and everyone in the company is engaged in constant dialogue to satisfy customer needs more effectively.

This all added up to Stanbridge Precision Turned Parts being well on the way to becoming a learning organisation in which 'learning equals working' and is not a separate activity undertaken by a training department. Learning is everyone's business and happens through the job, off the job and beyond the job. Thus Stanbridge prepare themselves to adapt to whatever circumstances lie ahead. They face the future with confidence and quality represented by Q1 is the key to this.

12. Growing People at Rothmans

The story of Rothmans, the international tobacco firm, is very much about quality from the people perspective. Teamworking is the key quality issue for them.

Colin O'Neill, responsible for people development at the two Rothmans plants in Darlington and Spennymoor in County Durham, outlined the Rothman priorities in quality:

> *Growing people, giving them accountability and responsibility, taking them from baby to full adult is the key activity of organisations, and managers are the people with the key role in this growing of people. In fact you can say they have no other function.*

This may sound a little extreme until you actually visit the plants and see how everything is shaped around the group working, which is characteristic of total quality management.

What's involved in the job

At Darlington and Spennymoor the physical configuration of the manufacturing departments is based on the need to get people working in groups. Each group performs a relatively independent set of activities which form a whole task with a visible start and finish.

Cigarette manufacture starts once the blended tobacco has been processed (it is called 'cut rag') and it is fed through pipes to the various workstations. There machinery links it with the paper which turns loose tobacco into cigarettes. From another group, the filters flow and are joined with the unfiltered cigarettes.

The completed cigarettes work through the machinery and are mechanically packed in small packages of 20 each, which are then packed into bundles of 200, as you would buy at a duty free shop. The appropriate labels are printed on them. Then a number of such bundles of 200 are put into boxes and collated into position by machinery. The boxes finally leave on the conveyor belt for the distribution area.

TEAM ENVIRONMENT

Some 18 people comprise a team or group, including a team leader who is known as the 'group manager'. In each of the two sites there are half a dozen making and packing groups. In the middle of the equipment on which each group is working is a 'bungalow'. It contains the group manager's office and the office of the administrator, responsible for ordering resources, and a small testing room for quality assurance. The biggest area is the rest area or tea bar, where the operators, fitters and other staff can eat and relax during breaks as well as using the area for meetings and problem solving. These rest areas are, wherever possible, designed by the workers themselves.

The areas of work surrounding the 'bungalows' are six large squares, or diamonds, each with a special colour to give group identity. The layout supports the interlinking of everybody's activities. Everyone belongs to a distinct group as well as to the whole plant.

KEEPING LOST TIME DOWN

The work of operators and fitters is concerned with keeping the machinery turning and producing cigarettes of the designed quality. Everybody needs a sense of urgency to avoid time lost: even a minute lost costs hundreds of pounds. Where it is lost they record it on input forms for computerised analysis. There is friendly competition between the groups to see who can get the best figures.

This group working creates a sense of ownership, which an impersonal full assembly line could not.

COMMUNICATIONS

The reporting structure runs straight from the group manager to the group members, with the group members themselves each accepting responsibility for being interchangeable and standing in for each other.

With such interlinking, communications are the most important aspect of the work. Everybody has to be clear about the objectives of what they are doing, have a constant supply of feedback, and have the opportunity to feed in the facts about the process and their interpretation of it.

As part of the communication need, everything in the group manager or team leader's office is open to anybody, not only what is displayed but most of the filing cabinets. Immediate information is also recorded by each machine, being later aggregated by computer.

STATISTICAL PROCESS CONTROL

Everybody has training in statistical process control, using a Ford interactive video package of four discs. It is associated with two case studies and after a test, leads to a diploma. Using statistical process control methods, everybody is involved in problem-solving. Instead of the group managers being there to solve problems for them, they are there to coach and guide the team in making their own analysis of problems and arriving at their own solutions.

MAINTENANCE

Maintenance provides an example of the way in which the team gets involved. Annually there is a major service of the whole of a machine, and the group workers take a keen interest in what is being done and use the opportunity to clean every part of the machine with great pride. There is no question of 'It's not my job'. This major service takes a full week.

There is a shorter service of eight hours every month. Prior to that service, there is a pre-maintenance meeting of those involved with the machine that is going to be serviced, attended by operators, fitters and a technical expert. It examines all the problems that have come up and helps to highlight where any special attention is needed. The problems are mainly breakdowns, faulty supplies, quality defects and bottlenecks. Multi-skilling makes it possible for a relief crew to stand in while such meetings occur. This is essential because of the continuous process nature of the work.

FAULT LOGGING

Areas of high downtime are continually monitored and faults investigated. Everybody is responsible for logging downtime if it is more than a few seconds. In fact, while I was there, somebody very quickly avoided more than three seconds downtime by rapid rethreading of some paper; another stopped a log jam of cigarettes descending into the machine.

If a lot of waste is being generated, the fault sheet, attached to each machine and maintained by the operator, will identify the nature of the waste. This is all logged on to a computer sheet and linked with other people's waste data. The figures are presented, not only in money and percentages, but in the actual number of lost cigarettes, because that is psychologically clear to the operators at a glance. These figures are discussed at weekly and monthly meetings.

If the problem appears to be one generated in the leaf and stem processing room, where the raw tobacco is cut and steamed to the appropriate moisture level, then discussions take place between the group and the Leaf Department about the nature of the cut rag that is coming through.

MOTIVATION

There are no incentive payments, although the salary rate is reckoned to be good. Everyone seems to accept that bonuses destroy group working. People will vary in their bonus, yet everybody's job is important, and with multi-skilling everybody tends to do each other's job.

Colin Dunn, a group manager, explained how BS5750 procedures were now being installed, and already accreditation had been achieved. BS5750 is itself an exercise in communication and can create a challenge. It is a matter of conforming to specification. The procedures themselves are made to come alive by the variables which the company feeds into them. I was shown the visual quality index, with 114 parameters which could earn demerits, and there was a great keenness to avoid these demerits.

There is also a keen interest in competitive comparison analysis. The analytical lab for the company as a whole will buy in samples from various companies, and compare the various group manufacturing standards with these external companies. There is a continual stimulus to beat the competition, both internally and externally. The demerits involved in such comparisons could relate to such matters as loose ends in the individual cigarettes. Problem solving involves thinking about things like this. Quality assurance specialists come in as part of the team to help investigate, but the prime responsibility for quality lies with the groups themselves. Some faults might need major changes and a managerial decision, but even then the operators would advise.

The involvement of the operators is quite different from the old days when the workers would simply have reported the problem and waited for decisions or actions to be handed down to them.

GROUP BUDGETING

The budget for the month and the year is all clearly set out and shared by everybody. This includes waste figures and estimated downtime; it includes time for maintenance, for cleaning, for training and briefing. The groups set their own budgets and submit them to senior management as covering their requirements. The budgets are always set on the basis of what is achievable, maintaining a balance between pessimism and optimism.

GROUP MANAGER AS TRAINER

As well as leading meetings the manufacturing group managers establish a positive working climate by involvement of the group through briefings and informal talks in such matters as:

- Budgets.
- Housekeeping.
- Safety.
- Absenteeism.
- Quality.
- Performance.

Training and development is part of the actual job rather than something separate from it. There is an ongoing educational process led by the group manager, involving everybody in the group in mutual education.

At Spennymoor I saw an example of this training element of the group manager's job in one of the groups. Bob Dolan, a group manager at Spennymoor, explained that they liked the style of the open group working areas because everybody could see what everybody else was doing – very much a part of the philosophy at Rothmans. Problems were not to be hidden, but exposed so that they could be solved.

FLIPCHARTS ON THE FACTORY FLOOR

The training activity that Bob Dolan shared related to the removal of special relief teams and he had a series of flipcharts which had been used at a meeting the previous day. The main flipchart indicated that with the dissolution of relief teams, all work was to be equally shared by all members of the group.

There followed a list of the jobs that had to be shared.

- Quality inspection.
- All aspects of group cleaning.
- Tray handling and trolley movement.

- Two-hundred bundle inspection.
- Rework and all stripping.
- Waste removal and recording.
- Assistance in brand change procedures.
- Preparation of BS5750 requirements.

TRAINING FOR EVERYONE IN BS5750

Another flipchart in Bob Dolan's office referred to BS5750. The reference manuals were there for all to look at, and anyone could initiate action to follow the principles.

This flipchart talked about getting things right first time by prevention and detection. It also emphasised continuous improvement and the fact that the next stage in the process is in effect, the customer.

DEVELOPING GROUP MANAGERS

We asked Dan Gibson, training consultant, how group managers came to acquire the skills needed to be able to exercise such influence in the teams. We began to understand a little of what Colin O'Neill had said at the start that organisations existed to grow people.

Dan Gibson said he had previously worked in production in Rothmans and after a period away in Scotland in other work, had returned to set up the pre-management cadre. This was a matter of developing, ahead of time, managers who would soon take over the role of group managers. Existing managers eventually retired or would be moved into other other types of work, at no disadvantage to themselves, to make room for new managers to cut their teeth.

In developing the themes of the pre-management cadre programmes, Dan Gibson took us back into the history of how Kingston Polytechnic had helped them develop the six principles of group working which are set out in a handbook.

THE SIX PRINCIPLES OF GROUP WORKING

The main objective that Rothmans hoped to achieve through group working is stated in the handbook as 'to create an environment which will encourage the involvement and commitment of all in the organisation toward achievement of the aims of the organisation to the benefit of both'. It considers that while the factory layout does not by itself achieve the objective, it does provide a framework and creates a climate which allows people to:

- Contribute to all aspects of group operations.
- Develop a sense of belonging and association.
- Develop themselves as individuals.
- Through dependence on and trust of other group members, grow into a strong and self-motivated team with the ability to achieve success.

It points out in its preface that people are what group working is all about. The position of the machines can help, but that is not the key.

The six group working principles are as follows:

Principle 1 – The basic organisational unit is the primary work group.

Principle 2 – Work group members share the same conditions of employment and have working conditions which complement group working structures.

Principle 3 – Each group is led by a designated manager possessing leadership skills.

Principle 4 – Working arrangements between members of the same work group are flexible.

Principle 5 – Each work group is, as far as possible, responsible for planning its own work, evaluating the results of its performance, and comparing these results with its agreed standards.

Principle 6 – Each group performs a relatively independent and significant set of activities which form a 'whole task', with a visible start and finish.

A key factor in the work of these groups and therefore of the managers is to find out what people think is wrong and seek their help in putting it right.

GROUP WORKING ACROSS CULTURES

For a time Dan Gibson had been operations manager at the Rothmans plant in Yemen. Although the culture was totally different, he found that teamworking and trust could be developed in this different environment. It was a matter of helping people to get a sense of ownership of what they were doing and to realise that they had skills that others appreciated. In the different culture the coaching and counselling had to be less overt, but it was still quite acceptable to develop the theme of using people to solve their own problems.

THE PRE-MANAGEMENT CADRE

The cadre is a matter of training in advance of vacancies; training for positions that don't yet exist. It was felt essential to do this ahead of forthcoming retirements. People were invited to apply for selection as group managers or team leaders. There was no age or craft limit. Anyone could apply. Some available information would be investigated about their timekeeping and attendance, because obviously it is essential that the group leader should set a good example. Flexibility and willingness to tackle anything is a key issue in selecting people to be part of the management cadre. One particular capability upon which great emphasis is placed is ambassadorial skill; the ability to interact well with others and represent the group or the company.

Those who passed the initial screening on these basic issues, and most did, were given a series of tests of verbal ability, then numeric and diagnostic skills (including lateral and logical thinking) before going on to interviews.

THE PRE-MANAGEMENT CADRE PROGRAMME

The programme of 30 days' training for the pre-management cadre was spread over six months and run by members of the Spennymoor and Darlington staff, some trainers from the Aylesbury HQ and some from a firm of consultants.

There was a lot of practical work as well as theory on the role of the manager, presentation skills, report writing, financial appreciation, team building, marketing and sales, planning, personnel, interviewing, selection and appraisals. High priority was given to quality assurance and total quality management, logistics, engineering, health and safety. There was a particularly long session on problem solving and decision making, linked with customer care and quality.

The idea was to give the group managers a tool kit with which to go back, and as soon as possible, start using what they had learned. They had to appreciate that they were first among equals and not remote bosses. They had to recognise the crucial role of teamwork in what they were going to do when they got their jobs as group managers.

INTERPERSONAL SKILLS

The very nature of group working means that interpersonal skills receive the greatest amount of emphasis. Everybody has to learn how to elicit information from team members, how to engage in open questioning, and to know the subtle differences between coaching and counselling.

Great emphasis is placed on the ability to empathise with other people. It is also important to be content not to seem infallible. The group manager does not know everything and will work *with* the team rather than impose solutions on it; nevertheless doing so without abrogating responsibility.

The role of the team leader as seen in Rothmans is one of taking chances on the ability of others and yet seeing that the group doesn't fall on its face. Initially this approach is more time-consuming but it is deep rooted and lasts longer.

Openness with problems

People at Rothmans are allowed to make mistakes as a means of learning. It is not shameful to have a problem. It is something to share with the group.

As part of the open approach everyone is encouraged to be involved with suppliers and, where possible, customers. On one of my visits a problem had arisen with the packing; the aluminium foil had not been up to standard. The group manager, through the Purchasing Department, arranged for the supplier's experts to come in to discuss the situation.

At the meeting the group leader summarised the problem, and then called on the operator to explain it in detail. This would not have happened in the past, but now the person on the shop floor dealing with the issue had the opportunity to lead the discussion. After all, people on the shop floor are best placed to assess their own problems. The operators are similarly involved in any internal discussions when problems arise with non-manufacturing groups or with the Leaf Department.

Common conditions of employment

Feeling is important as the reason for the common conditions of employment which exist at Rothmans. The 'us' and 'them' syndrome is disposed of.

- There is no reserved car park except for disabled people.
- There are no organisational barriers.
- Everybody receives a number of free shirts and trousers a year, with free laundering and replacement. This provision means that most people wear them, although it is not strictly compulsory, and it helps to remove barriers.
- Everybody shares the same restaurant.
- Everybody has the same sick pay.
- Everybody has the same pension basis.
- Everybody has the same private hospital insurance arrangements.

MAKING CHANGE WORK

Running a factory like the two in the north-east is, for Rothmans, a matter of making change work all the time and never accepting that finality has been reached. The process of involving everybody is the key area. If you get this process right, then the output will follow.

The job of the group manager is seen by Colin O'Neill as primarily counselling, coaching and helping people learn. Managers are managers simply because they have knowledge and experience to share. The rest of the team have the skills.

In order to be self-managing, groups need more knowledge; and it is the task of the manager or leader to give this, or more often to elicit it where it already exists in people. When people have a problem, the group leader doesn't say: 'Ah, this is what you must do', but rather discusses it, either collectively or individually, to get ideas out into the open.

LEARNING FOR THE GROUP

In traditional manufacturing, Colin O'Neill pointed out that the manager is usually too busy to listen to the shop floor workers. Then you get the manager saying the workers don't understand, and the workers saying that the manager doesn't listen to them. Actually the process of listening and sharing and benefiting from the shop floor workers' knowledge takes some of the load off the manager's shoulders. There is then less danger of being too busy.

Similarly, when it comes to decision making, too many managers jump straight in with solutions, instead of recognising that the person who raises the issue owns the problem and must own the decision. Therefore non-directive coaching is a sound way to handle the matter.

The purpose of an organisation like Rothmans is to develop people to enable them to work together to achieve a target and to maintain and improve quality. People development in this context is not about taking individuals and making them personally more effective, though that might be involved, but rather about making

147

the group more effective. Some individuals might go away and get information, knowledge or understanding on behalf of the group, but it is always group-orientated rather than individualistic. The objectives are related to the team and not to the individual. Knowledge is power and traditionally is often monopolised by people for their own purposes. In a proper group working approach, knowledge is gained in order to give it away, but the more you give it away, the more it grows.

A lot of the training consists of practical exercises to enable people to work together and support each other. Only the team can grow, not just the most skilful members.

PEOPLE LIKE LEARNING

Colin O'Neill told us that he never met anybody who really did not want to make a contribution. The trouble is that all too often we cap them, stifle their energy and curiosity and prevent them from learning; we then have a lot of untapped resources. Summing up the job of the group manager or team leader, and its impact on the team, he says:

> *'Every manager enables, empowers and facilitates. The manager is a team developer, a broad planner and organiser in conjunction with the team, a teacher of problem solving, a communicator and a releaser of initiative. The team learns and the team leader learns, and all are developed.'*

Everything that happens in the Rothmans plants is directed toward quality. It is embedded in the whole principle of group working. People need to own the principles of quality at all levels and they need to work together on their implementation. The well-led and largely self-directed team is clearly illustrated at Rothmans as fundamental to quality.

13. Braintree Means Public Service Quality

We might not immediately associate total quality management with the running of a large local authority in Essex (UK), but as Chris Conway and I interviewed employees, ranging from the chief executive to a refuse collector, we found the question of quality paramount. This chapter illustrates how public service can link with total quality.

The traditional image of a local authority has been of a rather impersonal organisation run by a lot of faceless bureaucrats. Even if this were ever true of some authorities, it's just not like this any more in many of them, and certainly not in Braintree. Charles Daybell, the chief executive, says: 'Braintree is a business and the local people are both the shareholders and the customers.'

British local authorities have been undergoing transformation from organisations which directly provide services to enabling bodies, ensuring that services are available. They have moved from hierarchical and central control to management by contract and influence; from direct management of services to devolved management; from uniform and standardised services to customer orientation, with emphasis on quality and choice; from standard to flexible employment structures. Many of these changes will find an echo in any business.

'BRAINTREE MEANS BUSINESS'

The district slogan is 'Braintree means Business', and when we went to see how they were doing, we found that everyone we spoke to who worked for the council had the same general ideal. They all spoke of the 'customers'. Everyone we met – telephone operator, chief executive, refuse collector, receptionist, personnel director, group accountant, swimming pool manager, planner, environmental health officer – shared the same approach. They all expressed how they saw Braintree in their own particular words, but there was a common thread. The variety of responses suggested that there was no question of an orchestrated response to our enquiries.

Braintree district comprises some 236 square miles from the outskirts of Chelmsford to the Suffolk border. It was one of the homes of the great Courtauld company and suffered the loss of 4,000 jobs when the company closed its local plant. Business opportunities have come to Braintree as a result of the council's attitude toward economic development and private investment.

The council is responsible for emptying 44,000 refuse bins a week, and for 38,000 housing repairs and 2,500 planning applications annually. There are 900 employees to ensure that a wide range of services is carried out, supplying some of them directly and ensuring that others are provided by outside bodies.

A GOOD PLACE TO LIVE AND WORK

Charles Daybell puts it:

> *'Our job is working together to run "Braintree plc". The authority is owned by the local people, represented by the councillors and served by all the employees.'*

The council's key objective is to ensure that the district is a high quality place to live and work in; to attract businesses to set themselves up in the locality and to encourage people to come and live there; and to support these aims by making sure that the environment provides the opportunity for a good quality of life.

After 'customer', 'quality' was the word most frequently used by all the people we interviewed. Peter Tattersley, assistant director of environmental services, said:

'Quality is doing what you say you'll do; and it goes beyond BS5750'.

Braintree is an authority which works to BS5750 in a number of fields, but aims to go beyond it in the search for quality, especially in areas where procedures and rules could impede action.

Trevor Jefferis runs the Riverside Pool and Squash Courts and the smaller swimming pool at Halstead. A down-to-earth London East-Ender, he explained:

'My job is to make people happy and this means looking after a lot of little things, which often give more pleasure than some of the big things – little things like fixing up bubble machines for the children in their small pool.'
'I see my job' he continued, 'as giving a complete leisure experience from the moment people drive into the car park to the moment they leave.'

He said you could measure this too.

'When people drive in there is no litter in the car park to make them feel they don't want to swim here. The lights are all on; there are no missing light bulbs; the sign posts are clear and the shrubs don't overflow on to the footpath; the windows are not broken and there is no graffiti. The receptionist is friendly; the showers aren't too hot or too cold; the keys in the lockers work; and the vending machine hasn't got a sign "out of order" written across it. It did happen once; so I had one of the attendants selling crisps to make up for it. I got told off for that by one of the accountants, but Charles Daybell tells us to have a go and even if you make mistakes you don't have to worry. You can always learn from them.'

We asked him where he learnt all this. He said it was a matter of common sense. You got on and did things and if they worked then you knew you were on the right track.

QUALITY IN THE PRINTROOM

Mike O'Shea, director of corporate services, illustrated what quality meant by the story of the printroom:

> 'It used to be rather tatty and the equipment was old. So we brought new equipment, but this meant halving the team of six. I consulted with them and they asked that all of them should be interviewed for the three jobs. Other jobs were found for the unsuccessful candidates. The whole place was refurbished. If you work in tat, then tat is what you get.'

The team felt so renewed by the new environment that they decided to call themselves 'Phoenix Printing'.

Mike said that the effect of getting the environment right was the same for the town as a whole:

> 'If you let the town get filthy, people develop a "don't care" attitude; you even get more crime.'

BRAINTREE'S MISSION

Braintree has a mission statement – and a vision statement too. They feel that if they write down where they want to be, this is a significant step on the road to getting there. The culture, the quality concern, the customer care, the people development will all flow from it – and people development in Braintree means everyone who lives and works there. So Braintree aims to:

- Secure the best possible conditions for all who live in our district to lead a high quality of life.
- Focus on our customers and provide the quality services they require.
- Ensure all our staff are given opportunities for development, through training, appraisal, respect and support.
- Operate the council in a business-like manner with clear accountabilities, and ensure that targets are met.

The Braintree vision

The vision is of a district which:

- is prosperous, clean and socially balanced;
- meets the basic needs of all in our community for affordable housing and a range of housing choice, for worthwhile employment and for security, health and welfare services and personal mobility;
- retains, respects and enhances its attractive environment, particularly its countryside, villages, historic buildings and conservation areas;
- while retaining its traditional character provides a range of modern industry on quality business parks, encourages initiative and enterprise as well as quality shopping, arts, leisure, education and welfare facilities;
- has thriving town centres at Braintree, Witham and Halstead. Town centres which are safe, convenient, accessible and attractive to shoppers and those who live and work there;
- meets the demand for efficient movement of road traffic, but not at the expense of safety and environmental conditions (particularly in the towns and villages) or the neglect of public transport;
- meets the particular leisure, welfare and housing needs of the young and the elderly;
- exhibits a real pride and respect on the part of all sections of the community, public and private, in its surroundings, with clean and tidy streets, parks and open spaces and property that is well maintained.

The Braintree vision illustrates powerfully how quality can be a key issue in a service industry, and indeed, in a public authority.

Quality in Braintree

The quality aim in Braintree is 'to deliver defect-free products and services to our customers, both internal and external, on time and within budget.'

Charles Daybell speaks of a 'defect-free district'. The district is on the path to total quality and to certification under BS5750 using in part Philip Crosby's organisation for training in quality. John Reeve, refuse collector and union convenor says:

'We are very concerned about quality control in the Refuse Collection Department. We accept BS5750 and think quality is very important in our job. The customers want all the rubbish moved, with none of it left on the path, and they want us to call every week. Things like that are what quality means for us.'

John also told us how the chief executive had spent a day on a dustcart with them and further days with other teams. This was good for the motivation of the team and no doubt good for Charles Daybell, too, as a member of a 'learning organisation'.

The 'Quality Improvement Award' scheme has been set up to involve all the employees in focusing on quality. Quality includes the way that customers are dealt with on the phone or face to face; anyone who telephones the District Office will straightaway hear the effect of the training in quality, by the way the phone is answered.

Peter Tattersley told us:

'In the Environmental Services Department we are developing quality assurance systems under the guidance of BS5750. We negotiate quality standards with the staff in a specific way. We have key service indicators to measure customer satisfaction. We actually encourage complaints so that we can put right anything that goes wrong. For every ten that grumble only one or two complain and so we don't find out. So we actually think it is good to get more complaints, at least to start with. Then we can make some progress to the defect-free standard.'

Braintree is realistic about quality though. Charles Daybell says that they do not provide gold plated taps when brass ones are perfect for the job.

An attractive brochure produced by Braintree District Council is the *Quality Life Catalogue* where the customers are informed of the services on offer for their home, their health, their environment, their leisure time, their rights, their community, their district.

Braintree District Council is not an elitist organisation. The district offices in the Causeway have an internal architecture which reflects collegiality between customers and providers alike. The general public wanders in and finds a welcoming style of furnishing. Rounded counters for receptionists and pay-in desks look comfortable; they have no sense of threat or officialdom about them. There is plenty of space and the children will be seen playing in what is after all *their* council office, but it is all so structured that the noise is not excessive.

The telephonists and the receptionists have genuine smiles to make everyone feel at home. The selection of people for these jobs has obviously been carefully carried out and they have been trained in quality service.

A CHANGE CULTURE

Quality doesn't mean standing still. Braintree sees change as of the essence in a progressive district. The change culture is fed by finding out what people want and responding with changed approaches. If quality is at best delighting customers and at least conformance to requirements, you need to know what will delight and what the requirements are.

The computer section ran a customer survey, prior to developing its first business plan. The customers were all the other departments in the council, emphasising the concept of the chain of suppliers and customers.

Robin Carsberg, responsible for the computer area, observes:

'We thought we were good at things until we asked, but we discovered a number of aspects needing improvement. One of the ways in which we responded was setting up a help desk and monitoring the way in which it has been used. We also set up user groups so that we could learn together how to establish a better service. Asking for feedback is now a regular feature of our work. It makes the customer feel valued too.'

DEVELOPING THE EMPLOYEES

Braintree takes a quality approach to the development of its employees. At any one time ten per cent of the staff are on educational activity, often with part-time day-release, in pursuit of various qualifications. In addition, some four per cent are engaged in any year in off-the-job skills training. However the emphasis is on the learning that goes on all the time as part of the service provision and the development of the new culture.

Training and development takes place at all levels for the Braintree District Council employees. You could say it is total employee development. The total quality approach in any case involves everyone, as does the related customer concept, which everyone we met talked about. While there is plenty of classroom learning it is likely that some 90 per cent of learning at all levels takes place through the job.

LEARNING TOGETHER

Roger Barrett, planning director, said Braintree was not a hierarchical organisation.

> *'It thrives on informal relationships. People are encouraged to network and work in teams across boundaries. The classroom training gives them the tools to make this effective, as in running meetings and generally communicating well.'*

The cross-function network is a valuable way of getting feedback about the impact of what you are doing, and feedback is fundamental to doing more effectively. Life in Roger Barrett's team means that business is not conducted by individuals in isolation.

In order to learn from the feedback and through everything they do in the job, Roger says that people have to be trusted and given a lot of scope for exercising discretion.

> *'A case officer now deals with a majority of planning applications that come to him without reference upwards and takes responsibility for*

making the recommendations for final approval by the council, with full backing from me.'

Delegation and trust are of the essence in 'learning through the job' so as to be capable of quality decisions. Mike Bailey was talking about learning through the job when he said:

'We are after continuous improvement in Braintree in everything we tackle. We have a system of job enrichment and we really believe in delegation. We give people scope to be entrepreneurial, to push out the boundaries, to test things out, to spread their wings and take on new things without fear. We've got an experimental environment where mistakes are there to be learned from.'

MANAGER AS DEVELOPER

Managers are all reminded that they have the prime responsibility for ensuring that training takes place and is relevant to the needs of the individual and the department or section. A quality approach is taken to training to ensure that it is 'fit for use', as one of the quality definitions puts it. One choice sentence in the handbook reads:

It is hoped that managers see training activities as priorities, even when faced with operational pressures.

All managers who feel they have some skills to offer are invited to take part in the delivery of the in-service training programmes. Before doing so, however, they are expected to attend the 'Training of Trainers' course.

No one comes on a course without having been briefed on the reason for attending. Great emphasis is also placed on debriefing, without which it is said that money will be wasted. Managers are made responsible for the relevance of the training. This makes for quality training.

STAFF PERFORMANCE APPRAISAL

Central to the development of staff at Braintree is the appraisal system. Everybody's progress in their job is assessed and their need for training analysed in discussion with the people to whom they report.

A well designed brochure is distributed, which begins with the statement:

> *Developing staff to meet objectives is crucial to the success and efficiency of the council. The appraisal system is a tool to help you, but its effectiveness depends on the importance you place on it.*

The approach suggested is honest and factual and offers help in giving and receiving appraisal. Its aims are as follows:

- To improve performance and job satisfaction.
- To identify training needs.
- To establish a framework in which targets for improvement are established and communication between the chief officers and their staff enhanced.

The process is similar to any good appraisal system, but the book gives appraisers some good advice, which begins:

> *Do you base your assessments on personality rather than on performance? Do you ignore the quiet person who contributes without fuss? Do you put haloes round your favourites, or black marks on trouble makers?*

It is an open system where the appraisee signs the form summarising the discussion and is given a copy. The form has to be typed or handwritten by the appraiser and not by any third party. There is nothing unique about all this, but Braintree does belong to the more open end of the appraising spectrum, as one would expect from its general philosophy. It does not follow the type of appraisal denounced by Deming as divisive and demotivating.

Peter Tattersley illustrates his use of the appraisal system for staff development:

> 'There was this redundant gardener with very little schooling. At appraisal he showed enthusiasm for a vacant post as dog warden. Under normal circumstances he would never have stood a chance, but appraisal brought out his suitability, by his attitude. It was then a simple matter to give him help by training him to write reports and letters and go and talk to schools. He is doing an extremely good job.'

Mike Legget, assistant director of housing, had this to say about appraisal:

> 'I see it as a two-way process. I learnt from one of my staff who told me at appraisal that I tend to move too fast on new things without winning support first. I found this useful.'

EVALUATING TRAINING AND DEVELOPMENT

Charles Daybell saw success in training and development of staff as going beyond particular aspects of training to the total success of the business.

> 'We evaluate business outcomes, as well as individual skills. The success of training and development is involved in the successful achievement of the corporate objectives. We set service targets and evaluate how far they are achieved – Are the rent arrears reduced? Are all the dustbins emptied? Is there a backlog of planning applications? What proportion of our staff have we retained? and so on. While we do set out to ensure that our customers feel able to complain, the overall numbers are less important than assessing how we dealt with the justified complaints. What did we learn? So it's rather what percentage of complaints did we successfully correct?'

Thus training and development is evaluated by its impact on the quality of the service given to the customers.

THE DUAL LEARNING ORGANISATION

There is an even wider sense in which Braintree as a district may be considered a learning organisation. Not only is work a learning and growing experience for the employees, but there is a sense of growth, improvement and learning about the whole business of Braintree. The council members, the council employees and the 'customers' served by the council are seen as part of one great partnership. This is made explicit by the council's attention to communications.

It is illustrated by what this study has described of the culture, mission, vision, quality service attitudes and business approach of Braintree. The authority is the enabler of wealth creation and the facilitator of quality of life development. It lies at the centre of a web of relationships between many of the elements which go to make up a community. It aims not to govern but to help release the energy of people to grow to the fullness of their potential; it provides an environment conducive to such growth.

QUALITY THROUGH COMPLAINTS

Two leaflets produced by the council deal with complaints procedures. This may sound a boring thing with which to end an exciting case study; but it sums up the Braintree approach.

First there is the guide for the people who live and run businesses in the Braintree district. It is attractively presented and entitled 'I would like to make a complaint'. It says that the council's complaints procedures

> are central to our philosophy of getting closer to you – the customer. We place great emphasis on the prompt and efficient handling of complaints, so that when you tell us of things which have gone wrong we can take action quickly to put them right.

The leaflet recognises that complete customer satisfaction may not always be possible, but the council aims to give a quality service and to respond to any complaints within seven days – and if this is not possible to keep the complainant posted. Precise detail is given about who to contact and what they will try to do, with a right of appeal to the local ombudsman. Each of the departments is described with a list of the directors; also a list of the district councillors and their addresses. There is a sense of positive encouragement to complain and a distinct will to pursue the path toward total quality.

Parallel with this green leaflet there is a red one for the employees called 'Our aim is quality'. It presents the *core values* of Braintree District Council:

1. *We are customer orientated.*
2. *We believe in the abilities of the individual.*
3. *We must be responsive and responsible.*
4. *We believe in quality.*
5. *We are action orientated.*

It then sets out a code of practice on complaints procedures for staff and a separate one for councillors, thereby joining the council members and the council employees together as one team. Both these codes give precise details of everyone's responsibilities and how to provide the best response to complaints. They are summed up in the introduction:

The council's aim is to give a high quality service to the public – OUR customers. The only job we have is to provide the best service we can. Customers are not a hindrance; they are our life blood. Without them we would also be without a job.

So we have adopted the five core values which we should all try to remember. You will see them on notice boards and flexi machines throughout the offices and they are listed at the back of this booklet.

What do they mean? In a nutshell they mean THINK CUSTOMER. Think of a way round a problem so that the customer benefits. Find a reason why we CAN do something, not why we can't. Imagine yourself on the other side of the counter or at the other end of the telephone. Because that's where complaints come in.

What is your first impression of someone with a complaint? A nuisance? But supposing it were you who were complaining. That would be different wouldn't it? There would be some justification then.

Well there's the truth of the matter. Everyone who complains feels he has grounds to do so. Not many people actually ENJOY complaining. To a customer with a complaint we owe the courtesy of investigating the problem, apologising if we are wrong and putting the matter right as quickly as we can. The more satisfied customers we have, the better our reputation and the easier our job will be.

The leaflet also implies that Braintree aims to be a learning organisation when it says that the basic aim of the new procedures is to ensure that

we deal with complaints efficiently and sympathetically, WHILE AT THE SAME TIME LEARNING FROM THEM.

No doubt when it comes to paying for the services Braintree people grumble like the rest of us, but they do appear to have opportunity to own the services and participate in their development. This chapter has emphasised that total quality is much wider than the manufacturing and engineering arena.

14. Quality and Teamwork Save Bedford

This is a study of quality as the key to saving a company and it illustrates the way in which trade unions supported the total quality approach to help save their members' jobs. This is also one of two case studies with Japanese input involved in the companies.

For ten years up to 1989 the old Bedford Commercial Vehicle Company had been making a loss. This was reversed and the launch of a new vehicle initiated. At a time when other companies were laying off staff, Bedford was overwhelmed by recruitment to get ready for the new product. This was in stark contrast with much of British industry.

Bedford has long been known as a manufacturer of trucks and vans. In 1986 it was faced with bankruptcy. There were problems associated with variable quality and industrial unrest and losses had reached £½ million a week.

Although it was owned by General Motors, there was a limit to how long the parent corporation could sustain the situation. With General Motors' 46 per cent stake in Isuzu, a joint venture was a natural development.

THE NEW COMPANY

A new company was formed in September 1987, fully independent of both General Motors and Isuzu but with General Motors having a 60 per cent share ownership and Isuzu having 40 per cent. The new company took the name Isuzu Bedford Commercial Vehicles, and is known as IBC Vehicles.

The board reflects the 60/40 split of ownership, but the Japanese influence is strong. There are four Japanese people involved at Luton, including the president. The other three are advisory, with no actual direct authority, but obviously a great deal of influence.

THE NEW CONTRACT OF EMPLOYMENT

When the new company was formed, there was some hard negotiation with the trade unions, but in the end £½ million a week loss was something that couldn't be argued with, and as a result, a new contract of employment, which introduced new principles, was agreed. Central to this new contract was a recognition that old attitudes of confrontation between management and the workforce must go. Written into the contract was a commitment to the principles of co-operation, openness and trust as the only way to ensure a quality product, which would sustain profit and jobs.

This was largely achieved, according to Phil Steele of the Personnel Department, although, of course, there were always some pockets of doubt. A major change of this nature could not happen overnight; there was still room for improvement.

TRAVELLING HOPEFULLY

Even when I met the late Tony Jackson, who was personnel manager, in February 1990, the signs for the future were good. Here was a man reared in the old fashioned school of personnel management, who in spite of a sickness which proved terminal, was radiating a joy at the transformation that had come over the company, and a resolution to do all that he could to inspire its progress.

He said that the circumstances, though radically changed, did not mean that perfection had been reached. It was always a matter of travelling hopefully. Business was never a matter of arriving, but constantly readjusting to the requirements of circumstances. In order to do this, you had to have a flexible organisation in which everybody was committed to work together to ensure the highest quality. The principle of continuous improvement was clearly appreciated at the start of the new era.

EARLY PROFIT

At the beginning of the new company a series of business plans were developed which envisaged a loss in the first year, followed by a small profit and then real progress. In fact, they made a profit in year one and doubled the anticipated profit in year two. Phil Steele puts this down to the totally changed way of working, though the move forward was not achieved without some pain.

SIMPLICITY OF APPROACH

A fundamental idea behind the new contract, which could only be a framework, was that the whole workforce should accept and own the new approach and see quality and customer satisfaction as their prime aim. There were initially 1,250 people, building up to 1,750 in the first 12 months. They had to want to be with the company; they couldn't be threatened into change. As Tony Jackson said in 1990, the hearts of the people had to be won.

The basic framework of the contract and of the agreements that flowed from it was one of simplicity. It did not attempt to cover every small thing by written rules. Great significance was given to day-to-day trust and to teamworking.

TEAMWORK

Teamworking became central to the new quality culture. The 1,250 manufacturing staff in employment in 1990 were divided into 130 teams, with up to 12 people in each, in all parts of the operation, press shop, body and paint, final assembly. Regular team meetings were established, team leaders were appointed with quality and efficiency to improve on a continuous basis as their key themes.

QUALITY: ACHIEVING EXCELLENCE

CONTINUOUS IMPROVEMENT

An inventory and production system was set up to concentrate on continuous improvement. Statistical process control was spread through the company with everybody gradually learning to understand it, use it and engage in the self-monitoring associated with it, just as the quality gurus have taught. 'Just-in-time' inventory methods were also adopted. A suggestion scheme was introduced and the company ensured that it actually worked, with financial rewards of a tangible nature being given. Even local managers had the right to make small awards in connection with the suggestion scheme if a particular suggestion was not quantifiable, but was moving in the right direction.

HARMONY

This teamworking approach reflected some of the principles which have proved so successful in Japan, but it was recognised that you could not automatically transfer a way of working, based on the Japanese culture, to a Western situation. In Japan the company is seen by the worker as an extension of the family, and the company president is the grandfather of the clan. Loyalty and effort to the firm is like loyalty and effort for one's family, and the pride that goes with that. So there is no complaining about half-hour physical exercise at the beginning of the day, nor about singing the company song.

In a British context, this would probably feel embarrassing. Nevertheless, many of the fundamental principles have been adopted and westernised. There is a meeting first thing in the morning as a means of getting into harmony, to use the Japanese word, with each other. This is a brief time when each team talks about the essentials of the day.

FLATTER MANAGEMENT

The development of teamworking has flattened the management pyramid and pushed decision making down to the lowest possible level, so that assistant managers have the authority to make many decisions previously made higher up the tree.

Where team leaders are eminently successful, then they may be transferred once their work is established, so that they can bring their new skills to bear in another team.

LEARNING THROUGH THE JOB

Training takes place at all levels of the organisation, and is considered a daily activity, particularly in the field of communicating. Training through the job is seen as vital. Communicating is a particularly important skill to learn as it is fundamental to the running of the teams.

THE TOP TEAM

The development of the team approach is not only for the shop floor, but is powerful at the top. Thirty top executives led by the five most senior, including the Japanese president and the vice president, finance, manufacturing and personal directors, have been going away at the beginning of the year for 1½ days to plan for the year ahead and discuss how objectives are to be achieved. The first of these meetings made decisions on capital expenditure for the future and how the small loss that might be incurred could be overcome, as any loss was bad for morale. In the event, of course, there was no loss.

The initial formation of the top executive team included an Outward Bound type of experience, where comradeship was enhanced by doing difficult things in the outdoors together. IBC Vehicles illustrates the point made by all the quality gurus, that top commitment is vital.

COMMUNICATIONS

The objectives worked out at the annual executive conference are cascaded down to everybody. Twice a year everyone in the whole factory stops work and comes to a conference room – the day shift in one meeting and the night shift in another – to receive a progress review of the company; the current situation, the future hopes, the financial background, and the opportunities for new ideas and new products. At the June meeting of the executive group, progress reports from all the other teams are considered. All this concern with proper communicating and the cascading of information is seen as developmental in itself, both for those at the senior level and for those further down the chain, who have to pass the communications along in the regular communicating, as distinct from the twice yearly jamborees. It also inspires a sense of belonging.

A positive approach

The company has talented management people, and Phil Steele said the aim is to take the shackles off them to broaden them and enable them to make further progress. There is no question of treating people as machines, because this would be a self-fulfilling prophecy. If high quality is to be maintained it has to be through people who understand what quality means and who are not satisfied with anything less.

The salary negotiations, although not agreeing the highest wages in the car industry, have been carried through with a minimum of problems and the company has lost no time of any significance through industrial action in the period since the changes.

Union representation

There is a company joint council of sixteen members, five managers and eleven trade unionists from five different unions. The only qualification about the union representation is that however many unions are represented, they will agree and speak with one voice and elect a single spokesperson. This is somewhat different from the traditional Japanese single union approach, but it expresses the same idea.

COMMON CONDITIONS

Similarly, the single status or harmonised approach to employment conditions is followed. There are no special parking arrangements for anybody, not even for the president. There is no clocking in. There is a sick pay scheme for the shop floor, as well as for the office staff, on the grounds that the one should be trusted as much as the other. Trust breeds worthiness of trust as, Tony Jackson said shortly after the new company came into existence. The staff all eat from the same kiosk areas and use the same microwave ovens. The pension is on the same basis. The only difference lies in the actual salaries paid. The move away from the 'them and us' attitude which used to characterise so much of British industry is a regular feature in companies which adopt total quality management.

PRAISE

The executive group who meet every January made some open resolutions one year. One of these very senior managers made the resolution, and made it public, that he would be careful to praise the good things all the time, and would not engage in any putdowns because these were demotivational and negative. Even if an idea is not particularly good, it should not be derided.

MANAGERIAL ORGANISATION

Of the managers below the 30 executives, 51 are assistant managers, and below that are the supervisors who now have a strategic input. Their ideas on the direction of the company and their particular part of the business are actively sought and received with genuine interest. The role of general foreman has been dropped, and team leaders have assumed a much greater role.

APPRAISAL

The appraisal scheme is not just for managers – all staff are involved. There are special awards for performance; training needs are analysed; readiness for promotion is considered. Training is available, not only to do what needs to be done currently, but to enable people to move on to the team leader role and more senior roles. People are sent on courses where appraisal reveals needs, but they can initiate a request to have some special experience.

In order to enable team leaders and supervisors to carry out appraisal discussions, everybody is trained in counselling and appraisal activity if it forms part of their function.

MULTI-SKILLING

Within the teams there is a move towards multi-skilling. The company would not claim to be there yet; it takes time to train people to widen their skills, but the attitude of flexibility and willingness to avoid the 'It's not my job' syndrome is making rapid progress. There are no job descriptions to shackle people, so that multi-skilling tends to grow organically rather than be imposed.

CULTURE CHANGE

All in all a culture change has been achieved, and the company is now much more open; problems are openly discussed. Phil Steele said that the personnel policies developed are no longer mechanical sets of rules, but rather an expression of what is felt to be right. In my discussions with IBC there was little emphasis on what would conventionally be called management development, but because of the need to nurture the culture change, the top 30, the next 51, and the supervisors were very much involved in activity which affected their own development.

The team approach means that everybody not only has the opportunity, but also the need to develop. At IBC it is very difficult to separate management development from people development and company development.

SHARED VISION

Because of the holistic approach to the activity of the company, IBC finds training and development integrated with the business itself.

The way in which the top management considers itself and its objectives annually by its away days and then shares the business objectives with all the employees, is certainly in the direction of the UK 'Investors in People' Initiative. (See Appendix A.) There is a vision at the top, and it is shared all the way down.

LEARNING EVERY DAY

The exercise of appraisal throughout the company for staff at all levels means that the training needs for everybody are clearly identified. Many of them are met through the job itself. The team approach means that every day is a learning experience in which people share insights with one another.

RIGOROUS RECRUITMENT

Recruitment is being taken very seriously to ensure that the people who join IBC are of a calibre whose skill can be enhanced by continuous development and training. Right from the start this is a matter of significant concern for all managers and team leaders, supported by the Personnel Department.

EVALUATION

IBC is pragmatic about evaluating progress in training for quality. The impact of specific training is linked with the great emphasis on communication, openness and trust. The existence of teams is seen as a way of daily learning and sharing. Collective synergies are developed by such teamwork, and it is very difficult to separate the training activity from the total trading activity. There is doubt as to whether any sophisticated evaluation techniques applied to specific training activity would add much to the effectiveness of the company.

However, everything that is done is constantly evaluated to ensure that the way the company is organised and the way people learn leads to continuous improvement in every activity. Where continuous improvement is an active policy permeating the whole company ethos and activity, then evaluation runs side by side with it. Individuals evaluate their own contribution, and their team leaders help them do this. If you know that things are better, that there is improvement not only in the bottom line, but in all the ingredients that weld together into the bottom line, then you know that you are on course.

A company like IBC that believes in continuous improvement, believes in teamworking, believes in communication and enhancement of performance, knows whether it is learning or not. Learning is its very breath, and the outcomes are clear to see – a quality product in the customer's terms.

15. Seaham Harbour Dock Company Takes the Long View

Those of us who like to sit on a cliff top and look far out to sea could find few better places than David Clifford's office at the Seaham Harbour Dock Company, where he is the managing director. The lovely Durham coastline stretching out for miles is a symbol of the envisioning of the future Chris Conway and I were there to talk about.

There has been a harbour at Seaham since 1828, when the Marquess of Londonderry built it as an outlet for the coal from his mines in the north-east. Today the port of Seaham (now part of Anglo United plc), is still thriving and handling a wide variety of products.

A SMALL COMPANY WITH BIG IDEAS

Although a small company (with a turnover of £4.5 million and 80 employees), it is the second largest employer in the area with about 700 jobs relying indirectly on its success. Devolution of authority and the development of people are its key routes to quality. This chapter shows how binding a company together with a sense of purpose helps to create quality service as perceived by the customer.

David Clifford believes that the development of the organisation is dependent on releasing the contribution of the whole workforce. This strategic view has not always prevailed at the dock. The 'us and them' attitude used to thrive at Seaham. The change is reflected in common conditions of employment for all the employees.

Management used to stay in their offices, we were told. But when David Clifford was appointed general manager in 1977, he initiated a new approach, by walking around the quays and talking to people. 'It was a long and painful process but it worked' and management by walking around is now the practice of all the managers at the port. It is the kind of business in which success depends upon that kind of relationship.

A MASSIVE DIVERSITY OF SKILLS

The 150 acre self-contained site encompasses many different operations and skills. Not only is there a lighthouse, but a coal disposal site, the dock itself and a five-mile railway system complete with engines and rolling stock.

There is also a wide range of crafts; electricians, fitters, boilersmiths, turners, stevedores and drivers of fork lift trucks, cranes and mechanical grabs. Also, there are the skills associated with the 200,000 square feet of warehousing, such as the computerised weighbridge, stock control and its management. Because of this diversity a multi-skilled and flexible workforce is essential to successful operation at Seaham. On one occasion, when they were shorthanded and had a deadline to meet, David Clifford donned his overalls and gave a hand in unloading a ship.

HOW THE DOCK IS MANAGED

The management structure of the company reflects David Clifford's belief that individuals should take responsibility for their own area of work.

The operations director, the company secretary and David as managing director form the management board of the company. In addition all eight managers act as a management committee which meets formally once a month and informally every week. David

Clifford has increasingly pulled back from the day-to-day activities of the port. On one of our visits his management committee was carrying out the annual round of wage negotiations while he talked to us.

This principle of delegating as far down the line as possible gives people a sense of responsibility for the quality of the work. It is in harmony with ensuring that all employees know they can make a clear contribution to the success of the business.

At the same time, flatter structures within the company have resulted in twelve grades being reduced to four categories of employee other than manager and foreman supervisor – craftsman, operationally skilled, labourers and trainees.

GETTING STARTED WITH A NEW STRATEGY

'We now have a more efficient and effective operation capable of responding and developing to meet future needs.'

These are the words of David Clifford on his organisation's search for a strategy for the future. In this search he was determined to involve as many people as possible in the process of developing and communicating a vision of where the company was heading.

To kick-start things, he decided that outside assistance was required. Thus, Seaham gained the distinction of being the first UK company to take up and complete the UK Employment Department's Business Growth Training Option 3 Initiative.

The essence of this scheme is that it provides substantial financial help towards securing the services of a management consultant over a one-year period. It aims to develop managers so that they have the ability to focus on key business issues and achieve business objectives.

Under the aegis of Option 3, Seaham acquired expert advice on planning for change as well as facilitating progress in a way whereby the employees feel a sense of ownership of the changes. Management training, both on and off the job, was designed and implemented.

THE DEVELOPMENT OF THE BUSINESS PLAN

In the beginning David Clifford and his managers held brainstorming sessions to identify their mission and then proceeded to divide up the objectives for further action.

From this a detailed business plan took shape. The next stage involved individual training and development needs analysis which started with the middle managers and went on to the supervisors during a difficult period for the company.

KEY RESULT AREAS REVIEWED

The process of creating a strategy involved identifying key result areas for individual managers, starting with the managing director himself. What does he have to do? To whom does he report? What does he delegate? From this type of question, a template was produced with which individuals could measure their own key result areas.

Each key result area was associated with the company's overall mission and objectives. People were asked if they had sufficient authority and resources to do the job. This determination to empower people to do things without constant reference up and with minimum supervision is a major aspect of the management philosophy at Seaham Harbour. The current phase of this activity is re-examining the company's objectives, reviewing everything that is done and evaluating success.

KNOCKING DOWN THE BARRIERS TO WORKING AND LEARNING

Some projects have been designed with the additional aim of providing an opportunity for teamworking, because as David Clifford notes: 'When people are busy, the barriers go down. It's when they have more time that artificial barriers often re-establish themselves.'

Every Friday there is a lunch-time meeting of the managers over sandwiches in David Clifford's office. They discuss the week's events and share information and opinions. It may be a specific 'hot topic' such as safety, but mostly the general operations of the port are discussed. The lunch period has been chosen because it tends to be quiet, and it provides the atmosphere of informality which aids free exchange of opinion.

The more formal monthly meeting provides the forum for reporting activities and receiving reports such as the financial figures from the finance director. The brief for the monthly meeting is prepared by each manager after they have met with their own managers and supervisors. Good ideas which have been generated are put forward to the monthly management meeting, and 'good ideas get put into effect so that people know that others are listening to them'.

This process is continually developing and improving the skills of employees which is central to being an investor in people. Development is not seen as an elitist activity, but as a matter of total employee development.

'We use our monthly management meetings as learning opportunities and giving people the freedom to make decisions, and by implication, mistakes – that's the best way to develop.'

Each manager brings a different supervisor to the monthly meeting on a rota basis, and this initiative has worked well, involving more people in the decision-making process at Seaham. In addition, the full minutes of the meeting are widely distributed all around the port. The minutes form a central element in communicating. They are written in a helpful way with sections, for example, on health and safety, quality, warehouse operations, engineering, in fact covering all parts of the harbour's operations. The minutes contain an open invitation to make suggestions (or indeed, complaints). This invitation has been readily taken up by the workforce who have made suggestions ranging from modifications to the dock's sea gates to the provision of litter bins on the site.

On a day-to-day basis, the foremen/supervisors are involved in organising the day's activities, and while, inevitably, there are variations in management styles between different departments, the foremen make a point of networking together to achieve a smooth linkage of operation between departments; they are customers and suppliers to each other. This method of working also enables employees to contribute to identifying and meeting their own job-related development needs. This development of the whole workforce is an enabling factor in bringing about major change within an organisation, not least in the pervasive issue of quality.

GOING FOR QUALITY

'Quality affects everything, really.' So says Brian Foster, the warehouse manager and quality representative. The motto of Seaham Harbour is 'total cargo care', and quality has been a key feature of the change programme which has transformed the business.

The warehouse operation at Seaham involves the management of the 200,000 square feet of warehouse space and ten acres of open storage. The work of these areas, together with the weighbridge, stock control and the bagging and palletising plant were assessed and passed first time by auditors from the British Standards Institute for the award of Part 2 of BS5750.

This standard requires all personnel to work systematically to a documented procedure. Brian Foster led the management team in the initial formation of the procedures of the warehouse, and now has a lead role in developing the quality initiative so that it will eventually take in all parts of the company.

WHAT QUALITY MEANS AT SEAHAM

The cargoes handled at Seaham are diverse; coal, coke, limestone, urea, fertilizer, dolomite, soda ash, scrap, pig iron, magnetite and grain are all exported from the dock. The imported products are anthracite, technical urea, coal, coke, ferrule alloys, refractory materials, fertilizer, sand, salt, phospate rock, sulphur and animal feeds. With this wide range of products being handled, a quality approach becomes essential.

The mixing of one product with another and the consequent

contamination could have serious consequences; a major quality issue is avoiding this. The dock handles animal feeds, which are inspected by the Ministry of Agriculture, Fisheries and Food (MAFF) who have strict regulations regarding their storage, and Seaham claims the best record in the United Kingdom for this type of storage.

One of the major potential contaminants of animal feed is bird excreta, which can cause the salmonella virus to develop in the feed. In their effort to prevent this form of contamination, the warehouse employs a contractor and his falcon to come in one day per month, and this is sufficient to frighten off the offending birds.

The quality approach at the warehouse involves a shared knowledge of the products handled, temperature control and the handling of potentially dangerous substances. It also means involving the customer who values the skill and knowledge of the warehouse manager and his staff. In fact, on many occasions the latter provide a sort of free consultancy to their customers.

QUALITY VERSUS PRICE

One of the problems which deregulation of the docks has brought about is that a small operator can quickly set up in competition and undercut on price. Seaham Harbour has found that the issue is not necessarily price – though it endeavours to be as competitive as possible – but quality. Quality concerns of an operational nature can have greater significance to the customer than financial issues. They ultimately have financial implications.

The quality of the products' storage means that the customer will return because of the reputation of the port. Brian Foster has said, 'We are working as a team and the result is that our customers receive a standard of service that precisely meets their specifications – you've got to be customer orientated now.' In this teamworking there is ongoing learning as the group searches continuously for more effective ways of maintaining the standards. It is a clear case of learning through the job and learning together to achieve total quality. It is also never-ending learning because it involves the search for perfection.

FORMAL RECOGNITION OF LEARNING

So how did Brian Foster get where he is today? He realised that his learning through the job needed to be supplemented. To achieve greater proficiency, he attended several events on warehouse management organised by National Association of Warehouse Keepers (NAWK). He has been able to take advantage of membership to keep up to date with the latest developments in this field, and also to network with other warehousemen in action learning groups.

This shared learning is further enhanced by Seaham's membership of the quality forum of the North Durham Corporation and the British Quality Association. Incidentally, Brian finds it necessary to order two copies of his NAWK newsletter as one always 'disappears' and is avidly read by his staff.

The penultimate word on quality is with Brian Foster.

'Quality is becoming a way of life for everyone here at the port. Due to the enthusiastic support and commitment we have behind us, from top management down through every department, our quality assurance programme has made a significant cultural impact on the company.'

However, David Clifford has given a firm indication of things to come on the quality front.

'The BS5750 registration achieved for the warehouse is only the beginning of our programme. Work is now well under way to extend this to cover all port and railway activities and eventually to achieve the ultimate goal of total quality management.'

ASSESSING THE NEEDS OF PEOPLE

It is no surprise to find training needs discussed as a regular standard item on the agenda for both the monthly and weekly management meetings. At Seaham each individual's training needs are assessed (as they must be under BS5750). The quality initiative has reinforced training and vice versa.

Another contribution has been from appraisal – not in the formal sense but in an ongoing review of key result areas with supervisors. This assists with the analysis of development needs. As an adjunct to this review process, through-the-job experience is enhanced by informal mentoring.

Under the earlier regulation by the National Dock Labour Board (NDLB) the sense of ownership and responsibility for the whole operation was stifled by demarcation and other restrictive practices. This atmosphere was not conducive to people being empowered because managers themselves felt helpless in the face of the legislation, which had become something of a controlling factor: 'You could only manage as far as they let you.'

The post-NDLB environment has meant a complete sea change for the management of the dock.

CUSTOMER RELATIONSHIPS

Commitment to the customer has resulted in flexibility and an enhancement of the staff's investigative skills, including new solutions to quality problems. People are seeing quality service as doing more than the customer expects and as an example, Andrew Ridley (Foster's assistant) has instituted giving customers the dock's internal record sheets so they can use them to reconcile their own stocks.

This open approach to customer relationships has involved the sea-going crews as well as the shipping agents who are based at Seaham. Customer complaints are taken seriously too: 'If you get a complaint, you do something about it.' Andrew reviews trends in complaints to see how the system can be tightened up. This propensity to innovation and initiative exemplifies what can happen when people's creative energies are liberated by a forward-thinking management.

Andrew Ridley's pride in the bagging plant, which he described to us with evident affection as 'my baby' evinced a desire to continue improving existing installations and procedures. For example, ten rather windblown acres of open storage are prone to dust problems – Andrew's solution was to invent his own sprinkler system which has considerably cut down this nuisance.

RELEASING PEOPLE'S POTENTIAL

Throughout his time at Seaham, Andrew has been the constant focus of his manager's attention in terms of his training needs and development. He has put Andrew into situations where he can learn through the job, whilst being actively supported and not just left to get on with it.

The commitment to continuous development is a central feature of what goes on at Seaham. This development is not confined simply to the managers of the port. When a person is recognised as having potential, that person is given a chance. David Clifford, for instance, insisted on promoting a telephonist to warehouse clerk as he saw her potential. She was given a period of time to acclimatise and learn the job before her performance was reviewed. Thus, faith in people based on sound analysis has formed a large part of people development at Seaham Harbour.

SEAHAM AND THE COMMUNITY

When a company has been established for over 160 years, strong links with the community are formed. Courage is then needed to introduce change. Changing the image of the port in its relationship with the community has been a major concern.

Quality management at Seaham also includes relationships with the community. An imaginative example has been the Seaham Harbour Coastal Centre. This building was formerly the Seamen's Mission and based on the quay has a good view of the port and the coastline. Used primarily to encourage local schoolchildren to learn about industry, it is also available for use by other interested parties such as further education students and adult groups. A schoolteacher is allocated to the running of the centre on behalf of the local authority and David's personal assistant administers it.

Another innovation has been an annual open day. In 1989 this featured ten NATO ships in the dock, and raised £8,000 for charity. The open day is an occasion when the townspeople of Seaham and the partners, children, and families of the dock's employees can visit the harbour and find out what goes on there. This understanding can be vitally useful in maintaining good relations between the company and the town dependent on it for its livelihood.

Seaham Harbour Dock Company provided many insights into a small company as a major innovator. The changes are real and not cosmetic. They fundamentally alter the way people perceive themselves and their jobs. There is a ceaseless search to contribute to the needs of customers and of the location as a whole, conforming to the requirements of the populace and seeking to exceed their expectations. This is quality for Seaham.

16. Quality with Texaco at Pembroke Oil Refinery

Texaco has a major oil refinery at Pembroke in Wales. Indeed it is one of the most advanced in Europe, and with capital costs high, and productivity critical to cost-effectiveness, quality in everything done is essential.

A QUALITY SYSTEM

An oil refinery is a process plant in which you get a very clear physical picture of what a system is about. Everything in the process flow affects everything else. A fault in one area can bring the whole plant to a stop. This is a clear analogy to understanding any business activity as a system. There cannot be little fortresses carrying on their part of the company's activities in complete isolation from each other. This is why the concept of the chain of customers and suppliers is so important in total quality.

So Texaco have built up an organisation in which the end product and the technical skills that stage by stage deliver the product are orientated towards quality. Quality in safety, quality in technical correctness, quality in environmental awareness. It was this preoccupation with quality that led the *Sunday Times* to commission the filming of a video on quality at Pembroke.

Quality is not related only to the main product, such as petrol. Getting more useful total product out of each barrel of crude oil is also a significant issue. It can make all the difference to the profitability, and therefore effectivess, of the company. Texaco can now convert almost 50 per cent of crude oil into petrol, with a further 40 per cent into other useful products such as jet fuel, home heating and diesel. This doubles the efficiency achieved in the early 1960s. This was borne out by a 1991 study of refineries throughout Europe. In four years the refinery moved from fifteenth on a rating of critical categories to second. This is a result of the co-operation of a whole range of people from designers and engineers to operators and technicians. It might be thought that using the word quality to describe overall business performance is stretching things a bit, but if the ultimate customer is to receive a product at a price that is acceptable, then productivity and efficiency matter too; they are part of the chain of quality.

SHUTDOWN 1990

All process operations, particularly where hydrocarbons (oil, fossil fuels, etc.) are involved, have a potential for danger. There are governmental regulations and substantial self regulation.

Whole areas of a process plant have to be closed from time to time so that major maintenance can take place. A key decision is how long these shutdowns take, and how often they should occur. Good quality preventive maintenance avoids unscheduled shutdowns, which lead to production losses.

In 1990 all production units were shut down in a phased manner to facilitate inspection and maintenance work. In addition, extensive revamp work was undertaken to increase the capacity of the refinery's catalytic-cracker unit.

It was decided to operate Shutdown 1990 as a project in its own right incorporating the quality management philosophy.

Total quality has to reach into every part of the company. It is not possible to have just one project on a total quality approach in isolation from the rest of a plant or company. The whole company and certainly the whole plant have to be involved in the total quality process. Pembroke are in no doubt about this.

PLANNING THE SHUTDOWN

In the case of the Texaco shutdown project, planning started 15 months prior to the operation, with the selection of people who would work well in teams. This is an example of a long timescale of preparation designed to save time when the actual work is done. These new teams followed the participative approach, thrashing out problems in meetings and learning to work together.

There was also a lot of listening to the staff, who operate the equipment every day. They were invited to be part of the project and to have a sense of ownership in return for which they gave expertise and commitment.

There was a detailed analysis of tasks, pre-planning of each part of the project and writing it down in detail.

Fundamental to all of this, and without which planning would not have achieved its objective, was making sure that full consultation occured continuously. Everybody, regardless of specialisms, shared the planning, listing and preparation. Nevertheless, there were specialists who could be consulted outside the individual teams. Information and knowledge was made available without the erection of barriers. This hierarchy went out of the window and individual responsibility came in.

IMPLEMENTING THE SHUTDOWN

The shutdown and revamp operation was also a success. It was completed on schedule (eight weeks) and within budget (£50 million).

Vast numbers of people were involved in the shutdown operation. Texaco normally employs around 650 staff at the plant, with 250 regular contractors, but at the peak of the shutdown period, working around the clock, close on 3,000 people were involved in the project. So high was the quality of the action that during the whole shutdown there was only one accident, a minor one where somebody's foot slipped through the scaffolding planks. It was felt that the reasons for this high safety record were the planning and preparation that had gone into the project. Most industrial accidents happen because people improvise, don't know where to get the right tools or from whom to seek advice.

The shutdown operation had a real impact on the normal work of the plant. Normal maintenance, part of the prevention aspect of total quality, is more effective because people became used to following fine detail in planning and using computerised procedures. Links were forged. People became more co-operative. They came to understand each other's jobs and work for other members of the team.

Measuring performance is involved in any operation. Texaco is already talking about and establishing even more challenging targets for the whole team to aim for.

BS5750 – TOOL FOR SUPPORTING TOTAL QUALITY

While total quality means an attitude of mind, it will not succeed just by good thinking, though that must lie at its root. Documented procedures are essential and can be achieved by following the BS5750 or ISO900 standards.

Areas of the refinery have been accredited with the BS5750 award, as they demonstrate written procedures and practices to ensure they operate to approved standards. Texaco believes this is important. It forms an excellent framework or foundation for a quality management system. However the company emphasises that it does not cover more than 30 per cent of what is involved in a total quality process. It covers what is often described as the 'quality assurance' element of total quality but does not involve all facets covered in this book, though it can be used to support them.

As at the end of 1991, Texaco's registration under BS5750 at Pembroke covered the blending, storage and testing of finished products, including gasoline, kerosene, diesel and fuel oil. Plant manager Guy Birmingham stresses that this achievement was a total team effort. Inspectors from the British Standards Institute visited Pembroke in October 1991, planning to spend three days auditing procedures and activities. But it took them only two days to be satisfied that the BS5750 requirements were being almost entirely met. Texaco was given 42 days to make good a few deficiencies, but within two weeks had met all the requirements.

David Harries, quality assurance manager, comments on the way in which the success was due to a concerted effort by all staff which operated across departmental boundaries. He sees the award as giving customers confidence that Texaco will meet their need – i.e., give them quality. Everyone has to be properly trained for their work and a yardstick against which to measure performance is provided. Harries sees BS5750 as a 'very powerful tool for letting us evaluate where we are and for *helping us move toward total quality*'. BS5750 is a tool to be used in the journey towards total quality. It is not the final goal.

THE COMPANY-WIDE TEXACO QUALITY PROCESS

This account of Texaco and its 1990 Shutdown has looked at a specific experience, but the challenge got total quality moving forward fast. It has removed barriers to communication, it has embedded the concept of continuous improvement, of teamworking, of ownership, commitment and collegiality. It is an example of the company-wide impact of the quality process.

In the company as a whole quality is inspired by top commitment. A quality council has been established with senior executives, aiming to practice as well as preach, as its members. Their programme includes the following:

- Developing a strategy and programme for continuous improvement.
- Setting up quality action teams (QATs) and employee involvement teams (EITs).
- Emphasis on teamwork.
- Helping everyone involved to define their roles and co-ordinate their activities.

Texaco's quality statement reads:

> *To create a continuous improvement process which unites Texaco in its commitment to a quality culture and focuses our efforts to meet or exceed customers' expectations by:*
> - *Inspired leadership*
> - *Employee participation*
> - *Teamwork*

Top management in Texaco are committed to quality. They are on record as saying:

> *Our renewed focus on quality leads directly to better productivity, improved service, and employees who discover a new-found pride in their company and themselves.*

They attribute the turnaround at Pembroke to the introduction of a total quality process. Previously people didn't have the spirit of participation needed. They were too used to being told what to do. Nothing more was expected of them. Total quality management can succeed only if everyone's mind is attuned and their contribution not only welcomed, but expected.

Texaco's top management declare that:

> *The customer is demanding better service, and the company needs to be in a position to provide it. The total quality process also generates productivity and quality improvements that contribute directly to the company's bottom line . . . and personal rewards . . . a pride which drives Texaco forward.*

17. *Quality with ICL*

This chapter describes ICL – Britain's major indigenous computer company, which has gone down the Crosby route on quality.

ICL employs approximately 27,000 people and operates in over 70 countries world-wide. The combined turnover of the group in 1990 was over four billion US dollars. The Ashton plant was opened in 1979 as the centre of ICL's mainframe production. Since then it has expanded and makes the complete ICL product range from personal computers to mainframes.

A MODERN FACTORY

The Ashton plant is a modern factory, using productive methods such as 'just-in-time' and 'flexible manufacturing'. 'Just-in-time' means that the material or components from the previous operation arrive just in time for the next operation. It is an example of a close customer/supplier chain. This makes each person in the chain responsible for supplying high-quality, defect-free products. It means that bottlenecks no longer build up because the material arrives too soon and in too great a quantity. Flexible manufacturing means that fewer people are dedicated to a single product. It also means that the production schedule can be changed at very short notice to cater for fluctuating customer demands.

All this is necessary to respond rapidly to customer requirements in the competitive information technology industry.

The factory has been so successful that in 1989 it was voted one of the best British factories in terms of quality, productivity, cost and customer satisfaction. This was followed in 1990 with a British quality award. However the company makes the point that the success of this factory can be understood only in the context of a company-wide programme launched in 1986, which has changed the face of the whole organisation.

QUALITY IN ICL

ICL recognised that if it was to survive in the 1980s and beyond, the quality and reliability of the product range must be second to none. This could not be achieved piecemeal; the whole company had to have a common understanding and a common goal.

A completely new quality management structure was introduced, led and monitored from the top by a steering committee of board members. A new post of director, quality was created and Joe Goasdoué was recruited to direct the programme.

Over the next four years a dramatic change occurred. Everyone in ICL went through a training programme so that everybody in the organisation, from operator to managing director now speak and understand a common language of quality. This is based on a policy which states:

> *We will provide competitive systems products and services which fully meet our internal and external customers' requirements first time, on time and every time.*

Supporting this, ICL defines four principles or rules of quality, based on the Crosby four absolutes:

- Quality is defined as conformance to requirements - not goodness.
- The system for quality is prevention - not appraisal.
- The performance standard is zero defects - not 'That's close enough'.
- The measurement of quality is the price of nonconformance - not indexes.

ZERO DEFECTS

ICL took the approach that zero defects was to be the objective, whether it took weeks, months or years. It meant measuring where you were, being clear about where you wanted to get to, and consistently reviewing the performance of the products to identify areas for improvement.

Zero defects in terms of ICL's approach means not producing anything which the customer would view as not conforming to requirements. Chris Hodgkinson of ICL makes the point that zero defects should not be confused with absolute perfection. This is sometimes misunderstood by people who think of it as an idealistic impossibility. Philip Crosby makes a distinction between defects and errors. He sees a defect as something which is wrong from the customers' point of view, which will be objected to when delivery is taken. Errors may be made, but are identified and corrected.

ICL follow Philip Crosby's approach quite closely and therefore you will hear in everyday conversation within the company, reference to the price of nonconformance. If you don't conform to the agreed specification which your customer, internal or external expects, there will be a cost associated with it. Everybody takes responsibility in a zero defects programme for doing their work right first time. 'Right' being conformance to customers' requirements.

Philip Crosby goes in for quite a lot of razzamatazz, as noted earlier, and this is part of the secret of his success. You might expect this to be alien to the ICL culture, but at Ashton alone, three zero defects days have been held so far. All staff freely sign a zero defects board which pledges their commitment to the goal of zero defects.

CHECKING YOUR OWN WORK

In the sixties ICL, like most of British industry, employed people to inspect other people's work. This meant that if anything was wrong by defined standards, delivery to the external customer would be prevented.

Inspection by people other than the person who produces the

component takes away responsibility for quality from where it really lies, that is with the person doing the job. You would often hear the phrase: 'It's not my fault, he let it go!'

The days of separate inspectors have long since gone in ICL. Now everyone is responsible for getting it right first time and checking their own work. Operators self-inspect so that errors are corrected at each stage of manufacture. ICL operators also have the power and ability to identify and suggest improvements to the process or procedures which affect the way they do the job. This new-found freedom means that employees find their job much more interesting and their pride in their work has been restored.

CONTINUOUS IMPROVEMENT

There are a number of ways in which staff can suggest improvements in the way the job is done. All staff have access to an Error Cause Removal system (ECR). When a person isn't able to solve the problem immediately, either alone or with the help of the supervisor, an ECR is raised. This identifies the problem and sends it up the line for resolution. The ECR stays open and is reviewed by the management team until it is resolved to the individual's satisfaction. This gives the individual operator a mechanism for alerting management to the need to make changes to the system and for contributing ideas to management. (For discussion of the variations which are systemic and require management attention as distinct from those which operators can handle themselves, see chapter 3.)

If the ECR is outside the scope of the division then an inter-divisional Corrective Action Request (CAR) can be raised. This is logged on a corporate computer system and again not removed until the problem is resolved. This contributes to a complete check on the total price of nonconformance.

At Ashton there are over 40 quality circles in operation. A group of people from the same department meet weekly for one hour to discuss and identify problems or introduce better ways of working.

Process improvement teams and corrective action teams also

operate across all layers of staff. They have a common aim, that of identifying ways to improve customer satisfaction.

At the end of 1990 over 60 per cent of Ashton workers were involved directly in quality improvement teams, the total of ECRs raised reached over 500 and 28 CARs had been raised on other ICL divisions.

INVESTING IN PEOPLE

Everyone in ICL is a 'member of staff'. The word staff was chosen quite deliberately, for in ICL there is no white collar/blue collar divide. There is no reserved car parking space, everyone eats in the same restaurants, no one clocks on or off, everyone works the same number of hours, and gets paid monthly.

ICL publicly recognises its people as one of its most important assets. The company invests time, effort and resources in developing them to their highest potential. Everyone in ICL has clear objectives set each year. These are reviewed every quarter. How you perform against these agreed objectives decides the level of your pay rise the following year. Some quality gurus are opposed to this approach: there is a need for some in-depth research into the detail of what actually happens in companies adopting it. There is also an annual appraisal which identifies the individual's ambitions and training requirements for the next year.

Also on an annual basis staff opinion is sought by a confidential survey. Management acts on the information to improve all aspects of the working environment.

TRAINING FOR QUALITY

The fundamental of this total quality approach is a well trained staff. Some 24,000 ICL people have received quality training which started with the chairman and managing director. At Ashton alone this amounts to over 16,500 hours in total.

The surprising fact connected with this training is that it was given by line managers and not by the training or quality departments. Line managers were first sent on a quality training course. They then coached their own staff in quality theory and practice. This cascaded learning approach has worked very well and has generated a real sense of ownership at grass roots level in the company.

The training courses were initially bought in from Crosby but since 1986 ICL has developed its own range of quality courses, for which in 1988 it received the training industry's highest accolade, a national training award.

THE QUALITY CHAIN

Jim Baglin, a production manager at Ashton, says that quality is a state of mind which now permeates the whole staff. He also identifies the customer/supplier chain as a significant help in the progress of the company. Everybody has a customer within the company who is waiting for the results of his or her activity. Thus the stores are suppliers to various sections who are their customers. If what is supplied is not of the correct quality, then the internal customer communicates with the supplier directly. The faulty item is not put to one side for another person to resolve. This reduces manufacturing time, reduces inventory and instils a sense of ownership of the problem at the lowest level in the organisation.

It also ensures that quality is attended to at each stage of the process by the people who find the errors rather than by end of line inspectors, where the task of providing a defect-free product to the customer would be much more difficult.

There is a readiness by management and other staff alike to halt the production process at any stage when the quality is not right. This goes against 'keep everything moving', which has been traditional in the manufacturing sector. The staff soon became aware that zero defects really meant that no product must leave the factory until it was right. This has extended to closing down production on more than one occasion in order to trace a fault.

Another prominent factor of the work being done at ICL is that labour costs have come down. In the early eighties materials cost about 50 per cent, and the other 50 per cent was down to labour and overheads. Currently the top of the range product cost is around 93 per cent materials and only seven per cent labour and overhead. This highlights the essential nature of 'just-in-time', flexible manufacturing and quality to the survival and prosperity of the manufacturing division of ICL.

Alastair Kelly, director of manufacturing, says that as more and more of the product costs move towards materials, then the investment in materials has to be kept to a minimum, because that's where most of the cost is. The product has to move through the factory as quickly as possible to reach the end customer. However, in spite of this there are no shortcuts on quality, as this would be counter-productive.

SUPPLIER RELATIONSHIPS

The quality emphasis involves other external companies in the chain. The chain is only as strong as its weakest link. Quality vendors have to deliver the right material just in time so that there are no inventory costs due to holding excessive stocks in the stores at Ashton.

ICL has a very clear policy towards sourcing components from other European companies wherever possible: the figure is currently over 60 per cent. The number of suppliers has been progressively reducing over a number of years. This means that ICL works very closely with its vendors sharing future strategy and new product information way in advance of what would have been considered a few years ago. Having established a mutual relationship based on trust and understanding, ICL are able to save time and money by not inspecting or 'shipping to stock' the vendors' product. It can be used in production right away; currently some 80 per cent of parts go through this system.

ICL operates what it terms a vendor accreditation programme; membership of the programme is based on business and quality credentials including Electronic Data Interchange (EDI) of essential information, for example, orders and production schedules. The suppliers are also expected to gain accreditation to BS5750 or ISO9000 or at least have clear plans to achieve it within a defined timescale. ICL operates similar schemes for its authorised traders.

The general manager of one of ICL's suppliers, Jarrobs Ltd of

Alsager, Stoke on Trent, tells how it took over two years to get the ISO9000 accolade. ISO9000 accreditation does not guarantee quality, of course, but it's a step in the right direction.

BS5750/ISO9000

ICL considers BS5750 registration to be a major element in its quality strategy in all areas of the company in the UK. In fact ICL is proud to be the first company to receive a corporate registration to the standard from the British Standards Institute in 1991 and plans to seek equivalent registration for all its subsidiaries world-wide.

RECOGNITION

Another part in ICL's quality jigsaw is recognition. All employees are encouraged to improve quality. Any member of staff who is seen to be doing a quality job can be recommended for a quality award. The cross-company scheme has three levels – bronze, silver and gold. At the highest level the gold winners, together with a guest of their choice, are taken away by the company for an all expenses-paid weekend where 22-carat solid gold medals are presented by the ICL chairman and managing director. All winners' names are included in the Excellence scheme roll of honour which together with quality stories, appear in the company magazine.

QUALITY CUTS COSTS

At Ashton, Alastair Kelly was the plant director during the time the quality programme was initiated. He was the driving force behind the plant's move to total quality. In 1980 the company was running at a loss and could not compete with Far Eastern suppliers either on quality or price. It had to get a competitive edge and quality was seen as the way. Alastair says that the ICL manufacturing division does not have the absolute right to manufacture ICL's products. If as an internal customer it cannot compete with external competition then the division will not survive. However, that day has not yet arrived. In the first five years of the programme ICL calculates it eliminated £163 million from the price of nonconformance (the cost of not getting it right first time). This supports the view that quality does not increase costs overall. Rather the reverse.

At Ashton the manufacturing cycle time is now down from 50 days to 12, inventory turns (the number of times stock is rotated) is up to 12.2 from 3.2 in 1985, goods in process time is down from 40 hours in 1985 to 0.5 hours now. At the same time operator efficiency and quality have improved dramatically.

QUALITY THE ICL WAY

ICL stresses that only by visible and total commitment by management will a quality programme succeed. The rules apply in bad times as well as good. You cannot expect an instant return on the investment. Quality improvement may take many years, but at the end of the day it is a matter of business survival.

What ICL has discovered is that there is no simple way to implement a quality programme, no single tool or off-the-shelf product will suffice. ICL aims to search out best practice tools and techniques and implement them to produce constant improvements in the quality of their products and services. Above all it considers that generating a new attitude throughout the company is fundamental to success.

18. Cameos on Quality – A Prison in London Japan in Plymouth Germany in Cardiff

This chapter shares a few glimpses of other organisations where quality and learning to improve performance are key principles of action. There is a prison at the leading edge of continuous improvement involving prisoners and staff in creating a better environment. There is a German company which has settled down in South Wales and a Japanese one in Plymouth.

QUALITY AT HOLLOWAY PRISON

You would not normally think of a prison as a place where quality and learning are key concerns of the management and of many of the inmates. So often the press reports what is wrong with our prisons that there is little coverage of valiant attempts being made to provide custodial services of a quality which will contribute to reformation; to ensure that the stay of the inmates is at least civilised; where the loss of liberty is seen as sufficient penalty.

Fresh Start
Quality in British prisons is defined by a programme of working called 'A Fresh Start: the new improvements.' It aims to bring about fundamental changes in all aspects of the prison service, from staff

employment conditions to the care regime for inmates.

Each prison governor has a contract with the prison service. Corporate aims and objectives are drawn up for each prison based on the statement of intent exhibited at the prison entrances.

> *Her Majesty's Prison Service serves the public by keeping in custody those committed by the courts. Our duty is to look after them with humanity and to help them lead law-abiding and useful lives in custody and after release.*

The governor has drawn up a statement of functions specific to Holloway Prison.

> *Through treating everyone as an INDIVIDUAL*
> *by encouraging good RELATIONSHIPS*
> *and providing constructive ACTIVITY*
> *to achieve the BEST CUSTODY AND CARE of prisoners.*

Clear guidelines are given for all the action necessary to turn these aspirations into reality, with details of how to make cells habitable.

Teamwork

Quality is as much a concern at Holloway prison as any other organisation, so is teamworking. The staff used to work as one big group with a daily allocation of individual jobs. People often had different jobs each day, responsible for different inmates. There was little continuity. When staff shortages arose, officers were often moved around from inmate activities, inmates were locked up for longer periods.

Now teams are organised around the main functions such as residential, visits, medical and admissions. Small self-monitoring groups work in continuity with each other and inmates. They pull together as a team when there are staff shortages.

They have changed shift times to fit in with work, education and prisoners' leisure pursuits and to avoid excess locking-up time. The inconvenience is outweighed by a better mood created in the prison.

Stable and continuous relations with prisoners are considered vital. There is a sense of sharing and belonging, which spreads beyond the actual teams to the inmates as well. There is a clear sense of having a line manager and a definite area of activity.

The quality of relationships with inmates

The prison officers are able to build up constructive relationships with inmates. Rapport is created. Whatever the prisoners have done they are people with interests, feelings and emotions who one day will rejoin free society. This approach fits the language of total quality. It goes beyond 'conformance to requirements or specifications' and approaches the definition of quality as 'fitness for use'.

Unfortunately the quality falls down when it comes to aftercare. The trust and familiarity that has established a tolerable human existence is withdrawn. For good reasons prison officers are prohibited from maintaining relationships with prisoners after release, yet they are the ones who have built trust and have often become the mainstay of the prisoner's life. In prison inmates have someone who will listen and have time for them. Once released they often feel isolated and forgotten by those who did care.

Some of the officers are concerned to find a way round this problem. They are loking for improved pre-release courses which will ensure that the prisoners have the skills to cope after they leave the prison.

Investing in people

A feature of quality companies in the commercial and industrial world is that they are, in the words of the government training award scheme, 'investors in people'. In the prison service every effort is made to motivate staff by investing in them, showing them that they are valued and respected, and that they are worth the investment of proper training and development, crucial to any quality programme.

In Holloway this philosophy is extended to the inmates. There is a major spending budget to provide them with adequate facilities. This is summed up by the comment of the previous hairdressing trainer, who transformed the drab training salon into a proper professional one 'If you want success you have to provide the right surroundings and resources.' This preoccupation with sound conditions for all does not mean that there have never been any problems. There was a period when there were strikes due to a breakdown in communication, which ironically came about partly because everyone was so busy setting up 'Fresh Start'. The shift system has been improved so that it is easier to get home leave, particularly important where officers work away from home.

Occupational health training is given to all staff and every effort has been made to ensure that the environment of a prison does not make the officers neglectful of their own health in such matters as diet and exercise.

Empowerment

The governor is seen around by staff and inmates and hierarchical status does not prevent any member of staff from going to him to talk about a matter of concern. He engenders a sense of trust and responsibility in the staff.

There are issues that need addressing. Of twelve governor grades at Holloway only one is a woman, yet it is a women's prison. Furthermore the change which has been brought about would have been more easily established if there had been more preparation. The change to teamworking requires a move beyond the purely functional skills to the interpersonal ones, which don't just grow automatically. A workforce prepared for changes can move forward more quickly.

The lesson has been learned; training in management and leadership skills has been introduced. Anyone made up to even a temporary senior role does not carry it out without preparation. The Holloway Training Department is working with Pentonville Prison to develop suitable courses. Feedback from staff on these is being sought and listened to.

Just as in the business world companies have feedback arrangements and suggestion schemes in order to generate participation, so in the prison. Suggestions are encouraged, even those from the inmates.

Arrangements also exist for part-time day-release courses to be attended by the prisoners. This helps them to establish links with the outside community which they will ultimately rejoin. In a six-month period 3,500 day releases were carried out, with only 14 run-aways. The inmates themselves help to control the situation; they assert peer pressure on their fellows, because they don't want withdrawal of privilege. The governor's attitude is: 'If it won't hurt give it to them.'

Everyone needs responsibility

This is difficult enough in quality commercial establishments. How much more difficult with prisoners. From the moment of arrival the tradition has been to take away all freedom to decide anything, from time of going to bed to time of rising. They are stripped of all decision-making rights and are taken over by the system. The attempt is being made to give as much responsibility as possible to the inmates. One officer told Corinne Seymour: 'We pass responsibility right down the line to the inmates' toes and right back up the line again.' Holloway Officers take this spirit with them when they move on to other prisons. Thus the new approach may spread. It is recognised that there is a long way to go. Money has to be spent on proper facilities. The demeaning task of slopping out, for example, has to be removed. There will then be a chance that a measure of respect from others will generate self-respect in the inmates, with good results when they are released.

It may seem strange to have a section on a prison in a book on total quality, but it shows that the nature of the product or service is not the point. It is a matter of ensuring that all action produces the result aimed at 'fitness for use'. If the prison experience could be of such a quality that fewer inmates returned, then the ultimate customers would be benefited, by fewer crimes and a safer society. In fact Deming's definition of quality as delighting the customer would apply.

JAPAN IN PLYMOUTH

British and Japanese cultures have been married in Plymouth by the formation and successful running of Toshiba Consumer Products (TCP), primarily manufacturing television sets. The synergy which has been created has developed a more effective organisation than one element alone could have produced.

Throughout the late 1970s there was a joint venture between the Rank Organisation and Toshiba, in which the 'jointness' was less apparent than under the new single banner. TCP was born as a totally new entity in early 1981 and so has a ten-year track record to look back upon. Three hundred of the 2,600 workforce, under new terms and conditions, were employed from the old joint venture which had faltered badly. Many of the former management team were re-employed, including the managing director. The aim was to operate Japanese policies, systems and procedures through a British workforce.

The whole design process comes from Japan, though local computerised design capabilities are now being developed. The production technology is Japanese and the company will remain linked with Toshiba's world-wide product planning.

Financial matters are mainly controlled from Japan. There is no autonomy here. Production costs and forecasts are tightly monitored and controlled. Human resource management is influenced by the Japanese philosophy of valuing people and investing in them. However there is no attempt to be prescriptive about the details. Cultural differences are recognised and there is freedom to adapt to the needs and outlook of a British workforce, so long as the people principles of the quality movement are observed. These require that workers should be encouraged to be 'thinking workers' and contribute to the continuous improvement of everything that is undertaken.

TCP's objectives
The company proclaims six major objectives and follows them in practice:

- Product quality (this is the prime consideration).
- Investment in employees (who create the quality).
- Fostering sound employee and trade union relationships.
- Working closely with suppliers (a key to quality).
- Close relationships with the local community.
- Support of the total corporate objectives and policies.

The overriding mission is to 'generate the highest levels of profit, in a consistent manner, without deviating from the high principles of Toshiba'. The high principles refer largely to the commitment that goes with quality. The word consistent is significant, because it is the essence of quality. If a company consistently delivers what it promises then the consumer has confidence and may even find delight! Customers need to know where they stand.

Further statements of objectives include the following:

To develop within TCP an industrial culture in which all members of the company:

- *willingly maximise their personal contribution;*
- *can identify with the objectives of the company;*
- *can develop and grow in personal terms;*
- *feel a joint loyalty to Toshiba as the parent company and to TCP as a UK operation.*

The language used might appear 'corny' in an old-style context. The British are happy to have extravagant loyalties to sporting teams, but similar language about working relationships are thought 'over the top'. The quality movement seeks to reverse this, and no country has been more successful than Japan in creating it in countries outside their own.

These objectives are built into the thinking of all employees; all policies and practices are geared to facilitate this. The company is sales driven and if outlets need more televisions, then more televisions must be produced, but without sacrificing quality. So high is the level of commitment that it is not an uncommon sight to see non-production staff on the factory floor assisting with production, and submitting to the instructions of operators. This contributes to an overall team spirit and enables new friendships and understanding to emerge.

Teamworking and communication

The impetus behind the success of the whole operation comes from the team concept. This link with the open-style management ensures a feeling of belonging to a great venture. When Corinne Seymour visited Toshiba, one team member said: 'We're a part of a family,' and it rang true. Commitment to quality means the sense of ownership and participative style. This is why so many of the Deming 14 points of quality contain people elements. Open-style management is based on clear communication. There is a structured approach to this.

- Every morning there is a five-minute meeting to discuss the previous day's performance and today's changes and targets.
- There is a monthly production meeting which discusses the effectiveness of feedback and the impact on production targets.
- Every six months the managing director addresses the whole company on performance and future plans.
- Briefing notes on all main meetings are prepared and circulated to all staff.

'MPs' on the Advisory Board

Staff also share in decision making through the company's joint Advisory Board. This meets every month under the chairmanship of the managing director, to discuss the operations, to advise on policy and planning and to reach decisions on collective issues. It is a forum for open discussion, listening to arguments and reaching consensus. It works on a constituency basis with elected representatives (as it were MPs) attending the meetings. The union could have

10 of these 14 seats, but it has never taken them up, leaving them to the elected representatives, who then have a free hand to express their views without a party whip. All are equally able to place items on the agenda. Emphasis is being placed on feedback mechanisms to the constituencies.

Many of the representatives have gained skills on the Advisory Board which have been useful in enhancing their promotion prospects, and they have been able to move up through the company. As the personnel director says:

> '*It is interesting to see them grow in confidence and become more rounded in their attitudes and approaches. They are exposed to another bit of the learning experience.*'

The representatives receive some initial guidance on procedures and processes and their learning by doing is supported by volunteer observers who are able to coach them in how to contribute more effectively.

Open surroundings
Alongside an open management style there is an open physical ambience. It is felt that closed doors foster suspicion and rumours; so the whole complex is on an open plan basis. Even the managing director sits out in the open and can be approached by anybody. This has drawbacks when space is required for quiet thought. There are places to go to for this, but it often happens anyway after hours. A case of the Japanese penchant for long hours unobtrusively finding a way in without edict. The few Japanese who work at the plant are, however, usually the last to go home and a midnight lock-up is not unusual.

One workforce
We have already met this in the earlier chapters. The concept of single status is essential to uphold the ideology of the valued worker. Simpler things like the provision of blue coats for all staff help. Many do wear them, although there is no compulsion. Tabards are also available for warmer weather.

Company cars are about the only difference between managers' and other employees' reward packages. Managers are not paid overtime either. Basic hours are 39 for everyone, but actual weekly hours vary according to seasonal demands.

There are few grades of staff and layers of management. This aids effective teamwork, with direct team leadership and responsibility for team members. Team results are published on quality, output and efficiency. The Japanese practice of visual images has not taken off among these British workers, so you won't see pink swans pinned on people in TCP.

Quality groups

Quality circles have not been universally successful. They tend to wane when a key member moves elsewhere. There is however the EQuIP group at TCP. This stands for 'Excellent Quality Improves Profitability.' The 'u' stands for 'you', to stress that the attitude of each individual makes a major contribution to quality. The findings of the group are presented to the rest of the company and ultimately in Japan.

The contribution of all the staff to improvement and beneficial change is taken seriously and everyone is encouraged to give feedback on what happens in their own job. Their views are valued and as far as possible acted upon, and certainly always acknowledged.

As one team leader put it:

'Each extra set out of the door will bring in extra profit to enable the business to grow; therefore we need to improve all the time. I am part of this.'

Soldering on

No, that is not a mispelling, I mean soldering.

Soldering is a key activity in the manufacture of television sets; so considerable investment is made in training and development in this skill. There are different grades of solderers, dependent on training and demonstrated competence. Every year two people from Plymouth and all other plants world-wide attend intensive training in Japan. They then come back and train people in their plants to a fixed time and procedure. They have to train 80 people in a two-year period. Others are then selected to attend the trainers' course. Those who train the trainers have themselves completed 800 hours training.

Competitions are held in soldering. A world-wide Soldering Olympic-style gathering is held to compete in all aspects of the art of soldering. This may appear incredible to the lay person, but it is taken extremely seriously by those participating and their plants. This approach has bestowed a high status on a key activity in the production of the television set. It is the reverse of Taylorism, which led to the belittlement of supposedly mundane activities.

Growing staff

Career progression through the various grades is facilitated in the company. All vacancies are advertised internally and internal candidates are preferred. People are encouraged to attend a wide range of training courses, inside and outside the company. For an accredited course the company will pay if the first year is successful.

All staff have an annual performance review which identifies improvement needs and supportive training. Training is continual and much of it is through the job itself. This too is characteristic of companies which go for total quality. So much of the learning is in the doing and the off-the-job components are rigorously linked to what goes on in the job. Team membership of itself creates training opportunity. Interpersonal skills and the art of communication and feedback are crucial.

The majority of the production staff in Toshiba are female. Women receive equal opportunity to move up through the company. There are a number of female engineers and a female production manager is already in post.

In the late 1980s TCP launched their sales drive into continental Europe. The manufacturing base grew tremendously and in 1990, 500 staff were recruited. As the company is sales driven, speed in recruitment and the related training and rapid absorption of the quality philosophy was essential. In fact turnover, overtime and absenteeism have grown because of the numbers recruited and the time lag in their grasping the quality approach.

What is a Toshiba supervisor?

All these difficulties are key areas of the concern for the supervisor, superintendent or team leader. In every work area charts clearly display to the teams the records of timekeeping and attendance. Peer pressure is thus stimulated, as absence affects the working and the pressures on the teams. They have an 88 per cent attendance rate, which though good for Britain has to be compared with 98 per cent in Japan! Absence tends to increase when the six floating days off have been used up toward the end of the holiday year. We mention things like this so that no one gets the idea that perfection resides in a quality firm like Toshiba. There is room for continuous improvement and supervisors and all staff are on the look-out for it all the time.

Many of the problems of attendance and timekeeping have genuine causes and superintendents are not quite sure whether they are supervisors as the term used to be envisaged, or whether they are really counsellors. Certainly the team leader role is much more concerned with people management and growth under the regimes we have been considering.

One supervisor says:

> 'The majority of my time is spent listening and trying to sort out my team's problems. Who else can they go to who knows them and will listen?'

The supervisor is not complaining. The company is there 'to provide the best possible working day for each person to enable them to give the best possible return'. It is thus not simply a matter of being nice to people but of creating personal conditions conducive to productivity.

No longer do supervisors or team leaders see the work of counselling and of helping people to sort out problems of any kind that are affecting their work as the job of the Personnel Department. Personnel cannot know all the people or have the time to help them, though some of the supervisors would welcome more training in areas such as counselling.

People whose needs are being considered and met are going to be happier. They will return this by commitment to the company.

The British senior production manager is totally committed to the way he has learned essentially from the Japanese owners.

'It is so simple', he says, 'a good day's work is expected of employees and together we prosper.'

This remark is not just a one-off from one individual. There is a spirit of enjoyment about the plant and a belief in the product. Staff take pride in their work and are continually striving to be the best. They feel valued and they are part of a 'we' culture, not an 'us and them' one.

GERMANY IN SOUTH WALES

Now we turn from Japanese companies and look at a German one which has settled in South Wales, near Cardiff. It is yet another illustration that the total quality approach is not peculiar to one locality or nation. It is a culture which can find root anywhere if properly introduced.

Bosch is over 100 years old. It employs 170,000 people in 130 countries. It is a private company with 93 per cent of the ownership held by a charity foundation for the support of medical and scientific projects and those for international understanding. The remaining seven per cent is with the Bosch family. There is therefore freedom from continual pressure to achieve higher short-term profits for shareholders or the need to worry about fending off takeovers.

Long-term investment and progress is the main concern. Research and development, capital investment and training are high among priorities. Solid growth and continual steady improvement are guiding lights.

Setting standards in total quality
That slogan is printed on all Bosch literature and documentation in Cardiff. It is not just a bland statement, but an attitude that impresses

you the moment you enter the new buildings. There is an air of excitement about the quality they are creating and aim to enhance. The ambience reflects this.

The Cardiff plant is a greenfield site, which is being established and nurtured largely by the efforts of Martin Wibberley, director of human resources. I first met him at a conference of the Institute of Personnel Management in the UK, where he stated that the total quality movement was the great opportunity for personnel specialists to use their skills in a way that was central to the business. He is certainly practising what he preached.

'Of all things the best'

This is another Bosch resolution, enshrined in the statement of corporate values.

1. *Commitment to total quality.*
2. *High priority to training and development, to achieve continuous improvement in quality, productivity and individual skills.*
3. *Meeting responsibilities to customers, employees, the local community and suppliers.*
4. *To establish single status among all employees to the maximum possible extent.*
5. *To create an organisational climate which encourages open communication, minimises hierarchy, invites involvement and partnership, and creates enjoyment.*
6. *To focus on the individual.*
7. *To be a responsive organisation – through flexibility and teamworking.*
8. *To maintain a long-term commitment to Wales.*

These objectives are not unique, but they have a flavour which is evident in all the best total quality companies. Although there are many task-orientated techniques, the essence of total quality lies in the people areas of communication, teamwork, reduced hierarchy, collegiality, partnership, commitment, personal responsibility, learning all the time and continuous improvement. Personal integrity lies at the root of many of these objectives and characteristics. After all that is what quality is about.

A learning climate

The Cardiff site was a greenfield one. The first six months after its inception were spent in training, developing and preparing the workforce. This ranged from the two-week induction programme through organizational and behavioural training to four to six months in Germany for technical training. This was not a one-time event but will be a continual cycle of investment in the workers. As Martin Wibberley told Corinne Seymour: 'Training is absolutely critical: it is the motor to achieving total quality.' The employees who receive training feel valued; it often contrasts with their previous work experience. As a cleaner put it, speaking of the induction programme: 'It was the best fortnight I ever had; no one has treated me like this before. I feel involved; I'm part of things.' The training has been thorough. For those who went to Germany there was a language and preparation course at a local college. A tutor was flown to Stuttgart with a video camera to gather materials for the course, which not only teaches the language, but familiarises the trainees with the area, the plant and city, so that their learning has a more relevant ring.

Organisation and status

There are five levels of employee grade; team member, team leader, group leader, department manager and director. And that's it. Single status terms apply to all employees in relation to pensions, eating places and everything except overtime. The most senior do not receive overtime payment. Manufacturing staff wear a uniform which they have chosen and other staff have a jacket of the same style provided for when they enter the manufacturing area.

The idea is to diminish distinctions and create a sense of unity, and there as elsewhere it seems to work. It is further supported by the banning of certain words from the company vocabulary. 'Semi-skilled' and 'unskilled' are out as descriptions of workers. Martin Wibberley feels that there is nothing more demotivating to a worker than to be called unskilled. All workers have some skills that can be nurtured. Organisations need all their workers to believe that they have skills to offer.

Union relationships follow a non-confrontational approach. There is a single union which works in partnership with Bosch and all the employees to develop and implement corporate values which they can own. After much discussion with a number of trade unions an agreement was reached with EETPU. The two most innovative elements in the agreement were:

- Total interdepartmental and interpersonal flexibility.
- Performance–driven pay for all.

Flexible teams

All contracts of employment reflect the flexible approach. The wording appoints people as 'working initially' in whatever job they start with. It implies continuous learning and changes of activity to meet personal and company needs. Everyone is expected to do anything they think they can do and or learn to do.

This means that manufacturing teams operate as integrated flexible teams. There is flexibility between manufacturing and technical skills and workshops are run to enable people to achieve this ability. Everyone is able to attend four modules over a period of six months (run twice to ensure accessibility to everyone). Credits are awarded at the end of each module so that employees can drop out for a time and then rejoin later. And it is all in their own time. There is no guarantee of promotion, but there is eligibility for promotion. Those who show exceptional ability are placed on the fast track for attendance on full-time courses of study. These are to be linked with accreditation through National Vocational Qualifications (NVQ).

Encouraging the learning habit

Currently the emphasis is on the functional, technical and behavioural training essential to the working of the plant. Later it is hoped to recognise that any learning from training and education helps to develop workers in the learning habit, with obvious benefit to worker and firm. However one step at a time.

Every six months there is a training and development review for all staff. This is completely separate from a performance review linked to salary, which is held six months later. Thus, twice a year at least, attention is focused on employees as individuals, on how they are doing and where they are going.

Before the development reviews the employees complete a summary of their concerns. Then a joint form is completed during the discussion. The review covers what needs to be learned and the changes taking place which will require new skills and career directions. An action plan is then completed.

Improvement

This is a key concept, both in relationship to individual work and the methods and processes by which the job is carried out. Better absentee and timekeeping levels are constantly sought by making the information available and then by peer pressure.

More significantly performance is reviewed against the extent to which people are improvement-orientated. The unions found this difficult at first, but now people are beginning to realise that they are responsible for thinking about their jobs and seeking to develop better ways of doing them.

'We want thinking workers, who continually strive to improve performance.'

So said Martin Wibberley, adding: 'After all no one knows better than the person doing the job.'

To elicit this knowledge from the thinking worker the techniques used are: problem solving through brainstorming, fishbone diagrams, Pareto charts, variation graphs and histograms. The aim is to get to the stage where quality is no longer inspected at the end of the line. As one team leader put it: 'We have to move to building quality in at the beginning of the line.'

In addition to the daily continuous search for improvement as the work is done, there are also off-line meetings to solve problems. Off-line but not off-job, because it is everyone's job to have ideas.

In the open plan meeting areas it is usual to see teams working through problems with a real enthusiasm to share ideas.

The team leaders are crucial to the success of these processes. They are trained to lead by total involvement with their teams, to coach and guide rather than merely to direct and order.

Other communication methods are employed; for example a Plant Council, with elected delegates, both union and non-union members, who are given training to enable them to contribute effectively. The delegates ask questions, gain information and inform the pre-decision discussions. The minutes of these meetings are circulated to all teams.

As in many companies who pursue the quality route there are daily meetings of the teams. At Bosch these last about fifteen minutes. Five minutes on the previous day's work, problems and today's targets; five minutes' feedback from the organisation and the Plant Council delegate and five minutes' hand-over from the previous team.

A multinational plant

At the time of writing there are 28 German members of staff although it is intended that in the end there will be only a handful. There will be a Welsh workforce operating a German company. The commitment to Wales is strong. The German staff have fitted in well, once they got used to the prevailing use of first names and other informalities.

There are Japanese ideas, German organisation, Welsh enthusiasm and a spirit which believes that anything is possible. There is also a ripple effect on other organisations.

19. Learning from the Case Studies

We have been looking at ten organisations doing things to secure a quality approach to business. It may be that none of the companies we reviewed would be called total quality companies or organisations by purists. Also, we have to recognise that how you set about ensuring quality in your organisation is determined by the situation.

However, if you pull together all the main ideas emerging from the companies we have reviewed, the key themes of total quality are all there, even though if we spent a few weeks in them we should doubtless find inconsistencies and non-quality examples. Principles are in action which could transform business.

CUSTOMER FOCUS

In all the companies described, there is a distinct focus on the customer as the purpose of whatever anybody does. This fits in with the quality concept which is all about either conforming to the requirements of a customer, producing something fit for the use of, or delighting the customer. Customers define quality.

In order to ensure that customers were getting the quality they required, a number of the companies we looked at had very clear links with their customers to ensure feedback on customer satisfaction. Beyond customer satisfaction and customer delight, they sought feedback on what customers might want in future. Some of this feedback was secured by customer surveys. We also had the case of Braintree District Council who, if they did not welcome complaints, certainly were very ready to learn from them.

We have seen the word 'customer' redefined to mean anybody who receives the result of your work. We have been introduced to the concept of the supplier/customer chain working its way right from the initial suppliers of raw material and components, through a factory or service operation to the outside world, ultimately landing in the homes of end users. This customer chain idea is extremely important and links together the people of an organisation into a system which is interlinked and interdependent. This is better than working in their own little fortresses interested only in maximising their own advantage. In the end this is self-defeating, because disadvantage to the organisation will ultimately mean disadvantage to the individual.

QUALITY DEFINED

Our studies also produced a number of definitions of quality. These came out incidentally from many of the people interviewed. There was 'consistency of product or service'. Somebody else said that quality was doing what you say you'll do. The leisure centre manager in Braintree said quality was making people happy. Somebody else called it a way of life. There was a warning about not providing gold plated taps when brass ones would do. In other words, quality is not a term that you use to describe mere superiority or excellence. Something can be too good for the requirement. Thus, somebody who wants a Metro or Ford Fiesta will regard those cars as quality products if they conform to specifications, if they do all that they say they will, and give thousands of miles of trouble-free driving. To somebody looking at that price range, quality does not mean a Rolls Royce or a Cadillac.

QUALITY TOOLS

Our case studies also showed how companies made use of techniques to support the attitude of mind which the word quality expresses. Stanbridge Precision Turned Parts was an outstanding example of this, because it had to have the techniques to demonstrate to Ford that it was worthy to fly the Q1 flag.

We have seen self-inspection replace inspectors looking at the goods after defects have already been built into them. We saw the responsibility for inspection restored to the people doing the job to ensure that what they do is correct.

We have seen shop floor workers involved in using problem-solving tools in order to enhance the quality of the work they were doing. At Stanbridge again we saw the computer system presenting graphs of statistical process control so that operators could look at visual display units and see any variations in the process.

The 'right first time' philosophy was adhered to in some of our examples, and the measuring of progress was significant. Others gave examples of working closely to share information with suppliers to ensure that there was a chain of quality from the suppliers' input, through the transformation process, to good quality output.

TRAINING FOR QUALITY

All our cases were deeply concerned to ensure a well-trained workforce from the newest apprentice to the chief executive. We saw Rothmans with their particular concern to ensure that their team leaders, or group managers, went through what they called a team leader cadre process, whereby a reservoir of team leaders was ready to move in and lead teams along the path of self-management.

We saw companies providing special training areas, whether this was for a purpose of learning how to use machines or to retire for an hour or two to work on a distance learning package. We saw flipcharts everywhere in working areas so that the workers could draw what they were discussing and clarify it visually. We came across the phrase 'total employee development' and we coined the phrase 'learning through the job' as the most significant way in which people learn. We preferred this term to 'learning on the job', because the preposition 'through' has a purposeful ring. Learning on the job may be accidental, and may suffer if not presented properly.

Phrases like 'releasing people's potential' and 'readiness to learn' and 'organisations exist to grow people' were frequent.

COMMUNICATING AND QUALITY

We found that all companies which went in for any degree of quality management were companies where there was a lot of talking going on. In fact we heard that in their early days, Rothmans plants were called talk shops. But when the talking finished, the action showed the resultant benefit. Thus it is the Japanese companies quite often take a long while before they are fully productive, but when the production starts to flow, it really flows.

In all the companies concentrating on quality that I visited, including some not in this book, boards displayed the results of the previous shift's activity and groups of workers would avidly consider them. No doubt with a degree of competition, not of the 'dog eat dog' type, but of the recognition that everybody's success was success for all the other teams as well. We saw how quality companies encourage networking, with people leaping across boundaries to learn from what others are doing. We saw shared vision from the top to the bottom, if terms like top and bottom were appropriate anyway. We saw respect for people. We talked to workers who obviously understood the key result areas for the company, and their own part in them. This enabled them to identify with company objectives.

We did see some companies in which quality circles existed, though often they were called improvement groups. They did not follow a rigid pattern. We realised that the early idea that Japan was offering the rest of the world, the concept of quality circles, was only the tip of the iceberg. Total quality goes well beyond quality circles. We noticed that in companies that concentrated on quality, answering the telephone clearly and promptly was a factor. When you consider that telephone answering is often the first contact with a company, it is worth spending money on training people to answer the phone in an effective manner. They are key ambassadors to the outside world for the health and quality of their company.

In the companies we visited we also met recognition that praise was worth giving and that people do not live by money alone. If they don't have it, they are dissatisfied, but if they do have it, and are never appreciated, they are still dissatisfied.

NEVER-ENDING IMPROVEMENT

We repeatedly met the word 'improvement', usually in tandem with the word 'continuous'. Quality means never being satisfied. When you have done everything to satisfy customers in their present frame of mind, there is always the opportunity to offer new satisfactions. These give a competitive edge over the company that has not discovered them. Total quality means being committed to a better way.

It includes knowing what your competitors are doing so that you can do it more effectively. However the Deming School suggests that it's much better to get on with doing what you are doing in a way that will delight any customer and let your competitors get on with whatever they're doing. If you do it right, you need not worry about them. There is something to be said for that.

The never-ending improvement approach encapsulated in the Japanese word *kaizen* is a responsive one. It welcomes change. It is ready with suggestions for new ways of doing things, and it is flexible.

Never-ending improvement was not part of Taylor's vocabulary as far as the workers were concerned. Improvement was the job of the management. In contrast total quality requires thinking workers, who recognise that even in little things they can make a big difference.

PARTICIPATION

If you have a thinking workforce who can make contributions to the progress of change; who can demonstrate daily that they are committed to improvement, then the things we have seen in our case studies are to be expected. We saw workers meeting suppliers along with their managers; the workers planning their own work. We saw less referring upward because people had the intelligence and the information to make the decisions that lay within their own competence. We saw self-monitoring going on, and people honestly recognising difficulties because the old 'management by blame' was out. We saw empowered workers with some control over their own destinies at work.

Linking with this were common conditions of service or single status where the old dividing lines between management and workers were disappearing – shared restaurants, common pension rights and private health insurance.

We also saw how the voice of the unions was consolidated so that the confrontational approach was being written out of the contract and a co-operative approach beginning.

TEAMWORKING

Of course in every company we visited teamworking was the high road to success. Groups of people, largely in charge of their own work, led by somebody who empowered them, created openness and trust. Whole task working was evident. Also people could operate on a multi-skilled basis where each could stand in for others.

In these teams there was no elitism, jobs were enriched, barriers were got rid of, knowledge and information were shared and there was a spirit of collegiality, with everybody listening to each other. All these qualities are essential to autonomous work groups with commitment to what they are doing.

LEADERS FOR QUALITY

We saw that managers became leaders in quality companies, with the manager as coach, counsellor and enabler. Colin O'Neill at Rothmans said this was all a manager had to do – but what an all. In the leadership style of the quality movement, hierarchies mattered little and example mattered much.

THE QUALITY MINDSET

All in all, the examples we have seen in the preceding chapters showed quality as an attitude of mind. The quality mindset is a learning one. It creates learning cultures where people can hardly distinguish between working and learning. They work as they learn, and they learn as they work, and this is fundamental to continuous improvement. Organisations exist to grow people who can do an ever better job.

The quality mindset enables people to have pride in their work. It believes in people's ability to deliver, it generates enjoyment of work, harmony of relationships and loyalty to a cause. It's a good environment for living and working, and it spans every activity – from the most complex engineering activities to the simple things like picking up rubbish and keeping the work environment tidy.

THE TOTAL THEME

This chapter has pulled together from our case study chapters some of the key issues illustrated by the visits we paid to organisations. All the themes that you will read about in treatises on total quality came out of the practical action of thinking workers seeking continuous improvement in organisations that might be described as learning organisations.

20. Total Transformation

Deming's fourteenth point in the 1986 version really sums up the whole theme of total quality and therefore of this book

> *Put everybody in the company to work to accomplish the transformation. The transformation is everybody's job.*

As I came to the end of a fairly intensive period of writing, it occurred to me that it isn't only about transforming individual companies and other organisations. It is about transforming society; it's a new philosophy of life, about working together. It operates successfully in a competitive environment, where market forces prevail, yet it encourages co-operation rather than confrontation. Even in the sharp battleground of competitive forces, it sees the benefit of collaboration over 'dog eat dog', recognising that if the whole market expands, then everyone is better off, rather than concentrating doggedly on market share.

TRANSFORMATION OF SOCIETY

However a little reader scepticism is in order at this point. The object of this penultimate chapter is to allay it by demonstrating 'a more excellent way' – giving customers what they want, rewarding lives for workpeople, self-directed teams in place of autocratic direction, pride in workmanship instead of unthinking obedience, learning in place of blaming, enjoyment in place of fear, profit instead of loss – for all the stakeholders, from shareholders to shop floor workers.

The total quality movement really is a revolution. It is about transforming working life, business achievement and customer delight. It must contribute to the transformation of the whole of society as it takes root and is therefore a subject that goes beyond technicalities of how to ensure products and services conform to requirements, important though that is. Never-ending improvement in the workplace, in the goods and services upon which the life of the community is based must contribute to the common good as well as to the individual benefit.

In this chapter I shall not try to restrain my enthusiasm, unfashionable though this might be in an age noted for cynicism. If Roger Harrison can talk about 'love in the workplace' and Deming about the 'joy of work' perhaps I may be forgiven for heeding the old song to 'spread a little happiness as you go by'.

A QUALITY JOURNEY ROUND BRITAIN

Quality is not a series of techniques or ways of working. It is a mindset, a way of thinking. This has been abundantly clear from everything we have considered. In the case studies in the second part of this book we saw organisations at work with a new zest as a result of adopting this mindset.

There was a little company like Stanbridge Precision Turned Parts winning the much coveted Ford Q1 award, with the prime minister's private parliamentary secretary unfurling the Q1 flag in the warm July sunshine. We sampled the vast amount of detailed work and statistical awareness that went into this achievement. We savoured Bob Knox's optimism and admired the way in which he could take on 10 per cent extra staff as an investment in the midst of a recession.

We visited Braintree in Essex and were infected by the quiet and resolute enthusiasm of Charles Daybell and his team as they served their customers – the inhabitants of a large rural area surrounding three substantial country towns. We shall not forget our visit to the Riverside centre, where the manager promised the 'complete leisure experience' and the refuse collector felt that quality standard BS5750 'didn't go far enough'. And all this was in the public sector!

At IBC Vehicles we saw how Bedford commercial vehicles had been saved from extinction by a union-supported move to teamworking and free communication, which won the enthusiastic support of professionals like the late Tony Jackson and training specialist Phil Steele, who had been brought up in the old regime.

The lovely coastline of north-east England attracted us at Seaham Harbour Docks, as did a company where the managing director, David Clifford, could talk to us while his team negotiated the annual wage round and a the professional falconer kept the seagulls from ruining quality storage.

There was Rothmans in County Durham with self-directed teams at work on machines surrounding their 'bungalows', sharing management responsibility with well-trained team leaders, even joining in discussions with external suppliers. We listened to Colin O'Neill describing the job of a manager as solely to coach, counsel and facilitate the efforts of the team.

We visited Holloway prison where the governor was empowering officers and inmates to find meaning in teamwork. Staff, without relaxing discipline, seemed to regard their job as a service supplied to society.

Then there was Toshiba where we saw how the Japanese approach to quality succeeds just as well in Britain as in Japan. It is not a question of a particular national culture; it is human to want to experience togetherness in pursuit of a shared objective. That way both company and individual prosper.

We saw Germany at work in Wales at the Bosch plant and caught some of Martin Wibberley's enthusiasm as he told of his banned words 'unskilled' and 'semi skilled' – just not applicable to any of the employees. Partnership, yet individual focuses were paradoxically emphasised at Bosch. The word 'enjoyment' of work came up again.

Pictures in the videos accompanying this book tell more than mere words of the quality approach of Texaco in Pembroke, particularly in the successful maintenance shutdown, illustrating the quality concern with prevention.

We went to north-west England and heard how the Ashton-under-Lyne plant had played a major part in the ICL turnaround, because of its conversion to the total quality approach. They went for zero defects, which to them meant not producing anything to which the customer would object. We also saw the quality chain of suppliers and customers, internal and external well established at Ashton and throughout ICL.

All in all it was a pretty impressive tour. I don't think it is extreme to say that it creates optimism for the future of Britain, particularly as we had time to explore only a small sample of what there is.

QUALITY MINDSET

We have seen quality in action as a route to excellence. We have pieced together the different aspects of quality emphasised by the varied range of organisations. It is indeed a matter of a mindset, a philosophy of life, as Deming would have it.

At the beginning of this book we listened to the wisdom of the gurus, Deming, Juran and Crosby. We can learn much from them. Their apparent differences of perspective are much smaller than the vast areas of their agreement. Inevitably one tends to respond to some aspects of their teaching more than others. I could not disguise the fact that I was especially attracted to the overall approach of Dr Deming. However, this was not to disparage the contribution of the others and a number of colleagues whose work is mentioned in chapter 21.

Deming's 14 points, in their various versions, gave me a means of holding the quality mindset in *my* mind and therefore afforded some structure to my writing.

I suppose a real breakthrough for me came in the attempt to write chapter 3 on an unpromising subject like 'Variations'. I came to understand how a statistician like Deming had arrived at a humanistic philosophy through an apparently mechanistic branch of science.

If random variation is a function of a process, once special causes have been dealt with, then the situation is stable and it is futile and demotivating to pressure people to do better, to blame the shop floor worker for poor quality. Further improvement can come only from improving the system and that is the responsibility of the management, guided and advised by the people closest to the action, the operators themselves. Nonetheless management have the authority to create the framework in which the rest of the staff operate.

Once these responsibilities are clear, then everything else in the 14 points is obvious: driving out fear, creating harmonious teams, restoring pride to work, liberating people's talents and uniting everyone under the banner of delighting the customer, who at the end of the chain pays the wage bill. If you are supposed to have an angle when you write a book, this for me was it.

The values that have grown for me during my professional life all chime in with the quality mindset. The combination of business discipline with caring about people come together. I found myself responding to the view that quotas and goals, over which one has little control, do little to inspire achievement. When linked with individual rating schemes they can be divisive and alienating, preventing the full growth of the self-directed work team.

More than ever I realised that what we want in business life, and indeed in life as a whole, is leadership which will enable us to do our own thing in concert with others, rather than to bow to the edicts of people called bosses, who can take away our freedom and order us to do what they say, without explanation or inspiration. In the quality movement I saw how these ideals could be and are being realised, without making business soft. Rather the reverse by insisting on high standards and high levels of personal responsibility.

COMPETITION AND CO-OPERATION

In particular on the broader front I want to pick out the issue of the possibility of collaborative competition. I do this with help from Rafael Aguayo's book, *Dr Deming: the man who taught the Japanese about Quality*. He expands the idea from the individual company to the wider business world, without proposing that market forces should be disregarded.

One of the contentious areas of Deming's teaching is his insistence on getting close to single sourcing as a realistic aim. He is not suggesting that you could move in one leap to having only one supplier for a particular ingredient of your needs. But it is certain that where firms have entered into close alliance with their suppliers, so that there is a family-like bond created. It has worked well again and again, to the business benefit of both parties.

The supplier has security of custom and can innovate and invest in order to meet the customer needs. The firm is assured of consistent supply of material of uniform and dependable quality. If difficulties arise they can work together as a team to overcome them. When new products are developed by the firm, the supplier is involved at an early stage working to ensure that both can benefit.

So is there wider scope for the co-operative approach, without getting dragged into the uneconomic ways of central planning or the equally user-unfriendly ways of monopoly trading. Aguayo is concerned at the loose way in which we use the word competition in our language. It is used to describe almost anything we do.

When a company develops and offers a product, we say that company is competing in the market place. Is there an alternative way of looking at it? Yes. A company can offer a product, and sales of that product may not detract from the sales of other companies. A product can expand the market without negatively impacting on sales of its 'competitors'.

Aguayo reframes the idea of market share. If the market expands by the activity of several competitors, (for example, people increasingly having second and third cars in a family), each company may have a smaller share of a larger cake. Why should they grumble at this? Aren't they all doing better? The firms are earning a good return and there are more satisfied customers.

The companies still compete and are thus stimulated to follow the route of continual improvement, but if one company triumphed over all the others, where would the competition and incentive to pursue continuous improvement be?

Rather than a headlong drive to increasing market share infinitely why not concentrate on quality, exceeding the customer's expectations, so that the market expands and there is more wealth for all? Looking for the niche, the something that your firm can provide uniquely is better than trying to grab market share by duplicating effort and trying to drive competitors out of business. Challenge them with superior products and the whole public benefits from your innovation and theirs as they fight back.

The quality mindset is about co-operation to please a customer. Deming suggests that we concentrate on this without always looking over our shoulder, seeing the competitor as an enemy. (I take it he would not object to our learning all we could about what is happening out there in the competitive world by competitor benchmarking, though not to the extent of taking our attention away from our own unique and ever better contributions.)

As well as ensuring consistent quality of input, single or near single sourcing reduces waste to the community as a whole without creating a conspiracy to keep prices artificially high. There is a place for sharing unused resources; more firms survive in the market place and then there is more constructive competition which will drive quality up.

The message is getting through to the business world as a whole, with the growth of joint ventures in specific areas, joint research activities, partial mergers and a whole range of organisational devices, which get the best of both co-operation and competition.

Aguayo proposes 'competing with' as superior to 'competing against'. This kind of competition can help everyone to improve. This approach is a wider way of applying Deming's 'drive out fear'. Many of the less acceptable activities of competition spring from fear – fear of losing, which often leads to desperate attempts to score, even to the extent, in some well known cases, of cheating.

Commenting on the futility of companies putting in their mission statement that they want to be first in some area, Aguayo comments:

A company's focus should be the customer. It should be looking to constantly improve its products, its people, its systems. It should be striving to improve the standard of living of society by meeting the needs of the customer. It shouldn't put its head in the sand and ignore what others are doing, but its focus isn't on beating the other guy. It should be open to any new ideas wherever they come from, including other companies, the customer or its own employees. Naturally if it's forever improving and other companies are not, in time it may offer such superior goods or services that some companies, its 'competitors', may find they can't 'compete' and may be forced out of business. But it would be a mistake to say it is 'competing against' anyone.

Perhaps this is the biggest lesson I have personally learned from studying the total quality movement. The widest implication of the quest for quality is that the spirit which substitutes internal collaboration for confrontation also substitutes win/win for win/lose in the outside world and in doing so often wins over those who practice only win/lose.

The Japanese share the secret of their success quite widely, confident in the knowledge that by the time we get where they are now, they will have moved on and still be ahead.

TOTAL PARTNERSHIP

While writing this chapter my optimism received a further spur when I heard Bill Jordan of the Amalgamated Engineering Union (AEU) speaking on the BBC programme *The Financial World Tonight*. He was describing a meeting of the National Economic Development Council which he had attended that day (8 January 1992). He, as a union representative, had put forward, in partnership with a British manager, a paper to the Council urging firms to invest in new Japanese–style production, following the lead set by Nissan and Rover.

Bill Jordan was delighted by the positive response his proposals met and the interest shown in the detail of his paper, which got the support of the three parties in the council – the CBI (Confederation of British Industry), TUC (Trade Union Congress) and the government. The paper had laid the emphasis on the need for partnership to apply these methods to achieve sustained growth for British Industry. Jordan said:

'My anxiety is that unless this revolution that's taking place is understood, unless these techniques are aggressively adopted by British

management, then our influence in engineering and in manufacturing will continue to decline. We don't think that's necessary; we think we have here at home now in Britain companies that are showing the way. What we need to do is to spread this doctrine wider, much faster; it can be done . . . and we're going to make sure that it is.'

This book aims to make a small contribution to the spread of this 'doctrine', as Jordan said, 'not through gimmicks, not looking for grand solutions, but through partnership in a particularly important job'. The meeting showed signs of a growing realisation that the total quality movement and other related changes do amount to a revolution in the way we do business and has to be taken seriously.

THE LEARNING ORGANISATION

Another quotation from Aguayo introduces another key lesson of the quality approach:

'Isn't trying to win necessary to achieve excellence? NO! Try keeping up with someone who loves what he or she does. What we need to cultivate is love of learning, love of work, love of playing. Love of what you're doing is what leads to mastery and excellence.'

To me this is one of the most significant statements in the whole of the now growing quality literature. Love of learning is implicit in continuous improvement, in self-directed work teams and in the whole idea of trying to exceed the expectations of the customer.

There is a growing literature on 'the learning organisation'. Writing this book and summing up what I have learned over the past three years from total quality companies has made it clear to me that the total quality company is the archetypical learning organisation. Everything is geared to learning to do everything better.

In a paper I gave at Ashridge in January 1991 at the AMED/ AMRG conference I said:

'When people are looking for a better way and finding it they are learning. When they are all doing it together, then you have a learning organisation. The slogan of the learning organisation is "learning together to do it better".'

I didn't know as much about total quality then as I do now, but I wouldn't change a word of it to describe a total quality company.

THE SYSTEMS APPROACH

A learning organisation is not necessarily a company which does a lot of training, though it will probably do a lot, largely 'through the job'. The whole organisation grows organically into a network of mutual understanding. Individuals still learn, but the whole learns through the interweaving of the parts.

As Peter Senge shows in his book *The Fifth Discipline*, the concept of the learning organisation is based on systems thinking. This is implicit in total quality, where everything that goes on in a company in the search for pleasing the customer is dependent on everything else. Every action is taken in the light of the whole, which was the thought behind Deming's point which urges us to break down barriers.

A key factor in any system is feedback. It is also prominent in the quality approach to business as we have seen in almost every chapter of this book. Everything from team meetings to process control charts is about feedback.

ORGANISATIONAL LEARNING

The learning which takes place is more than the sum of the individual learning. Something is added in synergistic interrelationships. Individuals think and talk and act. Organisations as such can't. It's the people in them who do. Peter Senge writes:

Organisations learn only through individuals who learn. Individual learning does not guarantee organisational learning. But without it no organisational learning occurs.

Dialogue is the hallmark of the learning organisation. The word dialogue in its original Greek form expressed the idea of 'meaning passing between people in the sense of a stream that flows between two banks'. In dialogue a group accesses a larger 'pool of common meaning' than can be accessed personally.

This is surely an appropriate analogy when we are talking about reflection. The team structure which has been so prominent in our consideration of the quality approach depends on dialogue. Some of the most important moments in the day may be when little seems to be happening. Thinking time is not idle time. Dialogue is not idle chatter. Total quality recognises this in its regular team meetings. Witness the early morning meeting at Nissan.

The chain of supplier and customer concept is implicit in the learning organisation. Everyone has to learn about the requirements of the next in line. This means dialogue with them as well as one's own team. One could could say that the sides of a learning organisation are elastic as they encompass neighbouring organisations involved in mutual transactions. Suppliers learn from customers and customers learn from suppliers.

OUR BUSINESS IS LEARNING

These ideas are well expressed in a Club of Rome report called 'No limits to learning' (Botkin *et al* 1979). A distinction is made between 'maintenance learning' and 'innovative learning'. Maintenance learning is shock learning – reacting to the unexpected, to crises, as in the special causes situation we discuss in chapter 3. Innovative learning is the planned attempt to learn and implement new things, as exemplified in continuous improvement. It implies an attitude 'characterised by co-operation, dialogue and empathy' according to these writers.

Pedler, Boydell and Burgoyne (1991) define the learning company, as they call it, as:

An organisation which facilitates the learning of all its members AND continuously transforms itself.

The purpose of learning is continuous transformation.

John Akers, former CEO of IBM, put the significance of learning very potently when he said of his company:

'Our business is learning, and we sell the by-products of that learning'.

That is exactly what any total quality company is doing. Whatever your job in a company, when you are working on your own and when you are working with others, the whole purpose is to learn and to put the learning into practice. There is no other purpose to work. As Bob Garratt has put it 'learning is the key developable and tradeable commodity'.

And what Peter Senge says of the learning organisation is true of all the concepts we have been considering in this book

As lifelong learners you never arrive . . . You can never say 'We are a learning organisation,' any more than you can say 'I am an enlightened person'.

Quality, too, like the learning organisation is a journey. In being so described it partakes of the very quality which makes us human.

Human beings are not static; being alive is all about development and change. Right from birth human beings are set on the path of change or development. There is a seven-year cycle of total physical change. From infancy to old age, every microsecond yields new learning to mind and spirit. Human beings can never say that they have arrived and that what they are now is what they will ever be. Perhaps we should stop calling ourselves human beings and speak instead of 'human becomings'. Life is a journey and we are always on the move; we are each of us 'learning organisms' and together can form ourselves into learning organisations. Continuous improvement is based on continuous learning and that is what quality is all about.

21. Come into my Study: an Invitation

NOT JUST A BIBLIOGRAPHY

It is normal at the end of a book which discusses issues which people may want to study further to supply an appendix listing books and articles which may help them. I will go beyond this and tell you a little about each book so that you have some idea of its usefulness for your particular needs.

I decided it was worth a chapter in its own right, though one which may well be referred to rather than read straight through.

I have not made a distinction between those books which I have specifically quoted and those which I have absorbed ideas from. In the text I mention a number of names and their works can be tracked down by reference to this list. Where it has been important to link a quotation with an author who is represented in this chapter by more than one book I have included a date at the appropriate point in the text. If only one book is listed here then that's the source of the reference. I didn't want to litter the text with reference signals.

So much for the mechanics of this chapter, which tested my word processing skills more than most. I hope you will actually find it not only useful, but also enjoyable as your eye runs down the brief descriptions and that you will feel it is not just a list. I hope it will lead you on to many new areas and ideas which will benefit your business life and indeed your whole life. The two cannot be separated.

WHAT'S ON MY BOOKSHELF

We will dive straight in. There is just one difference from my bookshelf. My shelves are not in alphabetical order. So what follows is a suggestion to me for some *kaizen* in my study. Physician heal thyself!

Aguayo R. (1990) *Dr Deming: the man who taught the Japanese about Quality*, London: Mercury Books.

> *One of the best books about total qualty as a management philosophy. It's in my top five. The principles of variation (my chapter 3) are clearly explained. The Deming 14 points are expanded. A key concept is co-operation all along the supplier/customer chain and even to the point of a non-confrontational approach to competitors. Total quality is about collaboration.*

Atkinson P. E. (1990) *Creating Culture Change: the key to successful total quality management*, Bedford: IFS.

> *A valuable handbook with lots of practical bullet points; emphasises that TQ is not something that can be created by a accreditation system; it has to be owned by everyone in the organisation. Practical ways of ensuring this.*

Botkin J. W., Elmandjra M. and Malitza M. (1979) *No Limits to Learning*, Oxford: Pergamon Press.

> *A report to the Club of Rome. Distiguishes between maintenance learning, to keep the status quo; and innovative learning to move into the future.*

British Deming Association (1989–1991) *Deming's 14 Points for Management and other pamphlets*, Salisbury: British Deming Association.

> *About a dozen pamphlets of 20 pages each, mainly written by Henry Neave, covering most of the issues in the 14 points. Very good on*

operational definitions where words are used in a specific way, clear on statistical process control and challenging on the rating type of appraisal. The Association also stocks technical literature on statistical process control, most of them written or co-authored by Donald J. Wheeler.

Byham W. C. and Cox J. (1988) *ZAPP! the Lightning of Empowerment*, London: Business Books.

A fun novel with a very serious purpose: people as individuals and in teams are given responsibility and respect with powerful effect on the way everything is done and benefit to the bottom line.

Carlisle J. A. and Parker R. C. (1989) *Beyond Negotiation: Redeeming Customer-Supplier Relationships*, Chichester: John Wiley & Sons.

Shows how to get customer/supplier relationships out of the adversarial mode, so that both benefit by a joint effort to provide the final consumer with products or services which will contribute to a high quality of life.

Carlzon J. (1987) *Moments of Truth*, Cambridge, Mass: Ballinger.

The president of Scandinavian Airlines tells the story of a turnaround based on inverting the hierarchical pyramid and giving responsibility to the people who face the public daily, with the top acting as support.

Collard R. (1989) *Total Quality: success through people*, Wimbledon: Institute of Personnel Management.

A wonderfully concise summary, which covers all the main TQ issues, from the views of the gurus to how to train teams in statistical process control (SPC) and problem solving. Quality as a people development matter.

Cox D. L. (1991) *Exploiting Change: By GABB & by GIBB*, Lichfield: WS14 0LD. Published by the author

A lively story of the turnaround at Ind Coope Burton Brewery, based

on self-directed teams and breaking down internal barriers. I have used his team diagram in chapter 7.

Crosby P. B. (1979) *Quality is Free*, New York: New American Library.

Many lively anecdotes and mini novels to back a clear expression of the basic TQ principles. ZD days and the tendency to sloganise may not suit all companies, and may not be appropriate where the problems are systemic. Crosby has a lot of successes and for many he is the introduction to the new philosophy, by his practical and down-to-earth approach.

Crosby P. B. (1984) *Quality Without Tears: the art of hassle-free management*, Maidenhead: McGraw-Hill.

Plenty of Crosby stories, but a very clear exposition of his four absolutes and 14 steps for implementation.

Crosby P. B. (1988) *The Eternally Successful Organisation*, Maidenhead: McGraw-Hill.

Another Crosby special which gets over the principles of quality by telling stories which are true to life.

Cullen J. and Hollingum J. (1987) *Implementing Total Quality*, London: IFS.

Sponsored by Coopers and Lybrand, this goes into detail about some of the statistical issues in a very clear way, while still linking in with overall philosophy. Is in favour of single source purchasing for each purchased product line, for better service and better price.

Dale B. G. and Plunkett J. J. (Ed.) (1990) *Managing Quality*, London: Philip Allan.

Twenty-four articles by various authors, combining case studies and guidelines for implementation. Less of the people approach, but a good account of some of the techniques which people use, including some I have only alluded to such as quality function deployment and quality costing.

Davis S. (1988) *2001 Management*, London: Simon and Schuster.

Future trends. Customers will get what they want at any place, at any time, with minimum physical matter and with the ecomomies of mass customisation. 'We are managing the consequences of events that haven't happened yet.' The book is called 'Future Perfect' in the States.

Deming W. E. (1986) *Out of the Crisis*, Cambridge: Cambridge University Press.

One of two or three classics. Written in a discursive way, yet very easy to find what you want. Loads of good little stories to illustrate every point. Hammers home his 14 points, his operational definitions theme and the principles of variation. It's a must.

Fiegenbaum A. V. (1983 3rd ed.) *Total Quality Control*, Maidenhead: McGraw-Hill

A classic by one of the group to which Shewhart, Deming and Juran belonged. Considered a 'bible' by many. To stick with him you have to want the facts and not an upbeat message.

Fisher R. and Ury W. (1991) *Getting to Yes*, London: Business Books.

A classic on negotiating in a way that will ensure that both sides win. It takes the line that the participants are neither friends nor enemies, but joint problem solvers. Separate the people from the problem. Focus on interests, not positions, and invent options for mutual gain.

Fraser-Robinson J. and Mosscrop P. (1991) *Total Quality Marketing*, London: Kogan Page.

The slogan on the last page sums it up. 'The customer is a holy cow; you don't milk a holy cow; you worship it.' 'Customer relationships, not individual sales or transactions, will become the unity of marketing currency.' Not much overt quality teaching, but an appeal to get rid of the mentality that was too preoccupied with 'closing the sale'.

Garratt B. (1987) *The Learning Organisation*, London: Fontana.

Succinct presentation from a top management perspective of what needs to be done to ensure that a whole organisation learns and not just individuals.

Garvin D. A. (1988) *Managing Quality: the strategic and competitive edge*, London: Collier Macmillan.

Harvard teacher challenges the failure of USA to live up to the quality mythology by a comparison between Japanese and American firms, particularly in the air conditioning industry. Continuous improvement is superior to acceptable quality levels (AQL) and stable internal standards in winning customers.

Groocock J. M. (1986) *The Chain of Quality*, Chichester: John Wiley & Sons.

One of the books which emphasises the internal/external chain at the root of customer satisfaction.

Hakes C. (Ed.) (1991) *Total Quality Improvement: the key to business improvement*, London: Chapman & Hall

A PERA International executive briefing. It's probably the quickest way for a newcomer to get to grips with the theme. Six key concepts, six management elements; six stages to launch it are the basis of the first main part with good diagrams. Then there is a 100 page 'dictionary' of all the main quality issues: B is for BS5750; C is for Cause and effect diagram; C is for Crosby; P is for Pareto analysis and so on. Finally some brief case studies. Another one of my top five.

Halpin J. F. (1961) *Zero Defects*, London: McGraw-Hill.

The classic which influenced Crosby. It expresses many of the TQ ideas of worker responsibility. It defines ZD as a constant, conscious desire to do any job right first time. People sign pledges to strive for this and a lot of promotional activities are proposed. However the concept of variation is not addressed, though people are given opportunity to make suggestions up the line.

Harrison R. (1987) *Organization Culture and Quality of Service: a Strategy for Releasing Love in the Workplace*, London: Association for Management Education and Development. AMED.

A consultant puts his career on the line by talking about love; tough love perhaps, but lifts the quality issues on to the highest ethical level.

Harrington H. J. (1987) *The Improvement Process*, Milwaukee: Quality Press.

A quality executive with IBM, he describes their quality revolution. Quality grows out of management style and not just a series of techniques or worker motivation. He gives a step by step detailed guide to implementing quality improvement.

Hasegawa K. (1986) *Japanese Style Management*, New York: Kodansha International.

Read this to understand the relationship of Japanese culture to management methods. A frank insider's view.

Hatakeyama Y. (1981) *Manager Revolution*, Cambridge Mass: Productivity Press.

The President of the Japanese Management Association talks of two aspects to managing; occupational and human. Within the first, like Botkin et al he sees maintenance and structural innovation. He addresses ability to influence higher management, enthusiasm for work, the joy of achievement, getting away from the role of judge, work as development and development by entrusting.

Hayes R. H., Wheelwright S. C. and Clark K. B. (1988) *Dynamic Manufacturing: creating the learning organization*, London: Collier Macmillan.

'People are the means by which control is achieved, not the thing to be controlled.' Everybody should be included in the learning process, because important insights arise at every level. Everyone in manfacturing thinking about their work and responding to feedback will ensure quality products. 'Learning is the bottom line.'

Heskett J. L., Sasser, Jr. W. E. and Hart C. W. L. (1990) *Service Breakthroughs*, Oxford: Maxwell Macmillan International.

Helps understanding the costs involved in poor quality service, well beyond rework, warranties and system audit. Deals with recovery of the customer when things go wrong. The service concept is defined in terms of results achieved for the customer rather than the services performed.

Hutchins D. (1990) *In Pursuit of Quality*, London: Pitman.

An update of the earlier Quality Circles Handbook puts quality circles and the responsibility of all employees in the context of total quality and culture change.

Imai Masaaki (1986) *Kaizen: the key to Japan's competitive success*, New York: Random House.

The standard text on continuous improvement as the umbrella under which all the quality concepts can be viewed. Emphasis on doing little things better, with specific examples. System improvement, not error correction is the true Kaizen area. Innovation is the larger scale, long term change.

Ishikawa K. (1985) *What is Total Quality Control?*, London: Prentice Hall.

> One of the Japanes gurus surveys the whole quality scene and stresses that people have more ability than they are given credit for, and want to do a good job if given the chance. The approaches and tools of enablement are described and the two kinds of variation recognised.

Juran J. M. (1964) *Managerial Breakthrough*, Maidenhead: McGraw-Hill

> The classic which saw the role of management as decisive, dynamic movement to higher levels of performance, not just controlling to maintain the status quo. Good changes must be developed as well as bad ones prevented.

Juran J. M. *et al* (Ed.) (1988) *Juran's Quality Control Handbook*, Maidenhead: McGraw-Hill.

> It's all there in great detail – 1,000 pages of it. A lot of statistics and essentially a reference book.

Juran J. M. (1989) *Juran on Leadership for Quality*, London: Collier Macmillan

> Detailed, but easy to find your way around. The Juran trilogy made clear: quality planning; quality control; and quality improvement.

Lessem R. (1991) *Total Quality Learning*, Oxford: Blackwell

> Transforming the substance of business by a synthesis of quality and learning so as to innovate. Lessem starts from a set of beliefs about the inner dynamics of being human and how these can interact in tough thinking and tender feeling.

Likert R. (1961) *New Patterns of Management*, Maidenhead: McGraw-Hill.

Classic motivational text. Introduces the ideas of interlocking teams with representatives of one contributing to another.

Macdonald J. and Piggott J. (1990) *Global Quality: the new management culture*, London: Mercury Books.

Valuable survey of the whole quality scene; all the gurus are there, the cultural context and the techniques and attitudes necessary for success. Thorough without being too technical.

Mann N. (1989) *The Keys to Excellence*, London: Mercury.

Very readable story of how Deming's thinking developed, with a good summary of the 14 points as a new way to manage business.

Mead G. H. (1962) *Mind, Self and Society*, Chicago: University of Chicago Press.

Founder of symbolic interactionism, which describes how, through the use of symbols like words, we are constantly recreated in our interactions with other people. Very relevant in teamwork and learning organisation thinking.

Neave H. (1990) *The Deming Dimension*, Knoxville: SPC Press.

This is another one of my top five. It deals with statistical issues so simply and conversationally, yet keeps them in the context of management. Urging people to do their best without the tools and systems needed is fruitless. Joy in work and win/win for everyone are other themes.

Oakland J. S. (1989) *Total Quality Management*, London: Butterworth Heinemann.

A thorough 'how to do it' handbook, covers most of the practical ground with less of the philosophy and context than some. Good for those who want facts rather than inspiration. Strong on simple statistics.

Pedler M., Burgoyne J. and Boydell T. (1991) *The Learning Company*, Maidenhead: McGraw-Hill.

First fifty pages give an excellent survey of what a learning organisation looks like. The rest of the book reflects on this and gives examples.

Popplewell B. and Wildsmith A. (1988) *Becoming the Best: how to gain company-wide commitment to total quality*, Aldershot: Gower.

A novel which I couldn't put down. The TQ truths gradually dawn on everyone in this company. Plenty of memorable discoveries, like 'everybody who is doing the job is the expert'; 'everybody is a supplier and a customer'; 'there's always a better way'.

Price F. (1990) *Right Every Time*, Aldershot: Gower.

An entertaining presentation of Deming's 14 points with interesting examples. Deals with the cultural climate in which quality tools are put to work. Not just 'how to do', but 'how to understand what you are doing'.

Robson M. (1982) *Quality Circles: a practical guide*, Aldershot: Gower.

Concentrates on how to run and gain benefit from quality circles.

Rosander A. C. (1989) *The Quest for Quality in Services*, Milwaukee: American Society for Quality Control.

A quality veteran applies it all to the services area. Distinguishes it from manufacturing and while believing in market research accepts subjective judgments of customer reaction. He applies the variation categories to services. Plenty of checklists, case studies. A valuable 570 pages.

Scherkenbach W. W. (1986) *The Deming Route to Quality and Productivity*, London: Mercury.

A concise and accurate exposition of the 14 points with the statistical aspect simplified.

Scherkenbach W. W. (1991) *Deming's Road to Continual Improvement*, Knoxville: SPC Press.

Sets about turning the theory of what Deming calls profound knowledge into practical methodology. Detailed techniques made simple, with plenty of examples.

Scholtes P. R. (1988) *The Team Handbook: how to use teams to improve quality*, Madison: Joiner Associates Inc.

A splendid spiral bound guide with details, methods and techniques for running successful self-directed teams. Any company based on teamwork should issue one to the team leaders and no quality circles should be without one.

Schonberger R. J. (1982) *Japanese Manufacturing Techniques*, London: Collier Macmillan.

Links quality with just-in-time and the range of innovations that have been adopted in Japan over the last decade or two. The link with flexible mass production is particularly close. It needs thinking people.

Schonberger R. J. (1990) *Building a Chain of Customers*, London: Business Books.

As the blurb says of the supplier/customer chain he 'shows how the universal adoption of this simple yet fundamental principle can replace destructive inter-personal and inter-departmental wrangling with a powerful and profitable synergy'. Every part of a company is united into being a cohesive learning organisation.

Senge P. M. (1992 UK) *The Fifth Discipline*, London: Business Books.

Will be an all time classic on the learning organisation. The whole company is seen as a system in which everything and everybody is interdependent and learns by feedback and communication how to achieve continuous improvement. It is one of the simplest expositions of systems thinking extant. Neither Deming, Juran nor Crosby is mentioned! But he's playing on the same field from another angle.

Shetty Y. K. and Buehler V. M. (Ed.) (1985) *Productivity and Quality Through People*, London: Quorum Books

Over 30 case studies covering the activity of companies in the quality and continuous improvement field.

Shewhart W. (1931) *Economic Control of Quality of Manufactured Products*, New York: Van Nostrand

By the man from whom Deming learnt. The real founder of statistical process control. You'll probably have to go to a national library to get sight of a copy.

Taylor F. W. (1915) *The Principles of Scientific Management*, New York: Harper and Row.

It lasted about as long as the Russian Revolution and like that its effects still linger on in many places.

Thompson K. (1990) *The Employee Revolution*, London: Pitman

If we are to have an internal chain of suppliers and customers, then internal marketing is a reasonable concept. Thompson warns about misconceptions on employees as if they are a homogeneous body who can be ordered about and who should respect authority, instead of being seen as individuals with a lot of talent to offer.

Townsend P. L. and Gebhardt J. E. (1986) *Commit to Quality*, Chichester: John Wiley & Sons.

Prefers the self-directed work team 'quality team' to the quality circle. Quality is everybody's business. Adding value and measuring it. Focus is on the service industry.

Trevor M. (1988) *Toshiba's New British Company*, London: Policy Studies Institute.

The full story of one of the companies reported on in chapter 18.

Walton M. (1990) *Deming Management at Work*, London: Mercury.

Story of six successful companies which followed the Deming route. A good chapter on performance appraisals and how to do better without them.

Webb I. (1991) *Quest for Quality*, London: Industrial Society.

An examination of Ford, Marks and Spencer, Nimbus Records and the National Trust and others as quality enterprises.

Weisbord M. R. (1987) *Productive Workplaces*, London: Jossey Bass.

Included here because he gives one of the best outlines of the founders of the participative approach to employment, with details of people like Kurt Lewin, seen as the founder of the learning organisation concept. A lot about Frederick Taylor too. Weisbord speaks from practical experience of scrapping productivity targets and going for quality.

Wellins R. S., Byham W. C. and Wilson J. M. (1991) *Empowered Teams*, Oxford: Jossey Bass.

About the clearest book on teams that from the start have been designed to be self-directed and to consist of all the people doing a particular job as a group. Its recipe is detailed and capable of specific application.

Whitley R. (1991) *The Customer Driven Company*, London: Business Books.

A handbook on the management of product and service quality, which emphasises their interdependence; the tangibles and the intangibles must be addressed as one issue. Referred to by Christopher Lorenz in the Financial Times, *10 January 1992.*

Wickens P. (1987) *The Road to Nissan*, London: Macmillan.

The story of how Japan came to County Durham and built up the most successful automobile plant in the UK, by following the total quality, people matter and countinuous improvement routes. One of the companies in the Ashridge research.

Wille E. (1990) *People Development and Improved Business Performance*, Berkhamsted: Ashridge Management Research Group.

The full summary of the Ashridge research for the Employment Department out of which most of the case studies in this book arose.

Wille E. and Hodgson P. (1991) *Making Change Work*, London: Mercury Books.

Thinking about change in general business terms was a useful preparation for writing this book, which has a more precise focus.

Womack J. P., Jones D. T. and Roos D. (1990) *The Machine that Changed the World*, Oxford: Maxwell Macmillan.

Based on in-depth study of the auto industry, lean production emerges as the way to mass customisation instead of mass production. It requires the total quality approach for its success.

Appendix A

INVESTORS IN PEOPLE – NATIONAL STANDARD
FOR EFFECTIVE INVESTMENT IN PEOPLE

An Investor in People makes a public commitment from the top to develop all employees to achieve its business objectives.

- Every employer should have a written but flexible plan which sets out business goals and targets, considers how employees will contribute to achieving the plan and specifies how development needs in particular will be assessed and met.
- Management should develop and communicate to all employees a vision of where the organisation is going and the contribution employees will make to its success, involving employee representatives as appropriate.

An Investor in People regularly reviews the training and development needs of all employees.

- The resources for training and developing employees should be clearly identified in the business plan.
- Managers should be responsible for regularly agreeing training and development needs with each employee in the context of business objectives, setting targets and standards linked, where appropriate, to the achievement of National Vocational Qualifications (or relevant units) and, in Scotland, Scottish Vocational Qualifications.

An Investor in People takes action to train and develop individuals on recruitment and throughout their employment.

- Action should focus on the training needs of all new recruits and continually developing and improving the skills of existing employees.
- All employees should be encouraged to contribute to identifying and meeting their own job-related development needs.

An Investor in People evaluates the investment in training and development to assess achievements and improve future effectiveness.

- The investment, the competence and commitment of employees, and the use made of skills learned should be reviewed at all levels against business goals and targets.
- The effectiveness of training and development should be reviewed at the top level and lead to renewed commitment and target setting.

Promulgated by UK Employment Department

INDEX